Angela

James Moloney

Annotated by Peter Bruck

Ernst Klett Sprachen
Stuttgart

For Leonie Tyle

> *"Older whites want war, older Aborigines want peace.*
> *Young whites want peace, but young blacks want war."*
>
> Noel Pearson, ABC Radio 1997

Annotations and additional material provided by
Prof. Dr. Peter Bruck, Lüdinghausen

1. Auflage   1 ^10 9 8 | 2014 13 12

Alle Drucke dieser Auflage können im Unterricht nebeneinander benutzt werden. Die letzte Zahl bezeichnet das Jahr dieses Druckes.

Internetadresse: www.klett.de / www.lektueren.com

Redaktion: Dr. Claudia Handwerker
Umschlaggestaltung: Elmar Feuerbach
Umschlagfoto: Corbis GmbH/Eliane/zefa
Fotos von Bobbi-Jo Brady und Emily: Peter Evans, Alderley, Qld., Australia.
Druck: AZ Druck und Datentechnik GmbH, Kempten / Allgäu
Printed in Germany.

ISBN 3-12-578162-7

9 783125 781627

Contents

Biography   4

Angela

Part 1 – Brisbane

Schoolies.   5

UQ.   36

Sorry Day   68

Part 2 – Sydney

Bankstown.   98

The Race.   144

The Gubba Man   164

Additional texts

Facts about the Stolen Generation   185

A review   186

Redfern Park speech (Paul Keating)   188

School project: Questions and answers on Angela   191

Author's note:
The name on pages 131 and 182 are inventions of the author. Any link with a specific Aboriginal language or group is coincidental.

Biography

James Moloney was born in Sydney, New South Wales, in 1954 but grew up in Brisbane, Queensland. He obtained a degree in educational studies at Griffith University and holds diplomas in teacher librarianship and computer education. He has been a teacher and librarian at a number of Queensland State Schools. In 1994 James Moloney received a Writer's Fellowship from the Australian Council. He has recently retired from teaching and is now a full-time writer living in Brisbane with his wife Kate and their three children.

James Moloney writes mainly for children and young adults. He has been awarded numerous prizes. Dougy, the first part of a trilogy, was commended for the Humans Rights Award for Children's Literature in 1994. Gracey, the sequel to Dougy, won the Australian Children's Multicultural Award in 1995. For A Bridge to Wiseman's Cove the author won the Australian Children's Peace Literature Prize in 1997. Angela, the last part of the trilogy, was highly commended in a UNESCO literary competition in 2000.

Part one

Brisbane

Schoolies

1

It was always the hottest day of the term. Last year and for three years before that, I had stood in the sun with the rest of the school as the Year Twelves paraded through our guard of honour. It was a Hamilton College tradition – like the woollen blazers we had to wear on special
5   occasions. The seniors, in those blazers and with their families hovering self-consciously around them, would come streaming out of the Assembly Hall and head for the marquee on the oval where morning tea was set out on starched linen tablecloths. They had to be joking! A cup of tea, in Brisbane, in November, with all the proud fathers in suits
10 and even the mothers too wrapped up in the occasion to wear something sleeveless and cool.

This year I would be part of that procession, part of the chattering crowd under the marquee, sweating inside my blazer. Already, the heavy beads of moisture tickled under my blouse and as for my
15 stockings, I could wring them into a bucket. Why couldn't they let us graduate in our summer uniforms, for God's sake.

There was no sign of that guard of honour as I hurried across the playground towards the hall. It would be an hour yet before the girls were needed and if I had not been so worried, I might have glanced left
20 and right to see their silhouettes moving about in the classrooms. This was supposed to be a day of memories, a day for looking back to when I was in Year Eight, Year Nine … But I stared straight ahead, walked straight ahead – and leaked perspiration.

---

schoolies (*AustrE informal)* the time of post-exam celebrations for year twelve students – 3 **guard of honour** a group of year eleven students who are standing in a line to greet the graduated students – 5 **to hover** ['hɒvə] **around** to wait close by – 7 **marquee** [mɑːˈkiː] a large tent used for social functions – 10 **wrapped up** *here*: involved in – 23 **to leak** to let out, esp. for fluids – 23 **perspiration** sweat

The humid breath of the hall blew into my face like a gust of cigarette smoke. The dull murmur of a thousand people seemed stale and hot as well. How was I going to find Mum amongst this lot? I had left her with Dad and the boys in the foyer ten minutes before while I headed over to the dormitory.

5 There was no need for them to stand around waiting, I suppose. All the girls were to sit in alphabetical order at the front while the parents and brothers and sisters and grandparents, if they had come as well, stretched out behind us. I stood craning my neck, trying desperately to see over and through the mass of bodies.

10 "Hi, Angela. Who are you looking for?"

I turned to find Karen at my shoulder. "Mum and Dad. Have you seen them?"

She shrugged apologetically.

"I have to find Mum. And quick. You couldn't give us a hand, could you?"

15 Another shrug, but she was a good friend and began to scan the crowd in the opposite direction. "What's the panic?" she asked, without taking her eyes from the job.

I was about to tell her, then thought better of it. She would only want to come with me when I went back to the dorm.

20 "Tell you tomorrow, when we're down the coast."

By that time she'd be too pissed to care.

"That's them, right in the middle," she called, pointing.

I was on my way immediately, following her outstretched arm. As I fought through the milling crowd, the hall became quieter and people suddenly

25 headed towards their seats. Looking up, I saw Miss Glencross mount the steps that led onto the stage. Damn, in a few seconds, it would be too late. I reached the row where Mum and Dad were sitting, my brothers David and Liam on either side. But none of them would look my way. There was only one thing I could do. As Miss Glencross waited at the microphone, like a

30 queen before her subjects, I plunged along the row, excusing myself as quickly as I slammed into the next set of legs. Most people were seated now and I knew half the audience was watching me, out of place back there with the families when all the girls were supposed to be at the front of the hall by now.

---

2 **stale** *here:* no longer interesting – 13 **apologetically** [əpɒlˈədʒetɪklɪ] showing that you are sorry – 21 **pissed** *(vulgar)* drunk – 24 **to mill** to move in a confused way – 30 **to plunge** to move forward forcefully – 31 **to slam** *here:* to run into

At last Mum saw me, her face immediately showing concern as I stumbled closer. Then I was standing over her. "What's the matter?" she whispered. Every ear within five metres was listening in.

I waited until I could lean forward, my lips almost touching the hair round
5 her temple. "It's Gracey," I told her softly. "She's in the dorm still. Says she's not coming."

I knew Mum wouldn't let me down. There, in front of a thousand people, she stood up, drawing every eye to her, even Miss Glencross's, and without a thought for the scene we were creating followed me back along the row.
10 At last we were free of the seats and through the exit into the blistering sunlight.

"Is Mrs Fielding with her?" Mum asked, tottering a little on her heels.

"No. Everyone's in the hall. Gracey must have hidden somewhere until they were all gone."

15 "Thank God you went looking for her then." After a few paces she stopped and threw her hands up wildly. "They should have guessed this would happen."

I stared back at her. No one knew Gracey better than me. *I* should have guessed.

20 We started towards the dormitory again, Mum still angry, and I realised that she was annoyed with herself more than anyone else. She knew Gracey too.

"I was worried when the other boarders told you what she was up to. Studying until two in the morning, night after night. When was your last
25 exam?" she answered herself before I could utter a word. "Yesterday morning, wasn't it? She's had twenty-four hours with all the pressure off and nothing to do but brood. No wonder."

The dorm was deserted. Our footsteps echoed in the stairwell, my own worn school shoes emitting a dull scrape while Mum's gave out a sharp tap
30 with each impact. At least it was cooler here. On the second floor I led her along the corridor to the bathroom and there was Gracey, just as I'd left her, still slumped on the floor in the long baggy T-shirt she slept in. Those powerful brown legs stretched out towards us, legs which had carried her to three State one hundred metre titles in four years and seen her dubbed

---

10 **blistering** intense, strong – 15 **to totter** to walk unsteadily – 15 **pace** step – 27 **to brood** to keep thinking about sth that worries you – 29 **to emit** [ɪˈmɪt] to make a particular kind of sound – 29 **scrape** an unpleasant noise – 29 **tap** a kind of sound – 30 **impact** *here:* movement – 32 **to slump** to sit down suddenly – 34 **dubbed** named

"Queensland's School Girl Champion" in the *Courier Mail*.

That was last year, though, before everything went wrong.

She didn't say a word when we came in, didn't even look up.

Mum did what I had done when I first found her there. She knelt beside
5 her and put a hand on her forearm. "Gracey. Darling," she murmured.

"I can't do it, Cheryl."

"Do what? Go up there to get your certificate?" Mum asked, soothing her.
"You don't have to," she added, surprising me. "It's just a ceremony. If it's too
hard then you can stay here."

10 Gracey seemed as surprised as I was. She looked suspiciously at my
mother for a few silent moments; then the tears started to well in her eyes
and the suspicion softened. Her whole face began to crumple, her brow
arching down over her eyes, her mouth opening to show the gritted teeth
and her bottom lip quivering heavily as she desperately tried to keep control.
15 But it was no use. "Mum was going to be here," she wailed. "Mum was going
to be here. She said she would."

"I know, darling," my own mother said, comforting her as she bent forward,
folding her in an awkward hug. "She'd be here if she could, prouder than any
of us."

20 "She wouldn't come to see the place all the years I was here," Gracey said,
each word an effort. "She didn't want to embarrass me. I know it. But I told
her, you see, I told her how they do graduation, with the whole school lined
up to farewell the seniors and how each girl goes up on stage to get her
certificate. She wanted to see that. She'd take the train in from Cunningham
25 for that, she said, whether I wanted her there or not. Oh Christ, how could I
make her feel like that. That she'd embarrass me. I loved her, Cheryl, I really
loved her."

"Of course you did."

"She should be here today," Gracey shouted, slamming her fists into her
30 knees and knocking her head back against the wall. The violence of it forced
Mum away.

What could Mum and I say to this? Gracey's mother had died early in the
semester while she was here at school. I had met her mother only a few
weeks before she died when I went home with her for the holidays, home

---

7 **to soothe** [suːð] to calm – 12 **to crumple** *here:* to suddenly look sad – 12 **brow** [braʊ]
part of the face between eyes and hair – 13 **to arch** to look like a bow – 13 **gritted teeth**
top and lower teeth pressed together hard – 14 **to quiver** to shake from fear or
anger

to Cunningham, a little town out west where her Mum and her two brothers were living. Gracey never did say exactly what killed her mother, though I remember the sound of coughing in the house each morning as we made breakfast. Then, as if that wasn't enough, her brother Raymond had taken
5 his own life, hanged himself with a football sock inside a gaol cell. That was as much as I knew because she would not talk about it when she came back to school. It was a miracle she'd come back at all.

Gracey's mind was full of these same thoughts. "Raymond would have come too," she said, finding enough calm to get the words out. "And Dougy.
10 It would have been like that first time we came to Brisbane, when I won my first State Title and Mrs Granello spoke to Mum about a scholarship. There would have been four of us, a family, like we were back then. Now Mum's gone and Raymond too. All I've got left is Dougy."

"You've been keeping this inside ever since you came back," Mum
15 whispered. "All that study. It wasn't just catching up on what you'd missed, you were trying to forget."

Gracey nodded, keeping her head down so that she didn't have to face us.

"Silly girl," Mum sighed gently into her hair. "You can talk about them now.
20 The exams are over. There's nothing to hold back for."

In the near silence a familiar sound drifted across the playground, the school song, raised up by a thousand labouring voices.

"They've started," said Gracey. "You should go. Both of you. No reason for you to miss out."
25 "It's just a ceremony," I said, echoing my mother.

"Go, please. I'll be all right now."

We were still on our knees. While Gracey struggled, fighting for control, Mum looked down at her legs and found the bathroom floor had ravaged one knee of her stockings, leaving the whole kneecap exposed. She stripped
30 them off and tossed them aside. Way to go, Mum, I thought. Later, if anyone dared a disapproving glance she would fix them with those hazel eyes, the ones that used to scare me, and dare whoever it was to look down at her bare, unshaven legs. The power suit helped, shoulder pads bigger than the footballer's I dated last year. If we did make it to the marquee after all, her

---

5 **gaol** [dʒeɪl] jail – 28 **to ravage** ['rævidʒ] to damage

natural poise would cancel out any creases and smudges from the bathroom floor. Having a mother like her made me stronger.

I took off my blazer and slipped in beside Gracey, hitching up my skirt to let a little air get at my thighs. I was better off than the rest of the girls,
5 packed into a stuffy hall, singing that dreary tune and wishing it was over.

The school song finished and for a minute or two there was silence until, slowly, Gracey began to talk. I thought it would be difficult to listen, that she would speak of those terrible weeks in Cunningham, of her mother's funeral or Raymond's tortured face when they cut him down. But no, Gracey wanted
10 none of that. She remembered her mother as a proud and healthy woman and Raymond as the kid she played with, fought with, looked up to.

We sat there for ten minutes, not that time mattered much. The sobbing eased and Mum asked, "How are you feeling now?"

"Much better," Gracey said simply and offered us the first tiny smile. "Look,
15 there's still time for you to get that certificate, Angela. And you, Cheryl. You should be there to see it."

"It's just a ceremony," Mum said again, without looking at me.

"But you've been looking forward to this, Angela," Gracey complained. "You told me yourself. What about Mr Watkins? You were going to wave that
20 certificate in his face, remember."

It was true. The teachers had always laughed me off as a party girl, an air head. Mr Watkins was the worst. 'You won't even make it into a cake-icing college,' he said once, when he dumped one of my assignments on the desk in front of me. But I had turned the tables on them this year and if I did make
25 it up onto that stage, there was an academic certificate waiting for me, my first ever – third in Accounting. Not exactly the Nobel Prize, but Gracey was right – I wanted my moment of glory, for a bit of smug revenge, if nothing else.

Revenge or not, it wouldn't seem right to leave without her, so I stayed
30 where I was.

"Now you're blackmailing me," Gracey moaned and she stood up suddenly.

"You're the black one," I said automatically, managing half a smile as Mum and I helped each other to our feet.

---

1 **poise** calm way of behaving – 1 **crease** [kriːs] line on clothes from folding – 1 **smudge** dirty mark – 3 **to hitch up** to lift up – 5 **stuffy** lacking fresh air – 5 **dreary** unhappy – 9 **tortured** *here:* looking painful – 21 **air head** *(informal)* silly person – 22 **cake-icing college** *(offensive)* college with a very low academic standard *(vgl. 'Puddingabitur')* – 26 **Accounting** bookkeeping – 27 **smug** pleased about one's success – 31 **to blackmail** to make sb do sth by making him / her feel guilty – 32 **to moan** to complain

Silence. For a second I worried that I had said the wrong thing. Then Gracey relaxed and, turning easily, wrapped herself around me. "You always called my bluff, Angela. From the first time I spoke to you, back in Year Ten. You were never afraid of the word black."

5 She let me go and stood in front of the mirror now, staring at her blackness. She was not the only Aboriginal girl in the school now and she had not been the first to be enrolled, but she was the first girl who had stayed – the first to stick it out.

I came to stand beside her so that we could both see our reflections side 10 by side. "You've never been afraid of it either," I said. "What did that Fenwick bitch say to you the first week you were here?"

"Old Lisa. Christ, I can remember word for word. 'Black sluts are only good for rooting blackfellas and making more little black bastards.'"

Behind us, Mum gasped. She had never heard that story, not what Lisa 15 Fenwick actually said, anyway.

Now it was Gracey who managed a smile into the mirror. "I can still remember her face too. You'd think she'd never been slapped before."

I was not a boarder, so I was not there to see it, the day Gracey went for Lisa Fenwick. But the fight had become part of Hamilton legend. Miss 20 Glencross took that Fenwick girl down a peg or two when the full story came out, but Hamilton was full of Lisa Fenwicks. Some of my friends had made bets about how long Gracey would last. One month, two. But not me. I had seen the way she stared us all down, that first morning in the playground. Mrs Fielding had brought her from the Transit Centre, driving the car right 25 into the yard just as the rest of the school burst out for morning tea. She stood there in an awful stretch-cotton dress one size too small for her as eight hundred white girls eyed her off. And she didn't flinch.

"I wasn't going to let those bastards beat me," she muttered now, as though she had read my mind.

---

3 **to call sb's bluff** to encourage sb to do sth he threatens to do because you don't believe him – 7 **to enrol** to officially join a school – 11 **bitch** *(informal)* insulting word for a woman – 12 **slut** *(offensive)* insulting word for a woman who has many sexual partners – 13 **to root sb** *(AustrE vulgar)* to have sex with sb – 13 **blackfella** *(AustrE offensive)* Aborigine – 14 **to gasp** to catch one's breath – 20 **to take sb down a peg or two** to show a person that he / she is not as important as he / she thinks – 23 **to stare down** to outdo in looking intensely – 27 **to eye sb off** to watch with curiosity – 27 **to flinch** to suddenly move because of pain or fear – 28 **to mutter** to speak in a very low voice

"And you didn't, Gracey," Mum said from behind us. "But if you don't get up on that stage, it will seem like you never really finished." There were three faces in the mirror now. Those hazel eyes again.

5 "Gracey," she went on, "you don't have to go down to the hall to prove anything. You beat the bastards long ago. And don't go down there for Angela or your other friends, even for this school." She paused, and reaching through between us, tugged at the blazer that lay across my arm. "But if you want to put on this uniform one more time, if you want to take that certificate
10 out of Miss Glencross's hand, then do it for Dougy and for Raymond ... and for your mother."

Then she stepped into the corridor, leaving the two of us alone. No, I thought. Mum can't leave the rest to me. I don't have the words.

"You deserve to graduate more than any of us, Gracey," I said, knowing
15 how lame this sounded. I would have to do better than that.

"Cheryl can hit hard when she wants to," Gracey said at last.

"Tell me about it."

"You're lucky to have her."

That shut me up. She saw me crumple a little and reached out to touch
20 me.

"No, I don't mean it like that – you've got a mother and I haven't. No, I mean Cheryl's pretty wonderful really."

I shrugged to show that I knew that too.

"I had this picture in my mind of what she would be like even before I met
25 her. Just from listening to you talk about her."

I must have looked surprised because she started to explain. "Remember the first time we got together ..."

"In the library, when you were sick of those boarders Miss Glencross had picked to show you round."

30 "Them! God. What try-hards. They played tag team on me, never left me alone. Then I got talking to you in the library that time. In five minutes I knew all about Cheryl, about the Italian tiles she imports and those terracotta lion's heads that spurt water into fish ponds. I knew she drove a Corolla and that your Dad had a Pajero but what he really wanted was a Porsche. I
35 thought a Porsche was a kind of dog. You even told me how to get round Cheryl if I had to ring you late at night. Christ, you could talk."

---

7 **to tug** to pull hard – 14 **lame** weak – 29 **to play tag team on sth** to gather around sb like a group of wrestlers – 31 **tile** a ceramic plate for floor or wall (*Fliese*) – 32 **to spurt** to pour out – 33 **Pajero** [pə'dʒerəʊ] a jeep, brand name of a Japanese car

"Mr Watkins thought so. When we wouldn't shut up, he gave me a conduct mark and sent me round the corner to work on my own."

"That's right. Then he sat down next to me and explained what a conduct mark was, like I was a five-year-old."

5   Gracey was smiling again. So was I. We looked at each other and those smiles silenced us. "So, was Mum like you imagined her?" I asked, trying to keep things going.

She shook her head. "First time I came to stay at your place, I was expecting this grey-haired old lady."

10   "She dyes it."

More half-smiles. "You saved me that first long weekend, Angela. Everyone else in the boarding school had some friend to stay with. The boarders were ready to pay out on me big time."

"Was that when we cut your hair?" I asked.

15   She turned to the mirror again, pulling gently at a few strands touching her shoulders.

"It still suits you, that bob. We had to do something with it. You still had your hair in a long plait, like a rope. Could have tied up an oil tanker with it."

20   "I needed a complete make-over, didn't I? And you were just the person to do it. You even stole that blue dress from your mother."

"Best thing I ever did. It was a girl's dress anyway – fitted top and that flouncy skirt. She only bought it because she turned forty-five and panicked. Wanted to prove she still had the legs. She wore it once then left it in the

25   wardrobe."

"I still don't understand why you didn't snaffle it for yourself."

"I wanted to but it just didn't sit right on me," I said.

"Didn't sit right on me, either. We had to stuff tissues down my front to fill it out."

30   "Not anymore," I said.

She looked down at her T-shirt and blushed.

"You stood in front of the mirror all night, trying to make the dress and your hair fan out when you twirled."

---

10 **to dye** [daɪ] **sth** to change the colour of sth – 13 **to pay out on sb big time** to give sb a very bad time – 15 **strand** a single thread of hair – 17 **bob** a short hairstyle – 18 **plait** [plæt] three sections of hair twisted together – 20 **make-over** a complete transformation, re-modelling – 22 **fitted top** tight upper part of a dress – 23 **flouncy** loose, not tight – 26 **to snaffle** *(informal)* to take something – 27 **to sit right on sb** to fit sb properly – 28 **to stuff** to fill – 28 **tissue** ['tɪʃuː] piece of soft, thin paper – 33 **to fan out** to spread out – 33 **to twirl** to turn around fast

"I did too," she replied, remembering.

We heard footsteps in the corridor and turned together, to find Cheryl standing there. She had not deserted me after all. Over her arm hung a blazer, the white of a blouse peeking out from under it, and dangling lower than both, we could see the pleats of a maroon skirt.

"These were in your wardrobe," she said simply.

Both of us stared, shocked at the audacity. My mother had sailed into the bedroom Gracey shared with Rachael McCormack, opened her cupboards, even her underwear drawer, I realised now, as I saw the bra in Mum's hand.

For a few moments none of us moved, none of us spoke. Then, before I could turn, Gracey's dark figure swept past me, taking the bra calmly from Mum's hand. She stepped away, turning her back as the T-shirt glided over her head. "I haven't got any stockings," she said suddenly as Mum came forward to pass her the blouse.

"Neither have I," Mum pointed out.

They both looked towards me. Should I, or shouldn't I. "It's only for another hour," I said and left my stockings on.

For the fourth time that morning, I marched across the scorching concrete of the quadrangle, Gracey with me at last. She was still doing up her tie while Mum folded down the collar of her blazer. There was no way we could sneak into the hall unnoticed at this stage, so we simply marched to the seats left vacant for us.

When the speeches were over, Miss Glencross began with the graduation certificates and awards. As a Riley, I had a while to wait, though there were plenty of my friends to applaud. The crowd had seen just enough girls across the stage to become bored with the endless clapping when Gracey stepped up for her turn. She waited briefly on the steps as the girl before her went forward, which allowed the entire hall to see who was next. When her name was finally called, it took quite a while to list off her achievements, Athletics Champion, Sports Captain of Leander House, second in Modern History, third in something else. Arms wide, Miss Glencross gave her a special welcome and the applause erupted with a new enthusiasm. Embarrassed, and holding onto a cumbersome trophy, Gracey tried to move off, but the Headmistress caught her by the elbow and brought her back to centre stage.

---

5 **pleat** narrow fold – 5 **maroon** dark reddish brown – 7 **audacity** [-'---] rude or cheeky behaviour – 19 **scorching** extremely hot – 22 **to sneak in** to come in secretly and quietly – 25 **award** prize for performing well at sth – 34 **cumbersome** heavy

A man near the front stood up, clapping still, and before we knew what was going on, we were all on our feet, girls, parents, the teachers, even the guests seated on the stage.

I could see Gracey fighting to hold herself upright. She looked for me and
5   I waved, then I saw her looking again, scouring the sea of faces. I thought of how much she wanted to find her mother's face in that crowd and how it must hurt to know she was not there. But she did find someone, and as I looked back, following her gaze, I knew she had spotted Cheryl and locked her eyes on her for just a few seconds. Then she was crying and Miss
10 Glencross offered a shoulder and held her there while the applause continued. Only when she returned to her seat did the clapping subside.

Later, my name was called. Angela Riley. I took the certificate and the murmured congratulations and, like Gracey, I looked back into the crowd, to where Mum and Dad were sitting. I wondered whether Mum would have held
15 out, whether she really would have missed this moment after all. Then Dad stood up, a lone figure amongst the crowd, but thank God no one felt the urge to join him. I was still smiling to myself when I passed Mr Watkins and so missed my chance to scowl. Besides, the old fart was smiling wryly and applauding especially for me.

20 We made it from A to Z and then paraded through the sweating guard of honour to the even sweatier marquee. But what I will always remember about that day is the long minute when everyone in the hall stood up for Gracey. Such moments can't be faked. They come spontaneously, when people recognise what it has taken to come through.

25 Gracey had come through.

2

Suddenly I was free.

At home, after the Graduation ceremony, I stripped off the Hamilton tie and blouse, unclipped the heavy pleated skirt and finally peeled off those stockings. Looking down at the untidy pile at my feet, a little voice spoke up
30 in my head. You never have to wear any of that again.

---

5 **to scour** [ˈskaʊə] to search carefully – 14 **to hold out** *here:* to have stayed away – 18 **to scowl** [ˈskaʊl] to look angry – 18 **fart** *(slang)* a stupid person – 18 **wryly** amused and displeased at the same time – 23 **to fake** to make a false thing look genuine or real – 28 **to unclip** to unfasten, to take off – 28 **to peel off** to take off

Then there was Schoolies Week.

Gracey could only make it for one night of Schoolies. She'd been invited to a special training camp at the Institute of Sport. Big deal, it was. Top coaches and the best runners in the country, names that
5 I recognised from the sports pages. She had to be in Canberra by Monday.

We spent Saturday night on the beach at Surfers where the Council put on a concert to keep us all out of the pubs. Not that it worked. Like the rest, I'd had a skinful by the time the music started and after a dance in the sand, I headed off to the dunes to let the noise drift over me mixed with the warm
10 ocean breeze. Before I could stop myself, I fell asleep.

I woke to find the band packing up and the beach deserted apart from a few stragglers huddled in clusters near the water's edge. Gracey was still there, though, nestled into the sand beside me.

"Oh, you're awake now, are you?" she teased when I rolled onto my
15 back.

"Sorry. How long have I ..."

"Couple of hours. I could have sold you three times."

"Were they offering a good price?"

"Enough to make me think about it."

20 "It's the body," I said. "All the guys are after it." I stretched my arms along the sand above my head, trying to wake up. This opened the gap between my skirt and the top I was wearing. Gracey poured cold sand onto my navel, making me squeal and stand up too quickly. For a second, the world spun around me and I fell against her.

25 "Not much of a drinker, are you," she laughed.

"Me! I'm sober as a judge," I snorted. "Didn't see you with a glass in your hand though."

"Usual excuse. Can't afford it," she muttered.

"Yeah, but someone poured you a glass of champagne this afternoon
30 and I saw what you did with it."

She knew I'd caught her out but stayed defiantly silent. Perhaps because I was light-headed, I kept at her. "You spilled a bit, *accidentally* then some

---

8 **to have a skinful** *(informal)* to be drunk – 12 **straggler** slowest person walking in a group – 12 **cluster** group – 23 **to squeal** to make a shrill sound – 26 **as sober as a judge** completely sober – 31 **to catch sb out** to find out that sb has done sth wrong – 31 **defiantly** [dɪˈfaɪəntlɪ] not accepting criticism – 32 **light-headed** dizzy from alcohol – 32 **to keep at sb** *here:* to continue to criticize

went into the ornamental fig and the dregs you left in the glass."

"OK, so I'm not drinking. It's not a rule, is it?"

"Of course not," I said quickly, surprised at her tone. I was only having a dig, after all.

5   We began to walk through the sand, towards the lights of Cavill Mall. Halfway there, she spoke again.

"It's Raymond. I can't forget the way those police went on at the inquest," she said bitterly. "Like it was the grog that made him hang himself and they had nothing to do with it. Feels like, if I have just one drink, I'm letting him 10 down."

"You were thinking about this while I played Sleeping Beauty?"

She nodded and for a moment we were back in the bathroom at school.

"Are you going to be all right in Canberra? Maybe you should just go 15 home."

"I don't know," she replied, throwing her face up towards the stars. "I keep seeing myself out there in the cemetery, standing in front of Mum's grave. How am I going to feel?"

"I can't imagine what it's like, not having your Mum," I said. "Look at 20 Cheryl and me. She still treats me like a little girl sometimes, but, well, you've got to have someone."

"Auntie Flo's my mother now. Close as I've got to one, anyway. Did you meet her?"

"That time I went home with you to Cunningham? I think so. She had a 25 huge bunch of kids in the house, enough to drive anyone crazy." I paused, remembering the hassled woman I'd met, winced as I thought of the way she shouted into the backyard, a crying baby on her hip. The kids were all so much younger than Gracey. "It's not the same, is it, when she's your auntie and not your mother?"

30 "Auntie Flo's all right. I love the way she bosses the blokes around and runs the house. At least that's how I think of her from before I came to Hamilton. You think *your* Mum controls *your* life. Auntie Flo's a tyrant."

We had stopped in the long shadow of the dunes while we talked. But she took off again, hurrying to be free of the sand, as though she wanted to feel

---

1 **fig** plant with soft, sweet fruit – 1 **dreg** last drop in a glass or bottle – 3 **to have a dig** (*informal*) to make a critical remark – 7 **inquest** police investigation of a death – 9 **to let sb down** to disappoint – 26 **hassled** troubled – 26 **to wince** to make a facial expression showing you remember sth unpleasant

hard ground under her feet. "I just want this year to be over," she shouted into the night.

It was a battle to catch up with her. When finally I managed to draw level she had reached the road and was waiting for a break in the traffic.

5 I put my hand on her shoulder, stopping her. "It's been the worst year for you, I know. Next year has got to be so much better. God, I hope we both make it into the same uni. What I really dream about is you and me in a unit together, doing what we like when we like."

"Tom and Cheryl would never let you do it."

10 "No, not next year. Besides, it's too expensive, but the year after maybe … What do you think?"

"Sounds great to me," she said. She did not seem as keen to escape now and turned back to me, listening for what I had to say.

"Look, the first step is a car. Everything I earn over Christmas is going
15 straight into the bank."

"Everything!"

"Well, might have a minor splurge but we've got to have a car. Wheels make you free."

"Free," she murmured, folding her arms around herself.

20 We could cross the road comfortably now. I stepped up, putting my arm over those tightly hunched shoulders, and led her towards the unit we were sharing with a bunch of Hamilton girls.

The next morning I walked with her to the bus station. "Will you make it back
25 to Cunningham in time for Christmas?" I asked.

"Only just. Can't disappoint Dougy. It means a lot to him, having me home, especially now that …" She left the rest unsaid.

Her younger brother Dougy was an amazing guy. Hardly said a word most of the time and it was easy to forget he was even there, but if you did take
30 notice, you could almost feel him thinking, turning things over in his mind, finding the good things in the world.

"Give him a kiss for me," I said. We shared a quick hug at the door of the bus. No sentimentalists, Gracey and me. I waved when she took her seat by the window and she reached up to flatten her hand against the tinted glass,
35 trying her best to smile. We wouldn't see each other again until uni started in February – at least, that's what I thought as the bus pulled away.

---

17 **splurge** spending a lot of money – 21 **hunched** bent

3

Karen celebrated Schoolies by having a little bear tatooed on her ankle and I got a sun tan where I've never had one before. Hardly a bunch of mad, bad rebels! A week long party and I was back home with a bag full of dirty clothes and desperate for a long shower without one of girls pounding on
5 the door and demanding that I hurry up. Just as I stepped dripping onto the mat, Mum knocked on the bathroom door. "Can I put these towels away, Angela?"

"Sure," I called and she came in, handing me one of the fresh towels to dry myself. She did a double take and eyed me off suspiciously. "Did you forget
10 part of your bikini, darling?" she commented. "Hope you used a sun screen."

I didn't need her permission to sit around on a beach and the way she said it was a real put-down. I'll fix you, I thought. When I had finished drying myself, I handed her the damp towel and sauntered back to my room without a stitch on.
15 The warm summer air felt good on my skin so I didn't bother with clothes until I'd dried my hair. It fanned across my shoulders as I swayed from side to side. Three years now I'd been wearing it like this. I pulled it back loosely behind my head to see what a shorter cut would look like. Mmm. Best to talk it over with the girls first. I looked at my naked body in the mirror. Not as tall
20 as Gracey but hardly short. I had inherited at least some of Dad's height, leaving Mum to live out her life as the shortest in the Riley family. Already she was refusing to stand back to back with Liam, my twelve-year-old brother. As for David, it was like living with a telephone pole in the house. You could use his shoes for the Sydney to Hobart.
25 Standing sideways this time, I checked the view again. Not exactly a catwalk model but the guys didn't seem to mind what they saw. Angela Riley, renowned heart-breaker and scourge of the lovesick male, stared back at me from the mirror. I didn't know if I wanted to be her anymore. I'd been out with a lot of guys in my time but I'd never been in love.
30 Two days after my return from the Gold Coast, I started full time shifts at Macca's. Seven hours a day at eight dollars fifty an hour, five days a week, right

---

12 **put-down** *(informal)* made to look a fool – 12 **to fix sb** *(informal)* to stop – 13 **to saunter** to walk – 13 **without a stitch on** completely naked –24 **Sydney to Hobart** a yearly sailing race between the two cities – 26 **catwalk** a narrow platform that models walk on – 27 **scourge** ['skɜːdʒ] sb / sth who causes great suffering – 30 **full time shift** working full time at different times of the day – 31 **Macca's** *(AustrE informal)* MacDonald's

through till Christmas. Even allowing for the break-out Gracey predicted, that was still over a thousand dollars towards the car.

I worked until my grandparents arrived on Christmas Eve. Grandma's arthritis had worsened and it was quite a shock to see her move about the
5 house so gingerly. Grandad was as lively as ever, though, with an opinion about everyone and everything, from the US President to the test cricket team.

Dad got onto him at the dinner table one night. "No matter what the issue, Richard, you always have an answer."
10 "Comes with the job," Grandad replied, laughing at himself. He was the minister at a church in Sydney, though I gathered from the conversation during their stay that he was about to retire.

They stayed for a week and when it was time for their return flight, Mum asked me to drive them to the airport. Last Christmas, I was still on a
15 learner's permit, and because Dad was too busy, it was Grandad who took me for extra practice behind the wheel. He was a patient teacher, I discovered, and when I passed the test (second time) he was the first person I phoned.

"You're driving very well, Angela," he said as we neared the airport, then
20 spoiled it all by adding, "Didn't close my eyes once." There weren't many people who could tease me and get away scot-free, but Grandad was top of the list.

While I was at the airport, Mum and Dad were frantically packing for the famous Riley family "holiday at the beach" which always began on New
25 Year's Eve. We dumped everything beside Dad's Pajero and stood there looking back and forward from the four-wheel drive to the bags and the loose gear, the snorkels, flippers, boogie boards.

"We'll never fit all this stuff in," Liam complained.

"Have to strap you to the roof racks then," David replied, shoving him
30 gently against the car.

I had a better idea. "We could take the Corolla."

But packing the Pajero was a challenge Dad couldn't pass up even if it meant the boys and I suffered like sardines all the way to the north coast.

---

1 **break-out** *here:* shopping splurge mentioned earlier – 5 **gingerly** carefully – 12 **to retire** to stop working because you have reached your pension age – 15 **learner's permit** first driving license which does not allow you to drive a car without an adult – 20 **to spoil** to ruin – 21 **scot-free** without punishment – 23 **frantically** hurriedly – 27 **gear** equipment – 27 **flippers** pieces of rubber for your feet to help you swim – 27 **boogie boards** short surfboards – 29 **roof rack** equipment on top of a car to hold things – 33 **to suffer like sardines** to have very little space

Noosa this year; three weeks of Dad watching cricket on tele, Mum reading, the boys surfing and me cruising Hastings Street for the perfect male. I had plenty of company in this quest. It seemed like half of my senior class had migrated to the same spot.

5 Dad had brought his mobile with him and checked our answering machine at home every day or two, just to make sure the world could really get along without him. Don't know whether he wanted it to or not. The second time he checked our messages, there was one from Gracey.

"Sounds a bit desperate," was Dad's comment.

10 I pinched his mobile and replayed the message for myself.

"Angela, it's me. I'm in Cunningham. Look, I have to ask you a favour. Can you send me a number I can reach you on? You'll have to fax it to the Post Office out here 'cause Auntie Flo hasn't got a phone. Is that OK?"

Who takes a fax machine on holidays? Not even my father. I would have
15 to go over to the Post Office in Noosa Junction and ... No, maybe I would get Dad to ring his partner and ask him to ... What a nuisance. In the end, I phoned the Cunningham Post Office and asked them to keep a message at the desk.

Gracey rang Dad's mobile the same day.

20 "What's wrong? You sound really worried."

"No, I'm all right, honest. Listen, can I come and stay with you for a while?"

"Sure, I'd love it."

"Would Tom and Cheryl mind, do you think?"

25 "Of course not. Come as soon as you like." Mum's head shot up at this. She had been hovering close by, trying her best not to look concerned. I mouthed, "Can Gracey come here?"

Mum nodded without hesitating, as I knew she would, but she had let her guard down and the worry was visible in her face now.

30 "I'm booked on a train tomorrow afternoon," Gracey told me. "Gets in to the Transit Centre in Roma Street at lunch time. There's a bus from there that arrives in Noosa about three." She rattled off the times and places as though she knew them by heart. Then she stopped and I could hear her breathing. "Is that all right?" she asked. This time, she couldn't keep the
35 pleading out of her voice.

---

2 **to cruise** [kru:z] to walk up and down – 3 **quest** search – 10 **to pinch** *(informal) here:* to take away, to steal – 28 **to let down one's guard** to stop protecting oneself – 32 **to rattle off** to say very quickly

"Sure. Is anything the matter? You sound like you're being chased."

"Oh, Angela. It's just that …" She stopped suddenly and I could hear voices in the background. "No, really. I'm fine," she insisted. "Sorry about this, but I'm on a pay phone and there's people waiting. I'll see you the day after
5 tomorrow."

So I walked down the steep hill from our unit to meet her in Hastings Street. Thank God she was travelling light. Mind you, all you need for three weeks in Noosa is a bikini and something to sleep in.
10 I told her this and she laughed. "Just as well I can sleep in my training gear," she said. There didn't seem to be any sign of the hassled girl on the phone a few days before. Not then, anyway.

"How's Dougy?" I asked.

"Doing OK," she answered as we set off. "He's not going back to school this
15 year. Not much point really – he's sixteen now." She yawned, reminding me that she must have sat up all night in the train. I took the Nike bag from her shoulder and looped it over mine. "You've had this bag a while," I said. "It's made a few trips out to Cunningham and back, eh."

"Yeah, more than a few," she said, as we passed a couple of tourists
20 making their way along Hastings Street. Not much older than us, they were weighed down by heavy packs and looking a little lost.

"I'm like them," Gracey said wistfully. "Only I'm back-packing through my whole life."

As she said this, the footpath narrowed and we began to climb the hill. I
25 went ahead, bent under the weight which was more than I was used to. Gracey trailed behind. I said something else that I can't remember now but there was no answer. She had stopped ten metres back, to look at the view I thought, so I trudged back down the hill. She glanced at me and I saw big tears rolling from her eyes. No sobs, no creases across her brow, just the
30 moist, shiny eyes. She wore those tears with the same shy embarrassment I had seen when championship medals were hung round her neck.

"Oh Angela, hug me," she said. "I've been so lonely."

"*Lonely*. You've just been home for a week."

She held on to me like a drowning swimmer until she calmed down
35 enough to walk the rest of the way.

Mum was all over her like a rash when we came in and this made it easier to disguise the half-dried tears. Dad even dragged himself away from the

---

17 **to loop** to put around – 22 **to back-pack** *here:* to not live anywhere permanently –
28 **to trudge** to walk slowly – 36 **rash** *Ausschlag*

cricket. Welcome, Happy New Year. There was a late Christmas present for Gracey lying under the potted fig, the nearest thing to a Christmas tree the unit could offer. Mum and I had slipped down to the boutiques in Hastings Street and chosen the gift. (I chose, Mum paid. No need to let sentiment eat a hole in my stash.) For years Gracey had been content to wear her school Speedos onto the beach but school was over now. Filled out over Gracey's brown curves, the pale yellow bikini I'd picked out for her would look sensational. Guys on the beach were going to burn.

Gracey struggled gamely to show her delight, but it was not the right moment. Luckily, Mum took the hint. "You must be exhausted, coming all that way," she clucked in her mother-hen voice. "Why don't you lie down until tea."

Gracey did more than that. She was fast asleep at six-thirty when David and Liam came back with the take-away. In the morning, she roused herself for breakfast then went straight back to bed.

"Not coming down with something, is she?" asked Dad. "Better check her temperature."

I put him off. I had seen this before. Gracey would drive herself and drive herself until her body just pulled the plug. She slept through most of that day, ate a little pizza with us and still managed to be asleep before me that night. The next morning I found her sitting on a banana lounge on the patio, taking in the view of Teewah Beach.

"You alive yet?"

"Sort of. What's the date today?"

"Ninth," I told her instantly. I knew what the question was about. We were waiting, same as thousands of other kids round the State, for a letter from the Tertiary Admissions Office.

"You'll get into Law," I assured her. There was no justice if she didn't.

Gracey might have been awake but she stayed listless, drifting like a sleepwalker. She said nothing more about her little crack-up on the way from the bus. I had held her until the weight of the bag pulling on my shoulder forced me to let go. No explanation. I put it down to her exhaustion, though what this had to do with being lonely, I couldn't understand.

---

2 **potted** in a container – 5 **stash** *here:* savings – 6 **Speedos** *(pl.)* swimming costume (Australian brand name) – 11 **to cluck** to make a sound like a hen – 14 **take-away** *here:* food from a restaurant which you can take home – 19 **to pull the plug** to defeat, to not function anymore – 27 **Tertiary Admissions Office** institution regulating your admission into a university – 29 **listless** without energy – 30 **crack-up** collapse

No point pressing Gracey. I had learned this over the years. If she had something to tell me, it would come out when she was ready.

"Come on," I said, slapping her on the knee. "There's a table in Hastings Street with our names on it."

5 On the way down the hill I did all the talking. When I'm like that, all my friends have learned to stay quiet and listen. Well, at least stay quiet, anyway. Sally, who was resident computer wizard at Hamilton called it my output mode. She added a few of those techno-head words as well that I didn't quite understand but everyone seemed to find so funny. Something about 10 data overload and stuff bypassing the CPU.

I led her to a little round table under an umbrella and ordered cappuccinos with two slabs of a completely obscene chocolate cake. Only then did I finally look at her face. It was empty. Nothing. There was no energy coming back across the table.

15 "What's the matter, Gracey? Are you worried about getting into Law? Is that it?"

"I'm sorry. I feel sort of … I don't know. A bit flat, maybe. Look, Angela, about uni. There's something I haven't told you."

She sounded so serious, I dropped the good-time mood and waited for 20 her next words.

"I've been offered a scholarship."

"Already! That's great. How come they let you know before …"

She put up her hand to stop me charging ahead like a bulldozer. "No, you don't understand. Not a scholarship to Queensland Uni or anything like that. 25 A scholarship to the Institute of Sport."

"In Canberra," I blurted out. Gracey in Canberra. It wasn't exactly what I had in mind for the year ahead.

"That *is* great," I heard coming from my own mouth. At the same time I told myself to snap out of it. This was terrific news and no one deserved it 30 more. "Wow, Canberra. Cold in the winter they reckon."

"Oh Angela, stop it," she snapped. "I haven't said yes or no yet."

"And that's why you're so down in the mouth, is it? You can't decide."

"That's part of it. I have to decide as soon as the Tertiary Offers come out. Apparently, I can transfer my course down to Canberra University, even 35 Law."

"So what's the problem? Be great for your running."

---

7 **wizard** *here:* a genius – 10 **CPU** central processing unit in computing – 26 **to blurt** to utter suddenly – 29 **to snap out of** *(informal)* to stop – 32 **to be down in the mouth** *(informal)* to be unhappy

She nodded without looking at me. "I'm thinking about staying here, though," she said softly. Then daring to lift her head, she added, "I'm used to Brisbane now, after so long at Hamilton. All my friends are here, you most of all. In Canberra I'd have to start all over again and, on top of Mum and
5 Raymond, I don't know if I can do it."

"Don't go then. It seems to me you win either way. Look, if it helps you, I'll come right out and say it. I want you to stay here in Brisbane. With any luck we'll end up on the same campus together. It's going to be so good."

She grimaced and I was lost again. What had I said? I tossed my hands
10 apart to show my confusion.

She pushed her face across the little table. "It's Auntie Flo, Angela. Remember how I told you she's like ... what do they call it, a matriarch, takes care of people. Well, she's no fool either. She guessed I would be studying in Brisbane this year so she's been onto this cousin of hers, lives in Kingston.
15 Got five kids. It's all teed up. I'm going to live with this family and go to uni each day."

"Shit. Kingston's a long way out. You'd have to get the train in each day ..."

"No, you don't get it. I don't care about the train. It's the family."
20 "You mean too noisy to study?"

"No! Not that." She let her head droop onto her hands. "It will be just like my auntie's place," she moaned. "Out there in Cunningham. I thought I was over that. Hating Cunningham like I used to, before Mum died." Suddenly she looked up, her face flushed with a desperate urgency, her voice pleading.
25 "I couldn't stay with them, Angela. Dougy and Auntie Flo, they thought I'd be around for weeks, right through to the end of January like I always do. But it was worse than going home when Mum was there. At least Mum asked me about school and how I was getting on and was I happy with my friends. They didn't want to talk about that at all. Just the life they know, in
30 Cunningham. And they expected me to slot back into it like I'd never been away. I couldn't. I don't fit in because I don't think like them any more."

She had said things like this to me before, but it had always come across as a kind of loving impatience, as though she wished all her old friends and family had come to Hamilton with her. I decided to meet her head on, even
35 if it sounded a little brutal. "You told me once your mum didn't even know what Hamilton could give you but she wanted you to get it anyway. Well, you

---

16 **to tee up** (*informal*) to arrange – 30 **to slot back** to move back into place

did, Gracey, in spades, and it's changed you. You're going to uni for a start. To do Law, most likely. How many kids out in Cunningham are waiting for an offer from Queensland University?"

"It's not going to uni, Angela. I don't mean that they're ignorant and I'm
5 the big-time student. It's the day to day things. Like …" She paused for a moment, thinking through the best way to explain. Her face came alive as she found what she was after, and she leaned across the table, her eyes wild and shiny with the tears that weren't far away. "Tell me the truth, Angela. What did you think when Jessica Turlington got pregnant?"

10 "Pregnant!" I responded, much too loudly. We copped a glimpse or two and no doubt set a few tongues wagging. But where was this coming from? What had she been up to in Canberra. Was she …? No, couldn't be. Gracey'd never shown much interest in guys, no matter how I pushed a few in her direction. I stopped trying to think ahead of her and thought about her
15 question. Jessica Turlington. One of those girls you met on the first day of Year Eight and the next time you noticed her, it's Graduation Day. Though Jessica didn't make it that far. She started to look a little out of shape before the June holidays and the rumours flew round. Come second semester, there was no sign of her.

20 "Jessica," I began carefully. "I suppose I felt sorry for her. That baby's mucked up her whole life."

"And how did her family take it?"

"Gracey! How do I know?"

"Well, take a guess for me. What would your Mum and Dad say if it was
25 you?"

I took a few moments to think about this. "They'd hit the roof," I said bluntly. "Not that I have any intention of letting a disaster like that happen to me."

"That's just it," she proclaimed as the eyes darted our way again. She
30 threw her arms wide, waiting for me to see the point. "That's what I'm talking about."

"Sorry. You've lost me."

"You called it a disaster. That's the way you'd see it. And your parents too, right?"

35 "Yes," I said uncertainly.

---

1 **in spades** *(informal)* to a high degree – 10 **to cop** to receive – 11 **to wag one's tongue** to talk, esp. about other people – 21 **to muck up** *(informal)* to ruin

"Well, I thought the same about Jessica. What a mistake! What a horrible thing to happen! Hope it doesn't happen to any of my friends. Hope it doesn't happen to me."

"But you haven't been sleeping with guys …"

5 "No, this is not about getting pregnant. It's about the way we look at things. Getting pregnant would be a disaster for anyone our age, right?"

I nodded again, even more confused.

Gracey swayed back in her chair, calming herself. "Did I ever tell you about Nerida?"

10 I shook my head this time, then a distant memory leapt up, half formed. "Didn't I meet her in Cunningham that time I went home with you? She'd been in your class at school."

"That's right."

"She had a little boy," I added.

15 "Stephen," said Gracey. "She came to see me after Mum died. She was pregnant again, and I thought, you poor girl. Two kids before you're eighteen. What a disaster. What a messed-up life, just like I felt sorry for Jessica. Well, Angela, I saw Nerida again at Christmas. Got a little girl now. But the thing is, Nerida's happy. Her mum and dad didn't storm around asking who the 20 father was. Stephen and the little girl are just kids or grandkids. They've got their place in the family same as the rest. Same as there's a place for me with Auntie Flo and my cousins and my brother every time I go home. That's what scares me, Angela. There'll be a place for me down in Kingston but I don't fit into that kind of family anymore. I was so scared when I thought 25 about it that I ran down to the station and booked myself on the first train out after New Year's, before I rang your place. If I couldn't get onto you, I was going to try Karen or Rachael. Anyone. I just couldn't stay there another day."

"You were lonely. That's what you said when you got off the bus."

30 She nodded.

"You don't need to be lonely, Grace. You've got me and my family. You're part of us now. We could almost be sisters. More like twins really."

"I know, I know. But it doesn't seem right."

"Look Gracey," I said, slowing things up a little. She needed to calm down 35 and what I had to say would cut deep. "Your mum's gone. It hurts to think about it but she just isn't there anymore. Dougy's the only close relative you

---

17 **messed-up** disordered

have and he's so different from you. If your mum wanted you at Hamilton, she'd want you at uni even more. She was so proud of you."

"Where am I going to live, though?"

"Why don't you come and live with us?"

5 "I couldn't. It's asking too much of your mum and dad."

"I'll talk them into it. And it won't be forever, will it? Remember what I said about getting a flat or something. By the time we're in second year, we might be able to swing it."

She let my words soak in and I saw a change in the way she was sitting.
10 Slowly the rag doll was coming to life.

"It will be years before you get over what happened, Gracey. It would be the same for anyone. It's not like you'll forget Raymond or your mother, but you've got a life here. It's going to be OK."

She shifted in her chair, folding both arms on the table and pushing her
15 weight down on the elbows. She tossed her hair back and finally looked straight at me, just as the shiny pools beneath her eyes broke into two enormous tears. They hurried down her cheeks. She smiled at me. Smiled at herself. I was looking at a face I knew so well.

4

"Angela, Angela," Mum shouted from the balcony. Gracey and I were in the
20 pool, trying out the bikini which she still refused to wear onto the beach. "Angela," Mum cried again, and she sounded so panicky that a dozen residents appeared on their little balconies, expecting an emergency.

"Carol's on the phone."

That was all I needed to know. Carol was our neighbour in Clayfield. She
25 was collecting our mail while we were away and we had asked her to look out for the letter. I was up the three storeys and into the flat before Gracey was out of the water. First time I'd ever beaten her in a race. "What'd I get? Has she opened it?"

The agony. I could hear paper rustling down the line. The Academy Awards
30 had nothing on this. ("The envelope, please.") She started to read the whole letter, a bunch of official-sounding paragraphs.

---

8 **to swing** *(informal)* to manage – 9 **to soak in** to take in, to understand – 10 **rag doll** a doll made of old pieces of cloth – 29 **agony** [ˈægənɪ] mental suffering

"Please," I begged her. "What course does it say?"

There was a final pause then: "Human Resource Management."

Clunk. There it was. My first preference had been a Bachelor of Business. The letter was offering me my second choice. When I didn't squeal and jump around the room, everyone waiting with me knew. "Human Resources," I said.

Dad took the phone and asked Carol to read the whole letter, while Mum wrapped her arms around me. "Hey, snap out of it. You're going to uni, aren't you?"

I was dripping water into a puddle at my feet. Gracey handed me the towel I'd left by the pool. "What campus?"

"I don't know. Forgot to ask."

"UQ," said Dad, punching the END button on his mobile. "St Lucia."

I started to brighten up after that. It might not have been the right course but it was definitely the campus I wanted. I broke out of Mum's embrace then squeezed her again myself. Dad joined in. "It's good news," he said. "Managing human beings is right up your alley."

Gracey stood by smiling and waiting her turn to congratulate me. Then it struck me. "Your offer must be in the mail as well."

"Oh shit," she murmured, putting her hand over her mouth when the words slipped out.

"Where did you have yours sent? What address?"

"Home, I suppose."

"Which home?"

"Well, I thought I would be in Cunningham."

"So it's gone to your auntie's house."

"Yes. Well, not really. There's no postman in Cunningham. Not on a motorbike like you have in Brisbane. People go to the Post Office to pick up their mail. But Auntie Flo only goes once a week."

"You can't wait that long," I insisted. "We've got to contact her." Then I had a brainwave. "It will be sitting around in the Post Office, won't it?"

"What?" said Gracey, confused.

"The letter, stupid."

"Oh. Yes. I suppose so."

---

2 **Human Resource Management** *Personalwesen* – 3 **clunk** deep metallic sound – 4 **to squeal** to cry joyfully – 8 **to snap out of it** *(informal) here:* to be more cheerful – 10 **puddle** small pool of water on the ground – 13 **UQ** University of Queensland – 15 **embrace** *Umarmung* – 17 **to be up one's alley** *(informal)* to be exactly what one likes – 31 **brainwave** *(informal)* sudden idea

I had Dad's phone out of his hand before he knew what was happening. For the second time in a fortnight I dialled the number for Cunningham Post Office. "Here," I said to Gracey, handing her the phone. "Ask if it's there."

It was, but the postmistress would not open it, no matter how much
5 Gracey begged.

"We've got to find your aunt," I told her.

"How? She's streets away and she doesn't have a phone. None of my relations do."

"Is there someone in the Post Office now who could let her know?"

10 "Angela! That's asking a bit much. I'll just have to wait."

"Could be days. Go on. Ask."

There was a bit of chat back and forth then Gracey said, "Seems like there is a man there knows Auntie Flo and he's gone to get her in his car. The lady says I should ring back in a few minutes."

15 "Tell her we'll hold on."

"But this is STD. Must be costing a fortune."

I looked at Dad. He was chuckling to himself. "Human Resource Management," was all he said.

It took nearly ten minutes but eventually Gracey's aunt was there in the
20 post office. By the sound of things, half the family was with her. There was the same rustling of paper as the letter was torn open, then a woman's hesitant voice came down the line. "Says here, you can do a … Bachelor of Law."

Our unit erupted in yahoos. "Ask her what campus," I told Gracey, but her
25 aunt didn't understand the word.

"Just says University of Queensland. That's all."

But that was enough. Gracey and I were going to uni together.

"Time for a little celebration," Mum announced.

Roll on, I thought. I heard the fridge door rattle and minutes later Dad was
30 there with a bottle of champagne and four long thin glasses.

"What about me?" David wanted to know.

"You can drink champagne when you get offered a place at university," Dad told him bluntly. David humphed and went to fetch himself a Coke. We moved onto the balcony and sat round the little circular table. "A client gave
35 me this before Christmas," said Dad. "Been saving it for today."

---

16 **STD** (subscriber trunk dialling) long-distance call – 22 **rustling** *Rascheln* – 24 **to erupt in yahoos** to explode with shouts of joy – 33 **bluntly** frankly, openly – 33 **to humph** to make a sound of dissatisfaction

He popped the cork and poured the champagne into each glass until the bubbles nearly overflowed. When they died away, there wasn't much wine left in the glasses. He gave a glass to Gracey and me straightaway then went on topping up the other two.

5 "Hey," I complained. "Full glasses, thanks."

"You can have a full glass the day you graduate. Cheers."

I swallowed a big mouthful. Gracey took a sip. "Ooh. It's sweet," she said, giggling.

As promised, I had not said a word about Gracey living with us. Now that
10 the offers were finally here, it would be easier to persuade Tom and Cheryl, but in the meantime I wanted to get the upper hand over something else.

I took the bottle and filled up my glass, ignoring Dad's glare, and after another swallow looked him straight in the face. "I've been thinking about uni. The practical things like getting out there each day. It will take an hour,
15 maybe an hour and a half to get from Clayfield out to St Lucia by bus," I lied. "And I have to get back as well. That's three hours wasted." I paused. Took another swig of champagne. "It makes sense that I get a car as soon as possible."

I stopped to see how this had gone down. Mum and Dad were looking at
20 each other. Not at me. Was that a good sign?

"A car," said Dad as though he'd never heard of them.

I swivelled round to Mum who was watching Dad's face and avoiding my eye.

"I've already saved a thousand dollars."

25 "A thousand dollars," Dad repeated, as though he had never heard of money.

"Gracey will have to stay somewhere, won't she? She'll need a lift from time to time and it's not as if I can use your cars, with you out in them all day."

30 "Angela, stop for a minute," Mum commanded. There was a glint in her eye and I wondered what I had missed. After a quick glance towards Gracey, she focused on me again. "Gracey will need a lift, it's true, particularly as the bus service seems to be so abysmal, as you say."

"What?" I asked, a little confused.

35 "But you just said yourself, darling. Buses from Clayfield out to St Lucia are not the best. And you see, Gracey's going to stay with us." Her

---

22 **to swivel** to spin, turn – 30 **glint** twinkle in your eyes, certain look –
33 **abysmal** [ə'bɪzməl] of very bad quality

face was unable to contain the smile she was holding back. She reached forward and took Gracey's hand. "For as long as she likes."

"But how did …"

"I had to do it on my own, Angela," Gracey confessed sheepishly. "Hope 5 you don't mind. I spoke to Cheryl about it days ago, while you were sleeping in."

I looked at her, amazed. "I'm going to kill you," I said.

She laughed. "What? Kill your own sister?"

But I wasn't finished yet. There was still the question of the car. I stood up, 10 my face flushed from the champagne and hot with my own excitement. "All the more reason for a car then," I said passionately.

"Sit down Angela. There's something else we want to tell you." Dad was laughing now, and if he was laughing it couldn't be that bad. I fell back into my seat, though I missed slightly and nearly went over backwards. "Your 15 mother needs a new car. That little Corolla is not up to the image her clients expect anymore, and besides, the air-conditioning has packed it in. We're picking up a brand new Mazda for her when we get home. But then there is the question of what to do with the Corolla."

"I'll buy it," I said suddenly, surprising myself. What was in that 20 champagne?

They both exploded as though I had said something hilarious.

"Make an offer then," said Dad, trying to look serious.

"Five hundred."

That fixed him. He gave me his stern business glare. "It's worth eight 25 thousand."

Slow down, I told myself. Think this through. There was one thousand, five hundred and twenty three dollars in my account last time I checked. I wasn't going to offer the whole lot – not yet, anyway.

"A thousand, then, but you have to do the registration and insurance 30 while I'm still at uni."

Mum and Dad were enjoying this. You'd think they were negotiating the price of coal.

"A thousand is all right but you pay the rego. We'll pay the insurance and you can get all your petrol on my business account. How's that?"

35 "Done," I said.

---

4 **sheepishly** embarrassed – 21 **hilarious** [hɪˈleəriəs] extremely funny – 24 **stern** hard, serious – 33 **rego** *(AustrE)* car registration

"And one more thing," Mum added, though she was smiling so I knew this last condition was nothing to worry about. "You have to take Gracey to uni each day."

Uni! And the rest. The guys would have to watch themselves. Gracey and
5 I would be hell on wheels.

5

Noosa was the place to be after New Year. No doubt about that. It seemed every time we walked along Hastings Street we bumped into someone else we knew. We hovered about the famously cheap fish-and-chip shop and at night gathered on the beach where someone always had a CD player. There
10 were boys we knew as well, guys we'd seen around since Year Nine, the type you could have fun with, knowing nothing would get too serious.

Maybe one day I'll be happier than I was that last week in Noosa but it will certainly be hard to beat. Gracey finally wore her new bathers onto the sand and the reaction was just what I expected. I could walk along the
15 beach stark naked and I wouldn't get as many looks as she did in that yellow bikini. I guess a figure like hers is the pay-off for all that training.

We met some guys. They were clowning around at a nearby table in the coffee shop, pretending they hadn't noticed us. Worst bit of attention seeking I'd ever seen, so I invited them over to tell them how poor their
20 performance was.

Gracey was so embarrassed she tried to slide under the table while I was calling to them. "Angela, what are you doing?" she whispered behind her hand, as though we were still in the library at Hamilton, on the lookout for Mr Watkins. As the boys brought their chairs over, I had to grab her wrist to
25 stop her leaving.

Rob and Michael. After an hour sussing them out, we challenged them to a horse-and-rider fight in the surf – girls against the boys. Gracey could match them but not me, so the boys became the horses and the girls the riders. This meant choosing a partner.
30 "I'll have Michael," Gracey said quickly, wading towards him and pushing her weight down on his shoulder to force him under. Well, well, I thought. That was fast. Michael was taller than Rob with long untamed hair that fell

---

18 **attention seeking** making other people aware of you – 26 **to suss out** *(informal)* to discover things about – 32 **untamed** *here:* untidy

across his face and the smooth tan of his chest. I had him picked out for myself, to be honest, even back in the cafe, and I felt for a moment that a prize had been snatched from my hands. I had seen Gracey go after what she wanted plenty of times but never a guy. She enjoyed herself too, swaying
5 around on his shoulders, shrieking as she came at poor Rob and me. They beat us every time.

No matter where she was, Gracey went jogging each day and since we were on the beach anyway, she would skirt along the water's edge until she was no more than a speck in the distance. In that final week Michael went
10 with her. Twice anyway. I think he was embarrassed that he couldn't keep up and after the second time claimed a sore calf muscle. Meanwhile, Rob and I soaked up the rays and pretended we weren't lazy.

The boys were as broke as Gracey, but at night we still found ways to string out our meagre dollars. Strolls along the beach don't cost anything
15 and there was always that army of familiar faces to be with. One afternoon, late in the week, the four of us picked our way amongst the rocks leading out towards Noosa Heads. The boys were leading, urging us on, just a little further, a little further. Not many people bothered to come this far. It was so obvious. Gracey knew what they were up to but she wasn't dragging her
20 heels, I noticed. Took Michael's hand at one stage. There, standing amongst the jagged rocks was the first time I ever saw her kiss a guy and she didn't look like she needed any lessons, either.

On Saturday morning we went for a last walk along the beach, just Gracey and me. It was a perfect Noosa day, a few clouds, a breeze coming in with the
25 waves that swirled around our feet. Out on the headland the high tide washed over the rocks where we had walked with the boys. I saw her staring towards it, brushing the hair from her face as though she was embracing the memory and holding it to herself.

"Did you give him our phone number," I asked.
30 She shook her head shyly.
"He asked though, didn't he?"
This time she nodded.

---

3 **to snatch** to take quickly – 8 **to skirt along** to walk along the edge of sth – 13 **broke** having no money – 14 **to string sth out** to make sth last – 19 **to drag one's heels** to be slow on purpose – 25 **headland** piece of land that sticks out from the coast into the sea

"God, I would have given him my number whether he wanted it or not. Didn't you see the way he looked at you. L-O-V-E."

"He was nice," she murmured then looked at her toes in the sand. "But a week is all I can manage at the moment. Love takes up too much of your mind and I'm all full up right now. Do you think I could book him up for next year?"

She was laughing at herself, but it was a funny thing to say, all the same.

"Different place next year," I said, knowing that I had somehow missed the joke. "Dad reckons if you have a great time in one place, then that's a good reason for never going back. Nothing will ever measure up to the first time. He laughs at people who go to the same place every year, same beach, same house, same things to do."

She was looking out to sea now and I thought maybe she wasn't listening, until she said, "Your family always go to the beach, though, don't they? Different beach, same ocean."

"S'pose you're right." I laughed meekly.

"Dougy's never seen the ocean. Did you know that?"

This took me by surprise. I'd thought she was drifting away happily on the warm memory of our days with the boys, of lying on the beach and wandering lazily back to the unit to eat mangoes and dream of the year ahead. But for Gracey, it seemed, there was never a dream that took her away from who she was.

"Dougy's never been in the surf, never felt a wave crash over his head, never tasted salt water."

"Bring him next year," I said rashly.

She laughed suddenly, a personal mocking chuckle that excluded me. "No, Angela, you don't understand what I'm getting at."

She did not try to explain and I was left wondering if this connection of Dougy and the sea, whatever meaning it held for her, had come to mind before that day. If so, she had never told me and I felt for a moment that nameless distance which sometimes fell between us.

Then Mum was calling us and in two hours we were back in Brisbane.

---

5 **to book sb up** to reserve – 17 **meekly** shyly – 26 **rashly** thoughtlessly – 27 **mocking** making fun of

UQ

1

While Dad and the boys unpacked the car (women are the brains in our family, men the brawn), Mum took Gracey and me into the house to settle an important matter. Whenever Gracey had escaped from the boarding school for a weekend, we put a mattress on the floor beside my bed for her
5 to sleep on. Hardly a long-term solution. "The question is," Mum wondered, "do we put another bed in your room, Angela, or do we give Gracey the room downstairs?"

That was tricky. Sure I wanted Gracey to live with us, but I had slept alone in my room since we moved here, twelve years ago. This was where I
10 retreated from Mum, Dad, two occasionally obnoxious brothers, David and Liam, and at times the whole world. When I closed that door I could get angry and cry and talk to myself, some-times dream for hours on end, curl up under the doona on a cold day, just me and a book. Everything was where I wanted it, the posters were mine, the odd little things on top of the
15 bookcase that no one could understand why I kept. But I couldn't say these things, so I gritted my teeth and put my trust in Mum.

It occurred to me that Gracey was ticking off points in her own mind as well, just as I was, but she didn't give herself away either. Sometimes, when she was nervous or uncertain, she would shove her hands into her pockets,
20 just to keep them still, I think. But in summer she lived in loose running shorts which offer no such hiding place. There in the hall, as we waited for the decision, she slipped her hands onto her backside, digging in with the heels of her palms.

Mum raised her eyebrows, appealing for guidance, and when there was
25 none from either of us, frowned as she said, "Gracey, how would you feel about sleeping downstairs?"

As soon as Mum spoke, we both relaxed. It was so obvious that the three of us burst out laughing, then it was down the stairwell to check out the guest room. Normally it was cluttered with junk that didn't belong anywhere
30 else in the house as well as the ironing board which never seemed to get put

---

2 **brawn** muscle – 10 **obnoxious** [əbˈnɒkʃəs] not likeable – 13 **doona** *(AustrE)* type of thick blanket – 16 **to grit one's teeth** *here:* to keep your mouth shut – 24 **appealing for guidance** *here*: asking for a solution

away. Not that day, though. The room had been cleaned out for Grandma and Grandad and there'd been no time for it to revert to its feral state.

Gracey walked in after Mum and me, staring at the single beds on either side of the room.

5 "I've never had a room to myself."

"You have now," I said. "This is all yours. Your place."

She was like a kid with a new toy. When David came looking for us in the afternoon to play tennis with him and Liam, she didn't want to leave.

"Come on," I had to beg. "Tennis is the only thing I can beat you at."

10 I could wallop David and Liam too, much to their disgust. They kept challenging me, hoping one day my form would slip. Not likely. They insisted on boys against girls and it ended up a pretty even affair. If that game was anything to go by, my brothers had already accepted Gracey as though she had lived with us forever.

15 Our plans for the year hit a snag, however, in the form of Auntie Flo. She rang a few days after we returned from Noosa, wanting to know when Gracey would be back in Cunningham.

"I'm not coming back before uni starts," Gracey told her. "Easter holidays maybe."

20 I didn't need to listen in on an extension to know how this news would be greeted. But that was nothing compared to the reaction a little later.

"No, Auntie. I don't want to stay with that mob in Kingston. It's too far from the uni and I don't even know them." Pause. "I know they're our relatives." Pause. "Yeah, all right, I suppose I will get to know them if I move 25 in, but ..."

Auntie Flo wasn't in the mood for buts. She made a long angry speech, her voice seeping out from the earpiece; Mum and I, listening anxiously in the background, could hear her tone.

Gracey was crying by this stage but they were angry tears. "You don't 30 want me at uni. That's your trouble. You didn't even want me to go to Hamilton in the first place. You said it to Mum plenty of times. She told me about it."

Auntie Flo ran out of coins and had to hang up, but she left Gracey distraught. "What am I going to do? She says I've got to be with other Murris, 35 but Cunningham's too hard and I couldn't bear it down in Kingston."

---

2 **to revert** to return – 2 **feral** untidy – 10 **to wallop** ['--] to beat, to hit – 15 **snag** unexpected obstacle – 27 **to seep out** to leak out – 34 **distraught** [dɪ'strɔːt] worried – 34 **Murri** term preferred by Aborigines, used mostly in New South Wales and Victoria, when referring to themselves

I took Gracey to my room and closed the door so that we wouldn't be disturbed. Though she had settled into the spare room, her room now, this was still where we felt most comfortable together, cross-legged on my bed. Here she told me what her aunt had said, filling in what I hadn't been able
5 to piece together. "I guess she knows how it hurt Mum when I wouldn't go home to Cunningham for holidays. Kept finding excuses. Usually to do with you. That's why she's making all this fuss, maybe. She doesn't know you, or Cheryl or Tom. It matters to her where I'm living. I'm lucky really to have someone who cares so much about me. Besides all of you, I mean." She
10 thought about this for a minute. "Lucky twice over. My own mother gone and I've got two women looking out for me."

Later, when I made the coffee, I went looking for Mum and found her hiding away in the little office she keeps off the main bedroom. Not that she does much from home, and somehow I knew that she was not concerned with
15 orders and invoices that night. She was writing a letter, I realised, not on her laptop but longhand. I guessed who it was for. At breakfast the next morning she handed the letter to Gracey and when she'd read it my friend went away to write her own. I sensed again the same connection between the two of them that had surprised me at Noosa. I wasn't invited to see the letters before
20 they were sealed inside the same envelope and sent off to Cunningham. A week later Auntie Flo rang again and spoke with Mum, who shooed us both out of the room.

We went down to Gracey's room this time. And waited.

Mum found us there, later. Instead of telling us the verdict straight out,
25 she looked around the room. "Not exactly girly colours," she said. "And it's looking a little shabby. Could do with a little sprucing up, maybe some new curtains."

This was answer enough. Gracey cried, but though it was partly through relief, I couldn't say they were joyful tears.
30 Mum was serious about the room though, and when she came home from work one day at the start of February and found us idle and apparently bored, she had an idea. "Would you two like to paint Gracey's room?"

What a total disaster that was. More paint ended up on us than on the walls. A tradesman would have been done in a day. It took *us* a week. When
35 we were finished we stood in the middle of what was now a corn-yellow

---

11 **to look out for sb** to take care of sb − 16 **longhand** ordinary hand-writing − 21 **to shoo** to make a sound to send sb away − 26 **to spruce up** to renovate − 29 **relief** *Erleichterung* − 31 **idle** doing nothing

room admiring the result and hugely pleased with ourselves. "We have to celebrate."

Gracey spotted the newspaper at her feet. "What about the movies," she said, digging her toe at the advertisements.

5 Dropping to our knees we scanned the possibilities. She went straight for the blockbusters showing at the big theatres in the city.

"Not those," I moaned. "They're just for air-heads."

"Oh thanks," she said. "I like being an air-head. Movies are for fun."

We'd had this argument before and I made a show of ignoring her. "There's
10 a new French film out. I saw it on *The Movie Show* before Christmas." It took a bit of finding but there it was, on at the Waldorf, a crumbling old cinema that specialised in films the others didn't bother with.

She picked one for herself while I stood my ground. "Great, how are we going to decide?"

15 "Flip a coin?"

Neither of us had one. "I'm not going to see that rubbish anyway," I announced. She knew it was a challenge. And it was on. She grabbed me before I could get out of the room. I was laughing so much I couldn't stop her tossing me onto the bed. I fended her off half-heartedly, grabbing her
20 wrists. "Watch out, you've got paint on your hands."

She looked down and saw a bright yellow blob on the end of her finger.

"Right," she said through her teeth and began to push down towards my face, the paint-splattered finger sticking out.

I held her off desperately, squealing. She was so much stronger than me
25 and slowly the finger came closer. "Don't, don't," I shouted, but I couldn't hold her off. Her finger was in front of my eyes now and I felt the cold touch of the paint as it made contact with my nose.

"I win," she crowed, relaxing the pressure.

I still had hold of her wrists, wondering what the tip of my nose looked
30 like.

"OK, OK. We'll see your movie."

Now the matter was settled, we paused, panting heavily, with the weight of her powerful body pressing on me still. "I'm glad you're here," I told her, suddenly serious.

---

5 **to scan** *here:* to look at – 6 **blockbuster** very popular film – 13 **to stand one's ground** to keep one's position – 19 **to fend off** to keep sth / sb away – 21 **blob** spot of colour – 28 **to crow** to cry out happily – 32 **to pant** to breathe heavily

"So am I, Ange. I had nowhere else to go."

I pushed her off the bed gently and she sat on the floor, letting her guard down. In a flash I had a dab of paint off my nose and onto hers and we were even, but the mock argument had set her thinking.

5 "Angela, in the boarding school I used to get sick of kids from time to time. Even friends like Rachael. I want to be here, it just feels right, but we'll be living in each other's pockets a bit."

"Yeah. I have to confess, I didn't want to share my room with you." The problem hung between us for a moment. "We know each other pretty well, 10 don't we? The signs." I sat up on the bed. "Look at this," I commanded and I crossed my arms, almost hugging myself, a scowl on my face that would freeze the Brisbane River.

"You're not that bad," Gracey protested.

"Not me, dummy. That's you. You're an exploder, a bomb that ticks away 15 silently and then *boom*."

"I am not!" Then after a pause, "Am I?"

"What about me?" I asked, curious.

She leaned back against the bed, considering. "You're not a screamer. You don't shout and swear." No surprises so far but there was one coming. "No, 20 you let your imagination run away with you. That's your problem."

"I don't."

"You do, Angela. I've seen you. You go quiet and moody, same as me maybe, but then you let things get out of proportion inside your head."

"Really?"

25 "Well, you asked. Oh, and you're stubborn like a mule."

I made donkey noises and we laughed, but as the laughter died away we were silent again and I knew she was thinking about what I had said. I was certainly thinking about her description of me. Then I remembered my brothers. "You'll get sick of David and Liam as well, you realise, same as I do. 30 When it gets like that, I just close the door of my room. Everyone knows what that means."

"Yeah, I suppose."

Before she could speak again, David appeared at the door.

"Knock," I shouted. "This is a lady's bedroom."

35 "Ladies," he sneered. "All I can see are two clowns with paint on their noses."

---

4 **mock** pretended – 7 **in each others pockets** closely together – 11 **scowl** a threatening look – 35 **to sneer** to say ironically

Gracey struck like a black snake, off the floor and holding him. I came at him too and before he knew it my smart alec brother had yellow paint on his nose as well, *and* his cheeks and his forehead and in his hair.

2

It was a blistering February morning when Gracey and I set out for the first
5 day of Orientation Week. The heavy traffic put me on edge more than I dared admit and there was no air-conditioner either. We had the windows down for a bit of poor man's air-conditioning, but since we hardly topped fifty Ks the whole way, there was no cooling breeze, just exhaust fumes and the humid breath of the city. We didn't care, though. We felt richer than any of
10 the businessmen who crept past us in their limos, invisible behind the darkened glass.

We reached Sir Fred Schonell Drive and suddenly the whole of Queensland University was spread out before us like some magic fortress. We both took in a sharp breath then laughed at ourselves.
15 The car park was full so I headed for those little corrals down near the river. Unfortunately, they all had signs saying which stickers were needed to park in them and threatening poverty to anyone who dared enter without one. Still, I lucked onto a free spot on the ring road that skirts the edge of the river and soon after we discovered the lake with its arching fountain, its
20 lily pads, its ducks and geese. We were past the lake and on the steep slope leading to the first buildings before my courage failed completely. "Oh God, I need a coffee," I gasped.

"Me too," Gracey croaked desperately. "Something wet. Anything. My throat's like a desert." She hadn't spoken much since we left the car and I
25 realised that if I was nervous she was petrified.

"The canteen is in this building." I said, nodding to our right.

"Trust you to know. You could smell the coffee, couldn't you? You'll end up the cappuccino queen of the whole place." Scared or not, she still loved a dig at me.

---

2 **smart alec** sb who behaves in a smart and annoying way – 4 **blistering** very hot – 8 **exhaust fume** poisonous gases produced when an engine is working – 18 **to luck onto sth** (*informal*) to be lucky enough to find sth – 20 **lily pads** leaves of a water flower – 23 **to croak** to speak in a low and rough voice – 25 **to be petrified** to be extremely frightened

We found the canteen, or refec as everyone seemed to call it; a sterile cafeteria with as much style as a pair of thongs. I hated it on sight. "Come on," I urged Gracey. "There's got to be a better place than this."

And there was, just around the corner, a proper coffee shop boasting
5 tables and chairs framed in thin black metal. Not bad at all. Better than your basic beige plastic, I decided, choosing the best spot. The coffee shop had an L-shaped outdoor section roofed to keep the sun away but open to the river breeze. I led Gracey to a table right on the corner where I could check out both legs of the L. This place had potential, no doubt about it.

10 With my nerves soothed by the coffee (Gracey had a Coke), we wandered round for an hour, in and out of the marquees set out like a school fete. I felt vaguely disappointed because it *was* so much like school – Debating Club, a hundred different sports touting for members. The only difference was no uniform. I was so sick of uniforms, not just Hamilton's but Macca's as well,
15 the striped shirt and shapeless pants. But as I checked out the other first years, I found I was still in a kind of uniform. Girls like me who'd been to a private school stood out a mile – tailored shorts, a Sportsgirl top, a pair of decent sandals or maybe deck shoes. The hair was the give-away though – a pony tail or a simple knot tied behind with a ribbon or some other splash of
20 colour. I took the scrunchy out of my own hair and let it fall free. Maybe a haircut was on the cards after all.

The place finally started to feel like a university when we passed the Gay and Lesbian tent pitched in the middle of the Great Court. Gracey and I joined the Beer Appreciation Society and, of course, the Chocolate
25 Appreciation Society. The queue for student cards stretched along two sides of Mayne Hall, all of it in the broiling sun. Not today, we decided, and headed instead for the bookshop. More bedlam but at least it was indoors. We bought a handbook and with this as a guide went in search of our textbooks. This brought Gracey the first shock of her university career. "Shit, look at the
30 price of these things. This one's more than a hundred dollars!" She moaned as she hefted a huge tome in both hands.

---

1 **refec** (short for refectory) a cafeteria – 2 **thong** *(AustrE)* rubber sandal – 4 **to boast** to show off – 13 **to tout** to try to attract – 18 **deck shoe** sailing shoe – 21 **on the cards** *here:* necessary – 27 **bedlam** noisy confusion – 31 **to heft** to lift up sth heavy – 31 **tome** a large, heavy book

"Do you get a free wheelbarrow to carry it around?" I asked, though I knew this was serious. She'd received a cheque for books and incidentals as part of her Abstudy but it didn't even cover her textbooks. She passed on a few of the less important ones, though how she decided between them was
5 a mystery to me.

The bookshop was only a short stroll from the outdoor cafe we'd discovered earlier so we reclaimed our table in the corner.

"Bloody money," Gracey said, staring at the pile of books. "This will be like school. Broke the whole time. I'm sick of it."

10 I bought the drinks.

Later in the week we returned for ID photos and to take our turn in the queue for student cards. Afterwards, I was held up talking to some girls I knew from the Grammar School and Gracey decided to go exploring on her own. "Meet you in the corner of that coffee shop," I called.

15 When I joined her there, she was so engrossed in a sheet of paper laid out on the table in front of her, she didn't even notice me arrive. I dumped the Hunt Leather backpack I'd bought as part of my Christmas splurge and still she didn't look up.

"You want a cappuccino? I'm buying."

20 The sound of my voice finally roused her, but for a moment I wondered whether my head had disappeared off my shoulders. Hey, come on Gracey, it's me! Then she seemed to snap out of it. "Oh. Not coffee. It's too hot. I'll have a Coke," and she pulled a five-dollar note from her pocket.

"My shout," I said.

25 "No. I've got money. It's my turn. I'm not broke yet," she added savagely.

I took the money and fetched the drinks. "What's so interesting?" I asked when she was still studying the paper on my return.

"It's some sort of flier about a group for Aboriginal students. A black guy gave it to me in the Great Court. Said I should go along. See what they can
30 do for me."

"Like what?"

"Says here it's a support group that helps you through your course. Lets you talk things through if you've got problems. Helps you study, that sort of thing."

---

2 **incidentals** *(pl.)* minor expenses – 3 **Abstudy** scholarship for Aboriginal students –
15 **to be engrossed** to be so interested in sth that you don't notice anything else –
24 **shout** *(informal)* one's turn to buy drinks or food

"You going to join?"

"Me. No. Not my kind of thing really. I've always got you to talk to in any case."

"I can't see you flunking, not after you worked so hard to get into Law."

5   She stayed silent for a moment, examining the leaflet again before slipping it into the side pocket of her bag. "It's just that ... Well, I've seen a few black students around the place." She glanced across at me, showing that timid, uncertain Gracey that only I was allowed to see.

"Well, if it's guys you want to meet, go right ahead," I said, tearing open
10 the little packet of sugar and letting the crystals rain down on the stiff brown foam. "Could meet some gorgeous black hunks."

She laughed. "Maybe I'll send you along first to check out the talent."

"Do they let pale-faces like me in the door."

"Non-indigenous students welcome, it says."

15   "That's me. Non-indigenous."

3

Orientation Week wound up with a twilight concert on the grass just down from the Student Union building. Gracey and I rocked along, feeling more a part of the place now. Then, on Monday, we started lectures.

   Through that first week, I searched the faces, picking out the smart, the
20 conchy and the losers who shuffled into each lecture hall looking as nervous as I felt. My timetable was pretty full but not as heavy as Gracey's. She had lectures right through the day with an hour off for lunch and the odd spare here and there through the week. The only decent break we shared came on Friday between midday and two o'clock.

25   "Ah, long lunch," I gloated when we stumbled across this piece of luck.

   Gracey moaned. "I can see you sitting in the corner of that coffee shop like a spider at the centre of her web."

   We liked this image and laughed about it between ourselves. The spot itself was soon shortened to simply "The Corner" and it became our meeting

---

4 **to flunk** to not pass an exam – 11 **hunk** an attractive man – 15 **non-indigenous** not Aboriginal – 20 **conchy** *(AustrE)* hard-working student – 22 **odd spare** occasional free hour – 25 **to gloat** to say sth with satisfaction

place. So the pattern was set – the tedious drive to St Lucia each morning, then we would separate, meet again some days for lunch or simply a quick hello, and in the afternoons share the journey home. It was just as I had hoped it would be when Gracey turned up at Noosa so desperate and afraid.
5 She began training again with the Queensland Academy of Sport, and when she couldn't cadge a lift with a coach or one of the other athletes I drove her out to the track.

In the third week of semester I got talking to a girl named Fiona Bennett whom I'd smiled at a few times during lectures. We ended up at The Corner
10 and before we'd even sat down Gracey turned up with a companion I hadn't seen before.

"This is Clare Manning," she said. "We're in the same tute."

To Clare she said, "This is my sister, Angela."

Both girls took the bait, staring at us with their eyebrows carving deep Vs
15 across their foreheads. "Sisters?" Clare dared to repeat.

Gracey and I kept a straight face. This was a trick we had played many times.

"You mean like, The Sisterhood," Clare prompted. "You know, sisters in the struggle for black rights. Feminism, that sort of thing."
20 "No, we don't go in for that bullshit, do we, Ange?" Gracey said dismissively.

Fiona tried her own explanation. "Different fathers, is that it? You're half-sisters."

"It would be news to Mum," I answered, trying for a look that mixed
25 surprise and insult. Fiona clammed up, afraid that she'd offended me.

Across the table Gracey went in for the kill. Behind her hand she whispered to Clare, "Angela's adopted but she doesn't know it."

Still the pair of them sat there like stunned mullets until we couldn't stand it any longer and burst out laughing. It took a little while for Clare and
30 Fiona to thaw out and realise they'd been done.

We were both meeting new people and, like Fiona and Clare, we dragged some of them along to The Corner to show them off, then we would talk about them on the long drive home. But with one of these new friends,

---

1 **tedious** tiring – 6 **to cadge** to beg – 12 **tute** *(informal)* tutorial – 14 **to take the bait** *here:* to be fooled – 18 **to prompt** to supply or suggest a word – 21 **dismissively** indicating that sth is not worth thinking about – 25 **to clam up** *(informal)* to suddenly go silent – 28 **stunned** too surprised to speak – 28 **mullet** type of fish – 30 **to thaw out** to become friendlier – 30 **to be done** to have been made fun of

Gracey shortcircuited the routine. She was late meeting me at the car and full of apologies but there was no hiding her excitement. Excitement! She was jumping out of her skin.

"I've just been to the Indigenous Students Support Unit," she said,
5 collapsing into the passenger seat beside me.

"I thought you weren't interested."

"Yeah, well I wasn't. Just thought I'd have a look around, you know what I mean?"

"So what's it like?" I said, feeding her the line. She was desperate to tell
10 me about it.

"It was great. I've never seen so many Murris in one room before. Not in Brisbane, anyway."

It was the word Murri which caught my ear, rolling off her tongue with an easy pleasure. "I never realised what I was missing, Angela. Just to be with
15 other people who ... who look like me for a start. Does that sound silly?"

"I didn't think that mattered to you anymore."

"It doesn't!" she wailed, then realised how she was contradicting herself. "All right, maybe it does. I don't know. The thing is, I met this woman," she babbled on. "Must be about thirty-five. She's doing postgraduate studies.
20 Postgrad, she calls it, like only a bozo would say it any other way. She was telling me what it was like for her when she started. That's why I'm late. We got talking and I lost track of the time. I'll bring her along to The Corner so you can meet her."

"Great. What's her name?"

25 "Rhonda. Rhonda Haines."

That was the first time I heard the name. A name I was going to hear many times in the months ahead.

4

After that first timid visit had turned out so well, Gracey dropped into the Indigenous Students Support Unit almost every day. It was just "The Unit"
30 now. I began to hear a lot about Rhonda Haines and it wasn't long before Gracey brought her along to The Corner. She was an imposing figure, tall, with a solid build and very dark skin. The pair of them towered over me.

---

1 **to shortcircuit** ['sɜːkɪt] *here:* to shorten – 20 **bozo** *(informal)* stupid person – 32 **to tower over** to be much taller

"Hello," I said, offering my hand. "Gracey has told me a lot about you."

"Yeah, I've heard a bit about you. Angela the angel," she said with a snort and then a half-smile that challenged me to take offence.

That was fine by me. I love a challenge. "Sit down, sit down," I said, turning on the Riley charm. "Would you like something? A coffee maybe."

"No, I won't sit down, thanks. I've got things to do."

But she stayed there, standing still, so Gracey remained on her feet as well. "Rhonda's doing her PhD," she told me.

"Oh really," I chirped. "What's your field?"

"Indigenous Australian Literature," she answered.

Oh God. Had I read any black writers? Wait a minute, of course I had. "We did *My Place* in Year Ten, didn't we?" I said, as though I'd answered a quiz question.

Gracey nodded, watching her new friend, who made a face briefly.

"There are better Koori writers than Sally Morgan," she said matter-of-factly.

This was becoming awkward. There were no easy hooks to hang a conversation on and we kept having to start again each time. When there was a sudden explosion of laughter from a bunch of guys nearby, Rhonda hunched her shoulders protectively. She looked as though she wanted to be anywhere else but here.

"I'm doing Human Resource Management," I offered lamely. Compared to a PhD in literature, this sounded like kindergarten. But my words were a dead loss. Rhonda simply nodded her head and glanced at Gracey. This was hard work.

I got her laughing in the end though. "Gracey only went to the Support Unit to meet guys," I said, winking at them both.

"No I didn't," she squealed in protest, lunging forward, determined to strangle me. I had to fight her off and admit it was a lie.

"She's getting a few looks too," Rhonda laughed. "You just watch out for yourself." She nudged Gracey in the shoulder, pleased with the girl's embarrassment and smiling again, a much easier smile than I had seen so

---

2 **snort** sound expressing annoyance and anger – 3 **to take offence** to think sb is being rude to you – 8 **PhD** abbreviation of the university degree Doctor of Philosophy – 9 **to chirp** to speak in a cheerful voice – 15 **Koori** (*AustrE*) term preferred by Aborigines, mostly in Queensland, when referring to themselves – 15 **Sally Morgan** Aboriginal writer whose famous *My Place* deals with finding her indigenous past – 27 **to wink** to close and open one eye quickly

far. She opened up a little after this, but I felt uncomfortable, as though I was pushing too hard and Rhonda didn't want to talk to me. I thought maybe it was the coffee shop itself and later, when she was gone, I mentioned this to Gracey.

5 "I've never seen her here, or any of the Murri kids for that matter. Food's too expensive, I think. They go to the refec sometimes but mostly they hang around the Unit to be with our own."

It sounded strange hearing Gracey say "our own". Rhonda was part of the gang she was talking about but I wasn't. It was the first time I had ever felt 10 excluded from a part of Gracey's life and I didn't like the feeling at all.

Gracey didn't spend all of her time at The Unit. She was seeing quite a bit of Clare Manning, the girl we had embarrassed along with my friend Fiona a couple of weeks before. They had been paired for a seminar which was due in Week Six and took it all very seriously, but when I ran across them in the 15 library they let me talk them into lunch at The Corner.

As we huddled round a table talking, my eyes wandered down the long leg of the L-shaped coffee shop. A guy was dodging his way amongst tables and chairs, staring at us and glancing down only long enough to find a new way through. He was very tall, his shoulders and arms bare under an athletic 20 singlet, his sun-bleached hair tied back in a pony tail. He was looking straight at me as he came on and I stirred in my seat. Things stirred inside too. What was he looking at me for? Did I know this guy? Oh God, I'd like to.

He kept coming, right to the edge of our table, and it was only when he was close enough to speak that his eyes seemed to leave me. "Clare," he said, 25 looking down at Gracey's companion. "I've been looking for you."

Well, I thought, Clare is a surprise packet. I had her pegged as the conchy type who went out once a month with a pimply boy in glasses.

She looked up, unconcerned. How cool was this girl? With a boy like this after her, she might have been a bit more enthusiastic.

30 But I had it all wrong. "It's Wednesday," the guy was saying. "Are you coming down to the courts?"

Clare checked her watch, grimacing at what she found there and I recognised a familiar complacency. "Sorry. I didn't realise the time."

---

20 **singlet** undershirt without sleeves – 21 **to stir** [stɜː] to move slightly – 26 **to peg** to consider – 33 **complacency** a feeling of self-satisfaction

Finally she sat back, ready to introduce Gracey and me. "Meet my brother, Jarred," she said as though she was introducing a vacuum cleaner salesman. Swinging away from me, she started through the motions. "This is Gracey, from my tute group and ..."

5   I was about to unleash the world's most dazzling smile when my chance was snatched away.

"Hey," the guy was saying to Gracey. "I know who you are. That's right, you're the sprinter. I saw you at the State Championships, year before last." For all he noticed, I might have been a steel post holding up the roof.

10   In the end I did get my moment of introduction *and* I tried the radiant smile, but the moment was gone and I registered about minus three on the drop-dead scale. When he left shortly afterwards, loping purposefully away amongst the tables, my eyes followed until he disappeared completely from view.

15   I turned back to the table and found Gracey watching me, an impish grin across her face. I raised my eyebrows and matched her smile.

"I have to go," said Clare, gathering her lecture pad from the table and shoving it into a huge bag. How did she manage to carry it? I've seen suitcases smaller than that.

20   She stood up and looked away in the direction her brother had gone. "Jarred's always doing something active. Wears me out just watching him sometimes. He hasn't worked it out yet, that's the problem."

"Worked out what?" Gracey wanted to know.

"Sport."

25   "What do you mean, worked it out?"

"Schools only invented sport to take guys' minds off sex."

Sounded odd to hear her mouthing off like an expert. I mean, she'd never heard of make-up and as for the top she was wearing, I wouldn't have washed my car with it.

30   I thought I should put her straight on the matter. "I've been out with a few guys who thought they were God's gift to both."

"Yeah," she said without offence, as though I might have a point after all. "Well Jarred, he's still into everything. If it's not running, it's footy or bloody tennis. He drags me down to the courts here every Wednesday to make up

---

5 **to unleash** *here:* to show – 13 **to lope** to run easily with long steps – 15 **impish** playfully bad – 21 **to wear sb out** to exhaust sb– 22 **to work sth out** to understand sth – 27 **to mouth off** to talk proudly – 33 **footy** *(AustrE informal)* Australian rugby – 34 **to make up** *here:* to complete

the numbers. Wish he'd wake up to himself. I've got stuff to do."

"Angela plays tennis," Gracey put in.

Clare was suddenly interested. "Do you? Want to join us? You can use my racquet. My shoes for that matter."

5 I was suddenly terrified. Tennis was my game, sure, but I wasn't exactly on the verge of Wimbledon. What if they were all champions? Gracey was grinning at me again, careful not to let Clare see her face. "You've got to come with me," I begged.

"Me! I don't even know which end of the racquet to hold."

10 "That doesn't matter. I can't go by myself."

"Oh, all right," she moaned, though I knew damned well she was enjoying every minute of this.

There were three people already on the court when we arrived, the beanpole Jarred standing out at one end while a boy and a girl shared the
15 other.

"Clare," a voice called. "Where have you been?"

They waited until the ball sailed over the base line before all three came across to meet us. I was nervous but there was a devil in me too, so when it was time for names, I jumped in. "I'm Angela and this is Gracey. Gracey
20 Goolagong Cawley." The heads snapped instantly towards her. Clare knew what I was doing and kept a straight face. Her brother knew as well and I watched him to see which way he would jump. The others wouldn't have a clue whether the real Evonne Goolagong had a daughter this age. We could have fun here, if this tall guy with the pony tail had a sense of humour. And
25 he did twig to what was going on because he held back, waiting as I did for Gracey to take up the deception, maybe launch in about her "mother" and the years of personal coaching she'd received.

But the gleam had gone missing from Gracey's eyes. She looked down at the cracked green surface of the court for a moment then threw her head
30 back, swishing that black hair loosely behind her. "Angela's having you on," she admitted softly.

We all laughed anyway and then got down to business. Jarred seemed to be in charge. "Clare, you play with Peter. Cathy, you're with me." Where I might fit in wasn't discussed so I sat on the bench beside Gracey.

---

1 **to wake up to** to start to realize – 14 **beanpole** *(informal)* tall, thin person – 25 **to twig** *(informal)* to understand – 30 **to have sb on** to trick sb

"What happened just now?" I asked. "We could have kept them guessing for ages."

She shrugged. "Didn't feel like it."

"You've got to admit we had them going though. You could see their
5   minds ticking over. Could it be? Is she?"

"No, well, I'm not, am I."

"Since when did that matter?"

"Since now," she said with a touch of heat in her voice and I realised too late it was time to back off.

10   She saw the concern in my face and backed off herself. "Sorry, Ange. I'm not angry about it. It's just … well, I just don't want to play these games anymore."

We left it at that and watched the game. Clare's heart wasn't in it but the other three played well, though not so well that I couldn't keep my end up
15   if they let me have a go. This came earlier than I expected when Clare limped towards the bench. "My ankle's not the best. Do you want to take my place, Angela?"

In Clare's shoes and with her racquet in hand, I took my place beside Peter. Jarred was serving and his height made the ball bounce wickedly.
20   There was no quarter given the girls either, I discovered, when he aced me on game point. Right, I thought. I'll get you.

Peter served out his game which we managed to win, then it was Cathy's turn. The first three times I faced service, I whacked the ball back hard only to see Jarred's lanky frame stretch across at the net and volley an easy
25   winner. It was hopeless. I couldn't get enough angle to stop him doing it every time, especially when he started to move even before I had hit the ball. But this early movement gave me an idea. When Cathy served to me again, I waited until I caught Jarred's movement in the corner of my eye. Then I calmly drilled the ball down the side line and watched as it landed inside the
30   tram tracks. Stranded in the centre of the court, he stood there with his racquet still in position across his body, waiting for the ball that would never come.

"Deuce," I informed him, moving into position for the next point.

Jarred and Cathy won the set anyway and we returned to the bench for a
35   drink. "We're going back to the library," Clare announced.

---

19 **wickedly** in a bad way – 20 **to ace** to hit your first service in tennis so well that your opponent cannot get it – 21 **game point** winning point – 24 **lanky** tall and thin, therefore moving strangely – 33 **deuce** ['dju:s] in tennis: score of 40 all

"See you at the car," I called to Gracey and she waved happily enough. There was no sign of Clare's limp now, I noticed as they headed off.

For the second set, Jarred suggested a change of partner. "You're not bad," he told me when we took the court. "The way you passed me at the
5 net before put me back in my box, didn't it?"

"It must be a long box," I said with a straight face.

He laughed. "Not as long as it used to be. I think you just cut me down to size." Then lowering his voice, he added, "Let's beat them, eh."

And we did.

5

10 "All right. Details," demanded Gracey when she joined me at the car that afternoon.

"Manning and Riley won six-two."

"And? Did he ask you out?"

"Give me a break!"

15 "Well, did they ask you to play next week?"

I shook my head in disappointment. "Seems like I was just filling in for Clare. Her shoes and racquet are on the back seat. Can you give them to her?"

"Clare hates it, you know. She'd be happy if you took her spot every
20 week."

I groaned, then when I thought of Jarred, felt myself brightening. "Tall, isn't he?"

Gracey shifted in the seat to stare at me. "I'm picking up rumbles on the Richter scale here." She made sweeping movements with her hand, up and
25 down, up and down. "You've got it wrong, Ange. He's a distance runner, slow and careful. You want to go for one of us sprinters, the volatile, passionate types. We're a lot more fun."

"Maybe I want something that goes on for a while," I murmured.

We were caught behind a bus and I had to change lanes quickly
30 to get past it. When we stopped at the next set of lights she said, "There's a track meeting on Saturday. You want to give me a lift out there? Might like

---

5 **to put sb back in his / her box** to put sb into his / her place – 7 **to cut sb down to size** to show sb that he/she is less important than he/she thinks – 14 **to give sb a break** to stop annoying sb – 23 **rumble** *here*: earth movement – 26 **volatile** ['vɒlətaɪl] lively

to hang around for a while and watch a few distance races."

"Yeah, maybe," I said. "And take that smile off your face," I added, without moving my eyes from the car in front.

Plans. They don't always work out the way they should. On Saturday morning there was a gentle tap on my bedroom door.

"Come in," I called, thinking it was Gracey.

David's head appeared. "Angela. Can I ask you a favour?" Normally David spoke as though he owned half the world and expected to have the other half by nightfall. There was none of that confidence today though. I sat up in my satin PJs, to make room for him at the end of the bed.

"I've got a problem, a big problem."

"What's up?"

"Scored a detention."

"Ooh, nasty," I teased. He was my brother after all.

"The thing is, the detention goes until twelve and my cricket match starts at one."

"So what's the problem? That's plenty of time to get out to your game."

"Yeah, but someone will have to drive me. You know, pick me up from school …"

Ah, now I saw the problem. "I gather you haven't told Mum and Dad."

He shook his head while those enormous feet swept about unhappily amongst my dirty clothes.

"You want *me* to pick you up from school and take you to the match."

"Would you? Please Angela. Say you'll do it."

I was about to say yes when I remembered the athletics. "Sorry, I'm driving Gracey out to the track."

"Yeah, but you could drop her off and come back for me."

"Not today. I want to watch her race," I lied, making my first mistake.

"But what's so special about today? It's not the State titles or anything."

"I just want to see how she goes."

"You can do that next week."

"I was looking forward to this week," I said wistfully.

---

13 **detention** punishment, where you have to stay at school longer – 32 **wistful** sad and thoughtful

He gave me a funny look. "Come on. Please do this for me. Dad will kill me if he finds out."

"Who gave you the detention?" I asked and this was my second mistake.

5 "Anderson."

The much detested Mr Anderson. I had heard about him from boys I went out with, even guys who had never been to David's school.

If he had made silly promises to be my slave for the rest of his life, it would have been easy to fob him off. But instead he just sat on the end of
10 my bed dejected and vulnerable. I'm a sucker for dejected and vulnerable.

"All right. I'll pick you up at twelve."

He exploded with a hissing "yes", and made a triumphant ball out of both fists.

At eleven o'clock I dropped Gracey at the track behind ANZ Stadium
15 where the events were already under way. By midday I was at the gate of David's school. He piled in and immediately began to strip out of his uniform, at the same time reaching for the cricket whites he had tucked away in his bag. "Not this way," he called when I pulled the Corolla back into the traffic.

20 "What do you mean? I know the way to your playing fields."

"My team's not playing at home. Our game's out at Ipswich."

"Ipswich! That's halfway to Uluru. Shit David, you should have told me this morning."

He stopped undressing. "Sorry."

25 But what was I to do? Stop the car and tell him to hitchhike? So I made a round trip to Ipswich and by the time I returned to the athletic meeting Gracey had finished her races. She had some bad news as well. "There was a really tall runner in the 3000 metres. Came third, it looked like to me, but he's gone home already. Better luck next time."

30 I let out a long sigh. "I suppose it would have looked a bit obvious."

"Since when has that bothered you?" she said.

"Don't pick on me, Grace. I just want to meet him again and sort of look a bit tennis-ish." I demonstrated a graceful backhand, trying my best to keep a straight face while she cracked up.

---

6 **detested** not liked – 9 **to fob sb off** to take no notice – 10 **dejected** unhappy – 10 **vulnerable** easily hurt – 10 **sucker** *(informal)* person affected by sth – 22 **Uluru** [ˈuːlʊruː] Aboriginal name for Ayers Rock – 32 **to pick on sb** to criticise sb – 34 **to crack up** *(informal)* to burst into laughter

"Do you want me to talk to Clare?"

"Don't you dare. Can you image what she'd say to him? 'That Angela chick is hot for your body.'"

"Well, it's true, isn't it?"

5 "No," I said indignantly.

"Clare doesn't seem to think he'd care much if you were."

"I don't know," I said dreamily. "There's something there."

I drove home thinking about what it might be.

6

There was no sign of Jarred early in the week and I certainly wasn't going to
10 sit around at The Corner hoping he'd show up. By Tuesday afternoon I knew
that I wouldn't be invited back for another game of tennis, though I must
admit I waited until the last minute before packing up and heading off to
my lecture.

As I was hurrying across the Great Court, a voice called to me, a familiar
15 voice attached to a waving arm and a beckoning hand. Gracey was sitting
amongst a bunch of black kids on a park bench thirty metres away. I was
hauled over.

"This is the girl I was telling you about," she announced to the group with
so much enthusiasm I felt a little embarrassed. She started to introduce me
20 around. "Tegan, Mia over there. This is Gavin," she said, pointing to a thickset
young man with a face wrecked by acne. He looked about twenty. There
were two other guys, Benny and Frank. Frank wore a Michael Jordan T-shirt
and did his best to look like an American basketballer. He was the friendliest
of the lot and kept talking to me even when I moved on to meet a girl called
25 Shirley and her friend whose name I didn't catch because Frank was
drowning out Gracey's voice. He was so funny, the type you couldn't help but
like from the first moment you met him. It was easy to chat out there in the
courtyard and they seemed like a great bunch.

Then Rhonda turned up. "Got yourselves a token white girl, I notice," she
30 said, greeting everyone. "Great, we can get into the whitefella's pub now."

---

5 **indignantly** angrily (*entrüstet*) – 15 **to beckon** to wave sb over – 17 **to be hauled over** to be made to come over – 26 **to drown out** to be louder than – 29 **token** alibi

They laughed and so did I though I could see a couple of faces turn my way to see how I would take this. Give me a break, I thought. As if I'd be upset by that. But I should have been warned. Rhonda told them she had some news, then turning to look straight at me, she called, "Got
5   some secret business to discuss here."

It was the term "secret business" that confused me. "Do you want me to go?" I asked seriously.

They all cracked up.

"She's just having you on," said Gracey, laughing with the rest.

10   Done like a dinner. I tried my best to laugh it off then slipped away to the lecture, but I was steaming just the same. I'd never let one of my friends do Gracey like that.

Gradually, as the weekly routine drew us on into the year, Gracey came less and less to The Corner. Not that it mattered. We spent so much time
15   together anyway, in the car, at home on the week- ends, there was no need. Friday was different though. Because it was the last day of the week, we used the two-hour break we shared in the middle of the day to rest and think about the weekend, sometimes on our own, sometimes with a new friend of Gracey's, though more often it would be Fiona Bennett or another
20   friend of mine.

It was during this long break on Friday, with Gracey and me sipping coffees like a couple of "ladies", that Jarred Manning turned up.

"Hi," he said shuffling towards the table. I realised it was shyness that was making him awkward. "You didn't come down for tennis on Wednesday."

25   "You didn't invite me," I replied bluntly.

"No, I suppose I should have been more up-front."

"Do you want to sit down?"

At this Gracey got to her feet. "I have to see Rhonda before I go home. She wants to give me some stuff to read." And before I could protest, she
30   was gone.

Jarred had ditched his athletics gear though his broad bony shoulders were still evident under the polo shirt. "You never told me what course you were doing," he said.

"You were so keen on downing poor Peter and Cathy, you didn't give me
35   a chance."

---

10 **to be done like a dinner** (AustrE informal) to be fooled – 25 **bluntly** direct – 26 **up-front** frank, honest – 34 **to down** here: to criticize

"Guess I'm a bit competitive." His long arm looped up like a monkey's and scratched the top of his head. When he saw me watching him he let his hand smooth down his ponytail self-consciously and grinned that I had caught him out. "So, what are you doing?"

5 "Human Resource Management. And you?"

"I'm doing Human Movements."

"Well, at least we're both human," I blurted out, cringing as soon as I heard the words. What a pathetic thing to say. I wanted to bite my tongue off.

10 He seemed to think it was funny though and started to relax. Maybe he thought that if I could say something stupid and get away with it he didn't have to worry so much. "First year, are you?"

I nodded. "What about you?"

"Third."

15 Third year. That made him at least nineteen. In the next thirty minutes I never did find out his age but I didn't care. He told me he didn't want to go into teaching with his degree. He wanted to do a post-grad course in America and end up running a place like the Institute of Sport. Most of all he wanted to coach elite athletes.

20 "Like Gracey," I said.

"Oh yes," he sighed, with an awe that could only be genuine. "I've seen her run. She's something special, that one. She could go all the way if she sticks at it."

"You're a runner yourself though."

25 "Of modest credentials." He chuckled, mocking himself and granting me the warmest smile. It was that moment which set me going, when he gave a glimpse of himself, free of pretensions and the clumsy attempts to impress that so many guys hide behind.

"So you will bring your racquet on Wednesday?" he confirmed and I

30 realised that he was getting ready to leave.

I didn't want him to go just yet. Tennis wasn't enough.

"Do you like Woody Allen?" I asked.

"Woody Allen?" he murmured.

Oh, no, I thought. Don't tell me he's never heard of the greatest film

35 maker in history.

---

1 **competitive** [-'---] determined to be more successful than others – 7 **to blurt out** to say sth without thinking – 21 **awe** [ɔː] feeling of great respect – 25 **modest** *here:* average, not brilliant – 25 **credentials** *(pl.)* abilities – 27 **pretensions** *(pl.) here:* making yourself more important than you really are – 27 **clumsy** awkward

"*Annie Hall*," he said. "With the subtitles. Saw it on video years ago. Really clever."

"*Clever*. It was hilarious," I said, setting him straight. "There's a festival of his films on at The Waldorf this weekend."

5 He looked mildly interested. "Actually, I like his more serious films," he told me, standing up and placing his large hands over the back of the chair. "*Hannah and Her Sisters*. I thought that was his best."

"It's the feature on Saturday night. Do you want to go?"

He looked at me as though it had never occurred to him that two people
10 might go to the movies together. "Yeah, I'd love to."

He rode a bike to uni but offered to pick me up in his father's car.

"No, I've got my own car. I'll pick *you* up." I watched to see how he took this news. Some guys didn't like to be driven, though there was no way I was backing off if he was one of them.

15 No worries. We made the arrangements and he strode away with the same purposeful gait I had seen the week before.

7

Here was a dilemma. Ever since our return from Noosa, Gracey and I had gone out together on Friday or Saturday night, sometimes both, but she didn't like Woody Allen much. "What's the point of a movie you have to
20 discuss afterwards to work out what it was about," she always complained. Besides, I didn't know whether I particularly wanted her to tag along.

Luckily, this ticklish situation was avoided when she announced, "There's a party Saturday night. A house full of girls I met at the Unit. Thought I might go." Her tone suggested that I wouldn't like it so I graciously didn't
25 press the point.

I drove her over to Taringa then headed for the address Jarred had given me.

Hannah and Her Sisters is such a great movie, we started arguing about it before we'd left the theatre. "Mia Farrow, she's so passive aggressive," he
30 insisted.

---

8 **feature** main film – 14 **to back off** to give up one's intention – 16 **gait** way of walking – 22 **ticklish** *here*: difficult

Passive aggressive! That was a new one, though I could see what he meant. "She was forced into that kind of role by her husband, though." To convince him, I tried my best to imitate Michael Caine's voice in the first scene. "She's so beautiful."

5 To my surprise he came out with the next line, though his attempt at Michael Caine was even worse than mine. "I just want to hold her and kiss her and take care of her."

I'd seen it enough times to know what came next. "Stop it, you idiot, she's your wife's sister."

10 It seemed a natural thing when he took my hand for the walk back to the Corolla.

"What a situation to be in though. Her husband and her sister, two people she loved."

We took the whole movie apart over coffee and again on the way back
15 to his house. Gracey would have been tearing her hair out if she'd come with us.

"See you down at the courts then" were his final words after he'd extracted his long limbs from the passenger seat.

On Wednesday, after Jarred and I had ruthlessly dispatched Peter and
20 Cathy once more, Gracey joined me at the car for the ride home. She was silent at first as we struggled to break free of the heavy traffic around the uni itself and I realised there was something coming. She was still wrestling with it silently when he reached Coronation Drive.

"All right," I said in mock exasperation. "Out with it."
25 "I don't know how to say it, Ange."

"Oh great! Now you've really got me worried."

"Shit, I'm making a mess of it and I haven't even started."

"So start!"

"OK, OK. It's Shirley. Do you remember her from that day in the Great
30 Court."

"Not really."

"It was her party I went to. She shares that big old house with two other Murri girls. There was a fourth but she left at the end of last week."

Still I didn't suspect, even though Gracey paused and stole a quick glance
35 at my face, as though she was waiting for me to guess. Finally she had to say it out loud. "They've asked me to move in."

I nearly ditched us in the river. "Move in? But what about ..." I managed to stop in time. To be honest, I was going to say "what about me", because that was the first thought that came into my head.

We had a plan going, with a lot of maybes and it was at least a year away, but it made an easy picture, Gracey and me, in a unit some-where, with friends dropping in and generally vegging out as we pleased.

"Do you mind, Angela?" she asked sheepishly. "If you don't want me to, I'll
5 say no. I have to tell them by Friday so they can look for someone else. Money's pretty tight and they need an extra person to spread the rent."

"It's your decision, I suppose." What a weak thing to say. The truth was, I was too stunned to work out what I really thought.

"Yeah, I know it's my decision but I wanted to talk it through with you and
10 Cheryl."

"I thought you were happy living with us. You know, sisters."

"I am, but ..." She couldn't leave that one hanging between us. She seemed to gulp air a few times then spoke again. "It's being round other black kids. Ever since I went to the Unit, I've felt so much better about being
15 here. It's probably hard for you to understand, Angela. You've never lived amongst people different from you, and it's not just the way I look, my skin colour. It's feeling at home, being with a mob who pick up the same things as me, little things like being looked at in the refec and having lecturers worried you won't be able to keep up."

20 "I thought you didn't notice things like that anymore."

"You always notice, Angela. It's just a matter of whether you care or not. Trouble is, I got used to being the only one. Now I'm not alone anymore."

"You were never alone, except for those first few weeks at school, maybe." I didn't like the way she sounded. There was no insult, no anger in her voice,
25 but I was unsettled, hearing her speak like this. "You've always got me."

"I know. And I'm grateful. You're my closest friend and that won't change. I promise. But I've met these other kids now and I like being with them, same as I like being with you. Rhonda says if I'm a Murri I should live with other Murris. Be good for me, after all those years at Hamilton."

30 So it was Rhonda's idea. And what was this about *after all those years at Hamilton*? Gracey had been happy there. If anyone knew that, it was me.

---

3 **to veg** [vedʒ] **out** *(AustrE informal)* to relax, do nothing – 8 **stunned** shocked or surprised

"I want to do this, Angela," she continued, convincing herself, by the sound of things. "It might help me with the way I feel about Cunningham and Auntie Flo and Dougy. Do you see what I'm getting at?"

"Yeah, I do," I said doubtfully. "But I don't think Mum's going to see it that way."

I was wrong though. Dad was away for a few days in north Queensland, so when David wandered off to his homework and Liam to bed, there was just the three of us. Slowly, choosing her words more carefully than with me in the car, she told Cheryl what she wanted to do.

Mum heard her out without interrupting, then, when I expected her to start in with stuff about Gracey being too young and needing to stay with a family that cared about her, all she said was, "It will be tough. You realise that, don't you?"

"So you think it's all right?" my friend asked timidly. Like me, she was surprised that the first reaction seemed so calm.

"We are not your parents, Gracey. Not even your guardians. If this is what you want to do, we can't stand in your way. But you shouldn't go into this all starry-eyed. Have you worked out whether you can afford it?"

"I've got my Abstudy. It covers the rent easily."

"Yes, but living in a house with other girls, there's more to pay than the rent." Mum turned to me. "Angela, get a piece of paper, so we can write down a few costs?"

Mum took the blank sheet of copying paper from my hand and slashed a rude line down the middle. "OK now. Income," she said, writing the word at the top of the first column. "Abstudy. How much is that per week?"

Gracey told her and she printed in the figure neatly.

At the top of the second column she wrote "Expenses" and immediately noted down "rent".

"My share is fifty-five dollars a week," said Gracey.

"Have they asked you for a share of the bond?"

"Bond?"

Mum explained.

"Guess I'll have to find out."

---

14 **timidly** shyly – 18 **starry-eyed** *(informal)* enthusiastic but unrealistic – 30 **bond** money given as security to the landlord

"It's a one-off payment, I suppose," Mum muttered to herself. She left a question mark beside the word then went to work on the rest of the column, repeating each item slowly as it was added. "Food communal, lunches at uni, other groceries, clothing, transport, athletic
5 expenses, personal hygiene." The list went on and there wasn't much Gracey or I could point to and say "don't need that one". Mum started again at the top of the list, working out an amount for each one then tallying the figures. It did not look good. Expenditure outstripped income by sixty dollars a week.

10 It was guesswork, of course. Gracey wouldn't really know how much she would spend until she moved into the house. But she was crestfallen, just the same. "I'll have to get a job," she murmured.

Mum leaned back in her chair, her eyes still on the paper. "It would seem so," she said, being very careful not to make this sound like *I told you so*.

15 "There's waitressing jobs sometimes on the noticeboard at uni," said Gracey.

"And fifty girls trying for each one," I added quickly.

Mum made a humphing noise to show her agreement. "Just so long as you know what you are getting yourself into, Gracey. You can always come
20 back here if things go bad."

That was it! It was settled. Mum sat there twiddling the pen in her fingers until she saw us staring at her and self-consciously placed it neatly on the sheet of paper with its ominous column of figures. Gracey was going to leave us, probably on Saturday morning, and Mum was acting as though
25 she had just finalised a business deal. Gracey stood up and for a moment it seemed she was going to head for the front door then and there. I made a whimpering noise, more out of shock than dejection, but it was enough to set Mum off. She staggered out of her chair, knocking it over as she grabbed for Gracey, pulling her close. I was on my feet too, making a three-way bear
30 hug, unsure of who I was holding. We sobbed until we laughed then sobbed again, composing ourselves only when David came out of his room to see what was going on.

Next morning Gracey appeared puffy-eyed.

"You look like you slept under a tree," I said.

---

7 **to tally** to compare – 8 **expenditure** expenses – 8 **to outstrip** to be greater in amount than – 11 **crestfallen** disappointed – 21 **to twiddle** to nervously move sth with your fingers – 27 **to whimper** to make a low crying sound – 33 **puffy** swollen

"Didn't sleep much at all," she admitted and we laughed as Mum watched quietly from the breakfast table. "I'm going to tell Shirley that I need a week to think about it."

"Sensible," Mum commented. She worshipped "sensible", my mother.

5 For much of that week Gracey stayed in the room we had painted together, studying the heavy tomes she bought in O week, though when I visited her each evening to say goodnight, and maybe have a little chat, there were always a few titles that didn't sound much like Law books. *The European Invasion of Australia,* was one that caught my eye.

10 "You're going, aren't you?" I said to her on Thursday night, after we had managed to avoid the topic for nearly a week.

She nodded.

Strangely, I didn't feel that emotional. Maybe having those few days to think it through was the best thing that could have happened. It was Mum 15 who went all weepy on Saturday morning when we loaded Gracey's few worldly goods into the Corolla and headed for Taringa. Around the familiar streets of Clayfield the car felt weighed down with the uncertainty of leaving, but after a few minutes the mood changed, as though the sun had suddenly appeared. This was an adventure, even if I was only allowed to go 20 part of the way. I glanced across at Gracey. "Are you having second thoughts?"

"What if I don't get on with them? Hanging around together at uni is one thing, sharing the bathroom's a bit different."

I decided it was time to hit her with another practical difficulty. "This 25 place hasn't got a TV, right?"

She nodded.

"That means no Melrose."

She looked genuinely stricken for a moment or two. Gracey was more addicted than I was.

30 "I've got the answer, though," I explained, smiling confidently. "Come home from uni with me each Tuesday, have dinner and we'll watch Melrose. Then I'll take you home afterwards."

"You're a genius, Angela," she sighed

I neglected to tell her that this was Mum's idea, probably so 35 she could keep an eye on Gracey, though she didn't quite put it that way.

---

6 **O week** week of orientation for new students – 27 **Melrose** short for *Melrose Place*, an American soap opera – 28 **stricken** overcome with sadness

We skirted the edge of the city, the ugly glass tower of Toowong Village growing bigger in the windscreen. I had only seen the house in darkness and still had in mind a vision of Gracey's new home as a big rambling house like ours, a little shabby maybe to give it character, with lino down the hall and
5 jungle for a backyard. When we found the street and Gracey told me where to pull in, this image was shattered. There stood a tumbled-down Queenslander perched on rotting wooden stumps not much more than head height. Most of the fence was gone and what remained fell back into the overgrown garden with a disgruntled air. The front veranda had been
10 built-in with fibro panels and louvres, the whole place daubed in a flaking pink-brown paint, walls, doors, gutters, the lot.

"You've got to be joking," I said to Gracey.

"It's OK inside," she assured me, though when we had lugged the bags up the front stairs, I wondered what made her think so.

15 "This is my room along here." We turned right just inside the door and Gracey led me into an alcove that was really part of the veranda with partitions in place to separate it from the rest of the house. There was a bed, a rickety wardrobe and a desk.

"You can't swing a cat in here, Gracey. You sure this is what you want?"

20 She looked around at the same things I had seen and shivered, not with disgust but with the pride of possession. "It will be OK to sleep in and do a bit of study maybe. Besides, the rest of the house is better. Come on. I'll show you."

In the hallway we met Shirley. "Thought I heard someone," she said. I
25 remembered her now, slim with tight black curls frothing all over her head and a permanent smile. She seemed an easy girl to like and I began to feel a little better about Gracey moving in.

"You know Angela, don't you Shirl?"

We exchanged nods. "Come on through. Wendy's doing the shopping but
30 Barb's here."

---

4 **lino** ['laɪnəʊ] short for linoleum – 6 **tumbled-down** old and beginning to fall down – 7 **Queenslander** wooden house standing on posts, typical for Queensland – 7 **perched** placed – 9 **with a disgruntled air** *here:* looking badly – 10 **fibro** *(AustrE)* ['faɪbrəʊ] cement-like building material – 10 **louvre** ['luːvə] similar to wooden shutters on a window to keep strong sun out – 10 **to daub** [dɔːb] to cover with sticky liquid, e.g. paint – 10 **flaking** small pieces of paint coming off – 16 **alcove** small part of a room – 18 **rickety** unstable – 19 **You can't swing a cat in here.** *(informal)* This is a very small room. – 25 **frothing** looking like foam or bubbles

So my best friend was now part of a foursome. Shirley, Barbara, Wendy and Gracey. I could smell coffee. I needed a coffee.

We made our way along the hall and since I was last in line I took the opportunity to stickybeak through each door. Typical students' rooms on opposite sides of the hallway. Couldn't see the floor in either of them for the dirty clothes, books, sheets kicked off in the night. The living room was tidy though, despite the stuffing bulging from an armchair and the column of bricks holding up one corner of the coffee table.

"What do you think?" Gracey asked me, knowing damned well I didn't think much of it at all.

"Bit run-down," I dared to say.

"A bit!" crowed Shirley. "It's a dump."

"Why do you stay here then?"

"'Cause the rent is two-twenty a week, that's why. If there was somewhere better for the money, we'd move – eh, Barb." She directed the last bit towards the kitchen.

"Bloody oath we would," the voice of an unseen Barbara replied. "Gracey, you want tea? How about your friend?"

Gracey called back. "Yeah, tea's fine. Coffee for Angela. Real strong. She's about to faint."

"No, I'm not." I laughed, pushing her. "It's just a ... surprise really. I was picturing something nice and cosy."

"Yeah, with a comfy armchair next to the phone and somewhere to put your feet up," she teased.

"Shouldn't the owner fix a few things up? Like that table," I said, pointing.

"Nah. Not worth his while," Shirley explained. "This house is going in a few months."

"Going?"

"Off the blocks. There's town houses being built here. Instead of pulling this thing down, they whack it on the back of a truck and take it some place, do it up, sell if off. No point touching it now though. That's why it's so cheap to rent."

The mysterious Barbara finally appeared from the kitchen and we all sat around the lounge room chatting. If I had closed my eyes, this was just how

---

4 **to stickybeak** *(AustrE informal)* to look secretly into – 7 **to bulge** to stick out from – 11 **run-down** in poor condition, not well looked after – 12 **dump** ugly and unpleasant place – 17 **bloody oath** *(vulgar)* swear-word – 23 **comfy** *(informal)* comfortable

I had imagined Gracey and me spending our time next year, if my vague plan had come off.

We were rinsing out the cups when there was a shout from the front door. "Anyone home?"

"That's Rhonda." Gracey bounded down the hall, calling a welcome. I expected them both to continue on into the lounge room, so when they hadn't appeared after a few minutes, I went searching.

"I'm just showing Rhonda my room," Gracey said as I joined them.

"Not exactly the Hilton, is it, Rhonda?" I suggested, winking at her.

"I wouldn't know," she replied instantly. "Never been in the Hilton."

Well, neither had I for that matter, not in one of the fancy suites. It was just an expression. It felt like I was on the tennis court again, serving an easy ball to warm things up, only to watch foolishly as Rhonda sent it whistling past my nose for a winner. I wanted to like this woman, especially as Gracey seemed to adore her. But, shit! She wasn't making it easy.

I wasn't going to give up yet though and the Angela Riley charm usually won people over in the end. "Where do you live, Rhonda?" I asked.

"Bardon," she answered. Nothing else.

"What, a house like this one or a flat?"

"House."

Oh Gracey, help me, I thought. But she wasn't paying attention. From one of her bags she pulled out a book and a pale yellow folder of photocopied pages. "I read all this," she said to Rhonda. "I cried all the way through it."

"Cried?" She was waiting for more, as though Gracey had let her down if this was all the reading had done to her.

"Angry too. I suppose I was getting more and more angry the further I went."

This seemed to satisfy her. They both stared at me for a moment before Rhonda took the book and the papers from Gracey's hand. "Got another one I thought you should look at. A novel this time." She took a thin, much thumbed paperback from her shoulder bag and held it out. Something about wild cats, I read from the title.

After that they launched into a discussion of yet another book Rhonda had given Gracey to read. No wonder she'd been locked away in her room

---

11 **fancy** decorative – 14 **to whistle past** *here:* to make a high sound while moving – 33 **to launch** to start

so much lately. I didn't want to be rude, but after five minutes of talk that went straight over my head, all political theories and something about language as oppression, I backed out of the tiny room and waited in the hall. They seemed to take the hint and followed me.

5   "You'll be happier here," I heard Rhonda say. To give her the benefit of the doubt, I suppose she thought I wouldn't hear her say this. But it was a damned cheek really. What did she know about Gracey and how happy she was living with my family?

   "You settling in all right?" Rhonda continued. "Anything I can help you 10 with?"

   "No. Not at the moment anyway. Angela brought all my gear over in her car."

   "That made it a bit easier for you then." I earned what looked almost like a smile. What did she think I was going to do? Make Gracey take the bus? I 15 was so uncomfortable.

   "It was the least I could do. We've been best friends since Year 10, haven't we, Gracey?" I said, taking a step closer, and then my judgment went completely haywire. If I live to be a hundred I will never do a more embarrassing thing. In front of this woman who seemed to rub me up the 20 wrong way just by standing there, I put my arm round Gracey and said, "Best friends forever, eh Gracey?"

   What can you do when you've just said such a stupid thing. I giggled like a moron, of course. Rhonda stared at me with a look of pity and even Gracey cringed. I straightened up and let my arm drop away. Oh God, why did I do 25 it?

   I just had to get out of the place now. I made a big show of noticing the time and how I had to pick up Liam from his cricket match. "See you on Monday, Gracey."

   "Yeah, OK Ange. Thanks for bringing me over. And don't tell Cheryl too 30 much about this place, will you."

   She had to cup her hands to the side of her face before she finished, because I was almost to the car. I have never left anywhere in such total panic before. I was so confused, I drove straight to Liam's cricket match, arriving when he still had an hour to play.

   I hate cricket.

---

7 **cheek** rudeness – 18 **haywire** out of control – 19 **to rub sb up the wrong way** to make sb angry – 23 **moron** idiot – 24 **to cringe** to be very embarrassed

Sorry Day

1

After Gracey moved into the house in Taringa, we saw more of each other during the day than ever. I think she was a little unsure of herself and needed to keep hold of comfortable, familiar things. That was me. Ms Comfortable. We had a coffee together in The Corner most days while she
5 told me about Shirley and Barb and that Rhonda Haines.

"Rhonda must think I'm an idiot, after the way I embarrassed myself in front of her."

"No, she's nice, Angela. She didn't say anything about it."

I wondered which was worse, to be laughed at or ignored.

10 "Rhonda's had a hard life, Angela. She was taken away from her mother when she was young." The way she said this, I expected more, as though she was going to tell me Rhonda's life story. But she looked away into the distance, distracted. "Maybe you can't understand how she feels."

As for me, well, I wasn't sure if I wanted to know Rhonda's life story.

15 I missed Gracey, missed having her in the house, there to talk to whenever I wanted, a companion in the car to make the slow journey to St Lucia more bearable. But in some ways I was set free, and the void left by her departure was quickly filled by Jarred Manning.

He was with me, the week after Easter, when Gracey came running from
20 the Union building, calling to me in The Corner and waving a shred of paper in her hand. "Quick, your mobile," she demanded.

My hand found it automatically inside my day pack. I used it so much it was always on top of the lecture pad and an occasional library book.

"What's the emergency?" Jarred wanted to know. I could see him looking
25 around for a fainted body on the concrete or smoke pouring from a window.

"A place in Toowong wants a waitress," Gracey whispered rather comically. She was so excited the whole cafe was watching her and heard every word. She looked down at the scrap of paper. "Cafe Carlo. I was at the noticeboard

---

17 **void** emptiness

just now checking out the jobs when it was pinned up. No one else has seen it yet."

By now she was through to the manager who was obviously just as bowled over as we were. Gracey listened for a while, breaking in here and there. "I'm eighteen" was one answer. Suddenly her face fell at something the voice said, but she recovered, biting her lip for a moment before she spoke. "Yes, I've had experience. I was a waitress at … er … Sizzler last year."

She rolled her eyes at me, her ear still glued to the phone. "Cappuccinos? Sure, no problem. They're my specialty. "

She made arrangements for an interview on Friday afternoon then ended the call.

"Specialty," I wailed. "You don't know the first thing …"

"Angela, you're the expert. You've got to help me," she begged, grabbing my collar. "This job is perfect for me." Suddenly her shoulders slumped in dejection. "The cappuccinos aren't going to be my biggest problem though, are they?"

"Your heavy tan, you mean?"

She nodded.

"Let's go round and look the place over anyway." Had to keep her courage up. "It's Tuesday so you're coming back with me for dinner – we'll get Cheryl to work out a strategy."

I took her back to Clayfield, via a brief stopover in Toowong, then laid the problem before my mother.

"Um, what were the waiters wearing?" she asked.

"Black pants and a black T-shirt with Cafe Carlo across the chest," I answered, "Oh yes, and a long black apron tied round the waist like those up-themselves French waiters."

"Wouldn't do any harm to let him know you'd checked out things like that. Got anything black, Gracey?"

"Jeans," she said. "Only black T-shirt I've got has an Aboriginal flag on it."

"Oh great. Sort of defeats the purpose, don't you think?"

We raided Mum's wardrobe and found a black top which Gracey put on.

Mum stood back for the full effect. "Neckline's a bit low but that won't do any harm, I suppose."

---

4 **to be bowled over** to be overwhelmed – 9 **to be glued to** to be fixed to – 28 **up-themselves** (informal) very proud or arrogant

As Gracey blushed, I joined Mum, adding, "We'll slick your hair back really tight, you can borrow my new silver earrings and add a splash of bright red lippy. Then it's up to you."

"Yeah, but I want him to give me a job, not ask me out."

5 We sat down to eat, and from the way Gracey attacked the plate, it was her first decent meal since her last visit. Afterwards, I filled her in on how cappuccinos were made. "The machine always sounds like it's about to explode, but there's nothing to it really."

Late on Friday I called for Gracey at the house and we did her hair and
10 make-up with the supplies I'd brought with me. At the cafe we walked in together and asked for the manager. "My name's Gracey. I phoned you about the job."

Her words hit him while he was still giving her the once over and I could almost see his thoughts tumbling through his brain. Waiter, black girl, very
15 pretty black girl, until finally, "Who's this?" he asked turning to me.

"Oh, sorry. This is a friend of mine. She drove me down here for the interview." As Gracey explained I backed away slowly.

They sat for a while talking, smiling once or twice, then she was taken behind the counter for a closer look. Gracey's body suddenly switched from
20 apprehension to excitement and I knew the answer, even before she swept up to me, dragging me outside.

"I got it," she shrieked to everyone passing in the street. "I got the job. Start tomorrow night."

"That's great," I said, feeding on her enthusiasm. "I'll be your first customer.
25 Check out your cappuccinos."

"Don't you dare. Not until I can do it properly. The boss sounds like a great guy. Name's Russell. I think he knows I'm lying about the experience but he says it's all pretty straightforward. If I do OK, he'll give me extra hours. For now, it's just Saturdays, four till midnight. Oh Angela, this is going to make
30 all the difference."

Difference to what, I thought, but there was no time to ask. I was picking up Jarred at seven and Gracey was on for a night out with the girls. It felt strange to part like that just as it was getting dark. Once we would have headed off together on a Friday night, but not any more.

35 It was that night I heard about Sydney. Jarred took me to a party where I happened to hear one of his running mates talking about a trip down south during the mid-year break."

"What's on?" I asked.

---

1 **to slick back** to put a lot of gel on your hair – 3 **lippy** (informal) lipstick

"University Championships. They're extending the season 'cause of the Commonwealth Games trials in August. Jarred can tell you all about it. He's going."

Was he now, I thought, and the wheels started to turn over.

2

I allowed Gracey two Saturdays to learn the ropes before Jarred and I descended on her. Once I took a good look, Cafe Carlo was trendy in name only. Sure, it had cute little tables and chairs on the footpath under a couple of impressive umbrellas, but inside it looked more like a milk bar. It was the kind of place you would go for a coffee after the movies if you were too lazy to look round for some place better.

"Oh hi!" she said with a tired sigh once she spotted us. She let me inspect her uniform – the same black jeans but now with a Cafe Carlo T-shirt. "Let me guess. Two cappuccinos, skinny for you, Angela, and heavy for Jarred."

"Do you have any cake?"

"Yes, but you don't want it."

When she brought the coffee, she sat down. "Russell says I can take a few minutes."

She talked about the job, though it sounded no different from mine at MacDonald's. Go, go, go, all the time. If the boss was a bastard you were no more than a slave.

We would only have a minute together like this, so I switched to the second reason I had come to see her. "Listen, I wanted to ask you about something. You too, Jarred," I added. They both stared at me suspiciously.

"Are you two going to the University Games in Sydney?"

"I am," said Jarred.

Gracey was not quite so sure. "I want to go, but it's a bit expensive getting down there."

"Why don't you both drive down with me. We'd have a great time – the harbour, King's Cross, all those shops." They both grimaced when I listed the

---

2 **trials** *(pl.)* test sporting competition – 4 **the wheels started to turn over** thoughts start going through your mind – 5 **to learn the ropes** to learn to do one's job – 6 **to descend on** to arrive unexpectedly – 6 **trendy** modern and fashionable – 13 **skinny** with low-fat milk – 13 **heavy** with full cream milk

last of these attractions. But there was no hiding their enthusiasm for the idea.

"Sounds great. Really depends on my training, but I'd love to see the bridge and everything," said Gracey after a brief pause to think it over.

5 Jarred was as economical as ever. "Sure."

The boss, Russell or whatever, caught Gracey's eye and she was quickly on her feet.

Jarred and I finished our coffees and headed off to see the latest James Bond movie. (All right, so I did enjoy a bit of escapism now and again.) My
10 last words to Gracey were, "See you at The Corner."

But she didn't come to The Corner. Not on Monday, or Tuesday, though she did drop by to tell me she couldn't make it for dinner. I was hardly alone, though. Jarred and I were now spending a lot of time together, sometimes in the library but more often in the coffee shop. He seemed to have forgotten
15 his lunchtime runs in favour of lunchtime with me. And I looked for him everywhere I went around the campus. It was easy to work out why, though I didn't dare to put a word to it. I needed to talk. I needed Gracey.

Calm down, I told myself. The chance would come. But on Friday, she didn't turn up at the usual time. I took a heavy book from my bag and began
20 to take notes, to keep Jarred out of my head as much as anything else.

It didn't work. My mind wandered back to Saturday night, to the movie and afterwards when we had strolled down by the gardens and found the moon reflected in the glassy surface of the river. Later, in my car, we had lingered over saying goodnight. No, "lingered" is not the right word.
25 "Passionate" or maybe "steamy" give a better idea of how we went at each other. There in the cafe I found myself doodling in the margin of my notes and then to my horror discovered I had been practising a signature: Angela Manning, enjoying the flow of my pen through all those "n's" and finishing the final "g" with a flourish. What was I doing!
30 At one o'clock a new batch of students spilled onto the paths heading for the refec, one of them Fiona who spotted me in The Corner and sat herself down. Before I knew it I was telling her what I longed to tell Gracey. "It's a bit scary feeling this way about a guy. Up till now I've always stayed in control, never letting anyone get too close."

---

24 **to linger** ['lɪŋgə] **over** to spend a long time – 25 **steamy** *(informal)* erotic – 26 **to doodle** to make little drawings while thinking – 26 **margin** *Rand*

Fiona considered my problems as though she was a regular agony aunt, offering a few comments here and there. But she knew she was there as a sounding board and I appreciated that. I liked her, though it was not the same. She wasn't the girl I trusted to keep my feet on the ground whenever my fantasies sent me floating away.

At five to two I packed away my unread notes and headed for a tutorial in the depths of the Forgan Smith building. As I hurried around the edge of the Great Court, I couldn't believe it. There was Gracey sauntering towards me with a friend on either side. One of them was Frank, the Michael Jordan impersonator, who was the first to spot me as I headed straight at Gracey like a cruise missile. He began to act up for my benefit just as he'd done the first day we met. I'd thought he was a lot of fun at the time, but my mood was different now and I ignored him rather pointedly.

"Where have you been?"

"At the Unit with these guys," she said happily.

"I was waiting for you in The Corner," I told her, and as soon as I heard my voice I regretted it.

The smile left Gracey's face. "I'm sorry, Angela," she said. "I didn't know you were expecting me. What, do we have a date now every Friday, like a meeting?"

"No," I answered, knowing how silly that sounded. I felt suddenly deflated, as though all the anger had disappeared with one sentence. "It's just that I need to see you. I've got a few things on my mind and well ... you're the one I usually talk things over with. I thought you'd be at The Corner today, that's all."

We had walked away from the other two by now, far enough for some privacy. Gracey took a moment to look back at them before she stared into my face. "Angela, I tried to tell you before. I can't afford to sit around in The Corner any more. You sort of have to buy something, a coffee or a Coke, or they start looking at you like you're taking up table space for nothing. It's too expensive. For what a drink costs in that place I can buy my whole lunch round at the refec. It's hard, Angela. Harder than at Hamilton. I've got to watch what I spend and I'm not working at Carlo's so I can drink cappuccinos here at uni."

I felt ashamed. "I didn't realise, Gracey. Is it really that bad? Mum and Dad could help out ..."

---

1 **agony** [ˈægənɪ] **aunt** newspaper adviser, therapist – 8 **to saunter** to walk unhurriedly – 21 **deflated** disappointed, feeling empty

"No, I don't want that. I can get by, if I'm careful. Trouble is I had to send money home to Dougy last week, so I've been a bit strapped. That's why I didn't come to The Corner. Look, if you really need to talk, why don't you come round to the house. Today's no good because I'm going over to Rhonda's, but tomorrow is fine, until I start at Carlo's at four."

Fine for her but no good for me. "Tomorrow I have a shift at Macca's. Sorry. Life's getting a bit complicated."

Gracey rolled her eyes in agreement and everything was OK between us again. "There's always Tuesday. I promise not to cancel this time."

What could I say? "Tuesday night then."

3

She was true to her word, and when I came out of my final lecture the following Tuesday, there she was, leaning against a sandstone pillar with a heavy bag at her feet. The weather was cooler now, heading towards winter. Her running shorts were gone and instead she had on a pair of khaki overalls with a black T-shirt underneath. Not exactly high fashion but she was on a tight budget these days so I bit my tongue.

She waited until we were in the Corolla before she told me about the meeting.

"Rhonda's mother is speaking. Shirley and the others are all going. Would you be able to drop me over there after tea?"

"Sure. Whereabouts?"

"A hall in West End."

The meeting was forgotten in the excitement of catching up. You'd think Tom and Cheryl hadn't seen her for a year. The boys were still clearing away the last of the dishes when Gracey turned to me. "Time to go," she said, touching her watch.

Mum heard her and looked a little disappointed. "Where are you off to?"

"There's a public meeting I want to go to. Angela's going to give me a lift."

"Public meeting!" said Mum.

I had to admit, it did sound a little strange.

---

2 **strapped** (*informal*) short of money – 11 **to be true to one's word** to keep one's promise

Gracey didn't flinch. "Yeah, there's a bunch of Kooris speaking tonight over in West End."

Suddenly Mum's face dropped its playful smile. "Is one of them Derek Campbell?"

5 Where'd she dig that name up from? Gracey didn't recognise it though, anymore than I did. "Maybe. I don't know for sure. I'm going to hear the mother of a woman I know."

"Who's Derek Campbell?" I asked Mum.

"Oh, he was in the paper this morning, that's all. Did you read the
10 article?"

Who was she kidding? She didn't seem in a hurry to explain the sudden seriousness though, so we left.

"How will you get home afterwards?" I asked when we were halfway there.

15 "Don't know. I'm meeting Shirley and the others at the meeting. We'll work something out."

"I was hoping to have a talk," I said. "There wasn't much chance tonight with Cheryl and the boys around. What if I come to this meeting and we go somewhere afterwards?"

20 "I don't know, Angela. It'll go for a couple of hours. You'll be bored out of your tree."

"What's it about?"

"Aboriginal business, really. Don't know if there'll be many whites there."

But as we pulled into the street beside the hall, it was clear that she was
25 wrong about that. Sure, there were plenty of Aborigines milling about and greeting friends, but there were just as many white faces.

When we linked up with Gracey's crowd, there wasn't just the three girls from the house, but Frank and another Aboriginal guy who stuck close to Gracey as we searched for seats. He ended up sitting beside her. We were in
30 one of those old school halls with a stage at one end, double doors at the other and dozens of windows along each side, all pushed out like wings. Every available inch of floor was taken up by rows of folding seats. The place was packed and so noisy we had to shout to be heard, until a woman on the stage rose from her chair, swinging the microphone lead to where it would
35 not trip her up. Her confident calls to order soon had the crowd quiet and she began.

---

1 **to flinch** to show a reaction – 20 **to be bored out of one's tree** (informal) to be extremely bored – 25 **to mill about** to move around – 35 **to trip sb up** to make sb fall

"Our first speaker tonight has been travelling around the country to meetings like this for weeks now. He's a busy man most of the time because he's the director of the Indigenous People's Health Support Unit. But he's taken time out from his job to speak to us about his life. He's going to tell us
5 his story tonight, so I'll hand over the microphone to Derek Campbell."

My head shot up at the name. So Mum did know what she was talking about. I looked across at Gracey to see if she recognised the name, but her eyes were focused solemnly on the speaker.

Derek Campbell looked a bit short of fifty, no taller than me really but a
10 ball of muscle under his baggy shirt. He took a moment, like the chairwoman, to swing the microphone lead around to where he wanted it and to gather his thoughts at the same time. Then he started to speak, in words I could barely understand at first, but after a while I realised he was telling us all where he came from. Not Sydney where he lived now, but where he was
15 born and where his family, his brother-cousins as he called them, could still be found. It seemed we had to know this about him before he could tell his story.

"I'm one of the children who was taken away," he began. "When I was four years old, they took me from my mother and I never saw her again. Never
20 heard from her, never knew who she was and after a time I even forgot what she looked like. Most of all, I didn't know who her people were. So I didn't know where I was from until I was much older – until I was an adult." He stopped there for a moment and I stole a glance along the row. Gracey and her friends waited eagerly for him to continue.

25 "I believed my mother was dead because that's what I was told. I was adopted, you see, by a non-Aboriginal couple. Their name was Campbell and they gave me their name. In time I forgot that I had any other name. They were very good to me, the Campbells and I suppose you could say I was treated like any other kid in the neighbourhood while I was growing up.
30 Because of that I keep the name Campbell, to remember them, because they are both dead now, God rest their souls.

But Campbell is not the name I was born with. I had to search out my original name – it was the first step I had to take when I finally decided to trace my mother. You see, she hadn't died when I thought she did – as I was
35 told she did. She lived for another twenty years after I was taken away. She

---

3 **Health Support Unit** *Gesundheitsfürsorge* – 9 **short of fifty** under fifty years – 34 **to trace** to find

was alive all the time I was growing up and when I started work, even when I landed a job in the Public Service down in Canberra. She only died in 1985. It's hard enough to know that I was taken away and very hard to know I missed out on meeting her again when I was grown up, but that's nothing 5 compared to what I found out when I did track her down." He paused significantly. "You see, for twenty years she had been trying to find me again and always she was beaten by the laws that stopped people like her finding out what happened to their children. No information was given out, no matter how many times she asked, no matter how much she begged.

10 So she was gone when I discovered my place, my people. She was gone, but not the rest of my mob. At the age of thirty-six I discovered I had a brother and three sisters and by that stage a dozen nieces and nephews. Got more now. Brother-cousins for my own kids. There were aunts and uncles too of course and that made a huge difference to my life – it was like 15 I was born again the day I drove out to meet them." He choked on these words, pausing, while every ear in the hall waited silently, the only sound the faint cry of a baby behind us and the gentle swish of cars passing in the street.

"This family, these people I didn't know I had, these people taught me 20 who I was and showed me where I belonged ..." He was overcome again and took another silent break to compose himself. "They told me about my mother. They say she died sooner than she should 'cause of her grieving, grieving for me that she was never able to let out and that festered inside her. That sort of grief will kill you. There's plenty of people here tonight who 25 know that."

He turned and made a small bow towards the other speakers behind him who were waiting for their turn. Then he looked out at the audience, which was still as quiet as in church and slowly swept his arm in an arc around the hall. It was an invitation, clear and irresistible, to share his mother's grieving 30 and immediately the silence was broken by a gentle weeping, one person in front of me, another behind. There were little pockets in every part of the hall. We had all been moved by the story and I looked around to see that many non-Aborigines were, like me, on the edge of tears as well.

Three seats along from me Gracey was crying silently amid her own grief, 35 remembering her mother, taken by death perhaps rather than human hands but taken just the same. She fought gamely, wiping the tears before they

---

2 **to land** *(informal)* to get – 2 **Public Service** *Öffentlicher Dienst* – 11 **mob** *(AustrE informal)* family – 15 **to choke** to gasp for air – 22 **grieving** suffering – 23 **to fester** to grow worse

escaped onto her cheeks and I heard Shirley beside her whisper, "Let it go, Gracey. This is the place." Shirley's hand was on hers, squeezing her fingers gently. I wished I was next to her, holding her other hand, but it was too far for me to reach. There were tears I could not hold back now, for Gracey's
5 mother and for Raymond whose despair had driven him to take his own life.

Other speakers followed Derek Campbell, each with a different story. Yet it was also the same story: of separation, of loss of family, of loss of country and of an overwhelming grief for what had been taken away.
10 Finally, Rhonda's mother took the microphone. Like the others, she had been taken away as a young girl. "We had a name for the men from the welfare board. The gubba men," she said, spitting out the word. "My brothers and sisters, we lived in fear of the gubba man everyday of our lives until finally he came for us, one by one. I was taken to an orphanage, hundreds of
15 miles from my people. Just me. None of my brothers and sisters were taken to the same place. Dozens of us black kids there were in that orphanage, dressed up in those starched uniforms, rules about everything and the strictest rule was this one. *Don't talk about your family*. It was like we had no past, as if we were only born on the day we arrived at the orphanage. When
20 I was old enough, they sent me off to be a servant in one of them big homes out in the bush.

"Of course it wasn't long before I had kids of my own. It was hard for me 'cause I didn't know my own mother, my people. When they took me away, they took these things away from me too, so I had to fight on my own to
25 keep my family together, fight against the reasons they had, the excuses for stealing my children, that the white way was better, that I couldn't take care of them, that I wasn't a fit mother. All lies. I was a good mother, I was!"

She shouted these last words into the microphone and I knew they were not just for us, the audience, sitting there. She was shouting at the men who
30 had passed this judgment on her so many years before.

"I was lucky, maybe," she continued. "Only one of my kids was taken and I got her back in the end. She's here tonight." The woman paused while she picked out Rhonda in the crowd. "But there's plenty who never got their kids back, never got to pass on the knowledge of their people and there's still

---

12 **welfare board** *Sozialamt* – 12 **gubba** *(AustrE informal)* name given by Aborigines to a white person, mostly if working for the government – 14 **orphanage** [ˈɔːfənɪdʒ] institution looking after children who have no parents

some who know their children are out there and don't even know who they are."

None of this quite prepared me for what followed. The chairwoman opened the floor to questions, and after an awkward silence a woman three or four rows in front of us worked her way timidly along the seats to the microphone stand in the aisle. In a trembling voice she began. "I don't have a question, actually. I just want to say something … for myself … to all of you who have spoken tonight." Her voice quavered and cracked as she was overcome by these words, but she fought her way back. "I want to say, I'm sorry that these things happened. If I could change the past I would, but all I can offer you instead is the promise, my own promise, that nothing like this will ever be done to you again."

Then she stepped away from the microphone, giving way to the emotion that she had suppressed long enough to get the words out. There was some spontaneous applause from a few in the audience, but when this did not become general, the embarrassed hands were quickly stilled.

As the woman reached her seat, crying openly now, a man rose close to the aisle. Again, there was no question, but an expression of deepest sorrow and regret. This man was followed by another and soon there were people standing all over the hall, ignoring the microphone to speak to whoever could hear them. The momentum built and for ten minutes it went on like this, without a word from the speakers on stage. When finally there were no more wishing to speak, the microphone was offered to Derek Campbell once again.

"When you ask politely for something to be done, decade after decade and still they ignore you, it's time to stop asking and start demanding. You have to protest, you have to grab their attention. We're going to do that, here in this city and all over the country, two weeks from now, on National Sorry Day. There's going to be a rally at the Roma Street Forum and then a march on your Parliament House."

This met with an enthusiastic cheer and after some details were outlined and we were all urged to take part, the chairwoman stood and thanked the speakers each in turn, Derek Campbell especially, and declared the meeting closed.

As we shuffled from the hall I felt light-headed as though I had been part of something unique and important. Gracey seemed to push through the

---

8 **to quaver** to speak in an unsteady way – 21 **momentum** force – 28 **National Sorry Day** special day in Australia to apologise to the Aboriginal inhabitants for doing them wrong – 32 **to urge sb to do sth** to persuade sb to do sth

crowd and when I saw Rhonda Haines in the distance, I realised why. When our group gathered round Rhonda and her mother, I was careful to hang back, feeling self-conscious. I had not set eyes on Rhonda since that embarrassing performance back at the house. I managed to stay pretty well
5 hidden until, after much respect and approval was heaped on Rhonda's mother, the talk turned to the protest rally and march.

"You'll all come on the march," Rhonda insisted.

Gracey and the others fell over themselves. "Of course we'll be there."

I stepped forward too, smiling as best I could. "I'll be there," I added. It
10 seemed like the least I could do and, in fact, I felt rather proud of myself, as though I was joining those people who had stood up in the meeting and expressed their sorrow.

Rhonda pricked my ballooning pride with a single glance. She didn't say a word, or even change the expression on her face. She simply didn't respond,
15 yet it was as though she had held up a sign: *What does she want to come for? We don't need her*. At least that was the way it seemed to me and the others picked up her disapproval instantly. It was an awkward moment but it passed, and still floating on the heady mixture of sadness and exhilaration that hung in the autumn air, we made our way to the car.

20 At the car I got more than I bargained for. Of course I was going to drive them home and I didn't mind that, but as well as the four girls, Frank and the other guy were there standing beside my little Corolla.

Gracey saw my frowning face. "What's up?"

"I don't know about this. I've only got five seat belts."

25 By that time Shirley was sitting on top of Frank in the back and Gracey was squeezing onto the unknown male's lap beside me. "Relax," Gracey urged, then turned to her friends and said, "Now she knows where the old expression comes from, "Full as a coon's Valiant."

The car rocked with laughter but it was at my expense. I felt off balance.
30 Dad would kill me if I was booked for overloading. Gracey paid a little for these sardine-can arrangements, though. Her overalls gaped open at the

---

3 **self-conscious** uncomfortable, very aware of one's doings – 13 **to prick** *here:* to destroy – 13 **ballooning** growing fast –18 **heady** exciting – 18 **exhilaration** [ɪgzɪlərˈeɪʃən] strong feeling of happiness – 28 **coon** *(offensive)* black person – 28 **Valiant** Australian Chrysler car, first built in 1962 – 30 **to be booked** *(informal)* to be charged (by the police) – 31 **sardine-can arrangement** overcrowded and tight sitting – 31 **to gape open** to come apart

sides as she squirmed uncomfortably on the guy's knee. "Stop it," I heard her hiss more than once and I couldn't help noticing where his hand had strayed. It set me wondering what she was up to now that she had a room of her own and a batch of new guys in her life.

5 What worried me more was the way the mood had changed since Rhonda had given me that disdainful look. As we drove off towards Taringa, talk in the back seat was mainly of the stories told on stage, especially Rhonda's mother's, but once we'd crossed the bridge, they moved on and the comments became more bitter, of white oppression and the petty racism
10 they all seemed to suffer each day. Now I knew how taxi drivers felt when I gabbled to friends at the top of my voice as though the cab was steering itself. It was getting to me. To hell with it, I thought. The night wasn't all misery and woe. "What did you think of the apologies?" I asked.

No one seemed keen to answer. Frank piped up first. "Sounded all right, I
15 suppose," he said sheepishly.

There was another brief pause before Barb's voice broke in. "Load of shit, if you ask me."

There was a murmur of agreement.

"But didn't they mean anything to you at all?" I said.

20 "Meant a lot of people wanted to unload their guilty consciences, that's what it meant," Barb replied.

"Yeah, what's the point of all those people standing up one by one," Shirley added. "Not going to change anything. Did you listen to that first woman? 'I promise it won't happen again,'" she quoted. "How's she going to
25 stop it. She's just one person, not the government."

I was stunned that the excitement I felt, the sense of being part of a moving occasion, had not touched them at all, or at least not in the way it had touched me.

"You know what I mean, though, don't you Gracey?"

30 She twisted on the boy's knee to face me. "Easy thing to apologise, then you go back to your nice comfortable home and nothing's changed."

It was obvious she meant my comfortable home and everyone in the car knew it. Outnumbered six to one I let it go. Oh God, it was taking forever to reach Taringa.

35 My passengers didn't so much climb out of the car when we arrived as fall out. "You coming inside?" Gracey asked.

---

1 **to squirm** to move around uncomfortably – 2 **to stray** to move, to wander – 6 **disdainful** full of dislike– 9 **petty** minor

I sighed. We had always said what we thought, Gracey and I. Things were better out in the open. "I don't know if I'm welcome," I said bluntly.

Her shoulders tightened, scrunching hard in against her neck as she stuck her hands in the back pockets of her overalls. "Try to understand, Angela. This
5 stolen children thing means a lot to us. It's very painful."

"I do understand," I answered quickly. "I'm just surprised they didn't pick up on how sincere those people were, the ones who got up and said sorry."

"It doesn't make the grieving any easier. You don't understand the grieving that's going on."

10 "I was there, too. I heard those people speak about their grief. I know how it must feel."

"You! You don't know what grief is, Angela. Not like Dougy and me or the people who spoke tonight, Rhonda's mum and the others. You've never lost anybody close to you. You told me yourself, the only loss you've ever suffered
15 was when your dog got run over."

Gracey was saying what she thought, observing our fearless rule just as I had done, and now she was paying me back in spades.

We had both said our piece now and normally the mood would have switched back again and we could relax. "I'm sorry if we gave you a hard
20 time on the way back here," she said. "There's a lot of anger in there right now. Maybe it would be better if you didn't come in."

"Yeah, well, I gathered that. But why do I have to feel like I've committed some dreadful crime?"

"The anger's not aimed at you, Angela. Until you've been angry at a whole
25 bunch of people, you'll never understand."

That was the second time she'd told me I couldn't understand something, as though I was blind and she despaired of ever showing me a sunny blue sky.

I gave her a sceptical look and headed home.

4

30 There was no sign of Gracey at The Corner on Friday, but somehow I'd known she wouldn't show up. Jarred sat with me for an hour until he had a class, and there were others buzzing by with a quick wave, some stopping for a chat. I still loved my Fridays.

---

2 **bluntly** openly – 17 **in spades** *(informal)* to a high degree

I was home by half past three. David usually went into town with his mates after school on a Friday, officially to use the CD Roms at the State Library but I doubt they even darkened the door. Liam sometimes went to Mum's showroom and caught a ride home with her.

5 An assignment was due on Monday and I had the notes ready to type up, but my mind wasn't on the job and after fifteen minutes I deleted the few rambling, meaningless sentences I had written and switched off the computer. Funny, really. There were times when I longed to have the house to myself. That afternoon though, I prowled around like a caged tiger. Dialling

10 Fiona's phone number earned me yet another of her father's corny answering machine messages. This one went, "We're all flat out like a lizard drinkin' but we're goanna be free soon, so leave your number after the tone." I'd strangle him if he was my father.

I tried Jarred's number though I had seen him only a few hours before and

15 I would see him again tomorrow. Mrs Manning told me he was out for a run.

So I went back to prowling, knowing that inevitably I would be drawn down the staircase to the yellow room. The ironing board was back in place and each bed had an odd collection of items showing the faintest layer of

20 dust. I picked the least cluttered, transferred everything to the floor and lay down with my hands behind my head. This was how I did my thinking.

The walls still looked freshly painted and why shouldn't they. It was only a matter of months. The yellow was everywhere, even on the tip of my nose if I crossed my eyes and concentrated on the fuzzy knob of flesh that

25 wouldn't quite come into focus. Come on, I told myself, Gracey had chosen what was best for her, what she wanted, and I was glad about that. This room was never more than a refuge for her, a holding station while she sorted out the panic of last Christmas.

That's what I told myself, but behind it all I couldn't deny what was

30 bugging me. I wished she had never gone anywhere near that Indigenous Students Support Group. As quickly as the anger flowed into me, I chased it out again with shame. Gracey had found something there. I hadn't seen her

---

7 **rambling** confused – 9 **to prowl around** to move around – 10 **corny** not original and therefore not amusing – 11 **to be flat out like a lizard drinking** (AustrE informal) to be fully extended – 12 **goanna** large type of lizard, common to Australia (Wortspiel mit **gonna** = going to) – 12 **to strangle** to kill with one's hands – 20 **cluttered** in a untidy state – 24 **fuzzy** unclear – 24 **knob of flesh** here: her nose – 27 **refuge** safe place to stay – 27 **holding station** place where you stay for a limited time only – 30 **to bug** to upset

so excited since she went off to the Australian Secondary School titles in Year Eleven. But that was just a few days down in Sydney and then she was back again. She wasn't coming back this time, not to this room.

The sound of the automatic garage doors broke my thoughts. Heavy feet on the floorboards above my head. At least one brother was home. No, that was too much noise. Both of them. After a few minutes I heard Mum's hard heels on the staircase and waited for her to appear in the doorway.

"Thought you must be down here," she said.

When I stayed where I was, apparently hypnotised by the ceiling, she stepped over to the other bed. I heard objects being moved, stood against the wall, put away in the wardrobe, and then the telltale sound of a body easing itself onto the mattress.

"She's growing away from us, Mum."

"Do you think so? She still comes to dinner on Tuesday, doesn't she? Only missed the once since she moved out."

"It's more than just getting together. I don't even know what kind of friendship we have anymore. We can't talk like we used to."

Mum shifted on the bed, and when I looked across, she had folded her arms behind her head, imitating me. When she was settled again, she said, "Some friendships last and some don't. Gracey's tied up with some powerful forces, most of them inside herself. In the end, it's got nothing to do with you."

"I know, I know," my voice pleaded, stretching out the words for emphasis. "I keep saying to myself, let her be. I don't have to be at the centre of her life. I just want to be part of it. But it's hard. I feel like I'm being slowly passed over for someone better, like a boyfriend, for God's sake. Now there's something. A new experience for me." I laughed bitterly.

"I wish I knew what else to say, darling. I was never as close to a girl as you've been to Gracey. It does seem strange to me, though. I thought you two would be friends till you were old and grey."

"Old and grey! Seems a long way off to me," I murmured. "Just the rest of the year would be fine." I was angry again and the words came quickly. "I'm being pushed out and it's not right. I'm better for Gracey than any of those others."

It was that bloody Rhonda Haines whose face lingered behind my eyes. Gracey was a different person when she was around.

---

11 **telltale** *here:* indicating sth – 35 **to linger** ['lɪŋgə] to stay, not go away

"Well, I don't know about that crowd she's moved in with," said Mum, "but I must admit, I thought it would be better for her if she stayed with us until the end of the year. It was like having another daughter in the place."

"Mum," I called gently. "Did you wish you'd had more girls?"

This brought an indignant humph. "One's enough trouble," she teased.

"No, I'm serious. Did you think about having anymore? After Liam, I mean."

"No, Liam was definitely the last." She was quiet then and I thought the topic was closed, until she turned on her side and spoke again. "To be honest, I did want another girl. I wanted David and then Liam to be a girl, for your sake as much as mine. I never had a sister myself." She hesitated for a moment before rolling onto her back again. "But we seem to have missed out, both of us, eh?" When I turned my head I noticed that her hands had slipped out from behind her head and lay like a blindfold across her eyes.

5

Mum's confidence about Gracey and Tuesday nights slipped a little when she cancelled the next week. Jarred was competing at a track meeting the next Saturday, and though I watched every sprint race, there was no sign of her. In fact, Jarred had some ominous news. "The word is, she went off the handle at one of the coaches at the Academy and hasn't been to training since."

When I finally ran into her on my way to a lecture, she looked tired, not just around the eyes but through her whole body. "Hi," she said, stopping to talk to me. The voice was bright enough. "How's the boyfriend?" she asked straightaway.

"Not as interested in sport as he used to be," I said smugly.

"Clare would agree with you I think." We shared a knowing smile. "Anything special happening?"

That was rather blunt, I thought, but I couldn't help grinning as I shook my head. "He's very tall and the Corolla's pretty small." I was smiling but this was closer to the truth than I wanted to admit.

"There's other places, you know."

---

12 **to miss out** to not have – 18 **to go off the handle** *(informal)* to lose one's temper completely – 25 **smugly** being pleased with one's behaviour

Oh yes, I knew. "What about you?" I asked. "That guy had his hands all over you in the car the other night."

"Huh, he wished." She made a face, a hard, humourless grimace that worried me. "Gracey?" I said gently. I didn't like the look on her face at all.
5 "What? Tell me."

"Look, don't make a big thing out of this, Angela, but well…that same night after you went home, he just wouldn't take the hint. He disappeared after an hour or so and I thought, good, he's gone home. Then later, when we were locking up and I went to my room, there he was, in my bed with all
10 his clothes piled on the floor."

"You threw him out, didn't you?"

"Of course, but it wasn't easy. Thank God Frank was still there and he persuaded him to go without a fight, but what got me was the way he stood on the steps arguing. 'She's black. Why doesn't she want to fuck me?' Can
15 you believe that?"

"Are you safe in that house then?"

"Yeah, we're fine. Look, I told you. Don't make a big thing out of it and for Christ's sake don't tell Cheryl."

The mention of Mum's name punched a hole in the conversation. "She
20 misses you," I said at last. "Will you come round on Tuesday night?"

She didn't answer at first.

"Bet you could do with a decent feed and a night in front of the soaps," I added and that seemed the clincher.

"Get Cheryl to do a roast, eh! Shirl and the rest are a great bunch but they
25 can't make toast without burning it."

So she came home with me to Clayfield one more time. Dad would never admit it, but he missed Gracey as much as Cheryl and I did and he managed to monopolise her for the first ten minutes after we arrived. I was afraid he would make one of his smart-arsed remarks about the overalls which
30 seemed to have become her uniform lately. But she was flirting with him so furiously, I doubt he noticed. Then dinner was on the table and for an hour it seemed as though Gracey had never moved out. It all came to an abrupt end though – all because I opened my big mouth.

Dad was still high on Gracey's attention and decided to tease me about
35 Jarred, trying to make me squirm in front of Gracey and the boys. He could be a clod at times.

---

29 **smart-arsed** clever in an irritating way – 35 **to squirm** to feel embarrassed or uncomfortable – 36 **clod** *(informal)* awkward or stupid person

"Angela spends more of her Saturdays watching races than she did when you lived here," he told Gracey.

"Not this Saturday," I countered. "Jarred's on his own. I'm going into town for National Sorry Day."

5 "Sorry Day. Haven't heard of that one," said Dad. "What's it about?"

It was Gracey who jumped in, speaking quickly, as though she was quoting a slogan. "The government's refusal to take responsibility for the stolen generation," she told him. "There's a rally at Roma Street Forum then we're marching to Parliament House." She leaned forward to look down the table

10 at me. "So you're still coming, Angela? I wasn't sure. You don't have to, you know."

Why did she add that last little bit? She didn't sound very encouraging, but I put this aside and nodded enthusiastically. I was wondering what Dad thought of his daughter on a street march.

15 To my surprise he pushed back in his chair and gave the table an enthusiastic slap. "Good on you. Hope it goes well."

Mum, on the other hand, didn't seem quite so sure. "I suppose that's one of the things students do," she said. "We went on a few marches when we were students, eh Tom. Didn't seem to matter what they were about."

20 My parents looked at each other from opposite ends of the table and I saw a silent message pass between them. Then Dad looked down at his hands. "I suppose if we were fired up by the cause we didn't care about the detail," he said, and I sensed a change in his attitude, as though the hearty support of a few seconds ago had withered away.

25 Gracey's antennae were out as well. "This is a serious protest," she said indignantly. "And I can assure you I know exactly what it's about. You should listen to Rhonda Haines when she gets going on it. It was a systematic policy of genocide and the politicians have to realise that."

"Now wait a minute, Gracey," Cheryl cautioned. "Genocide is a nasty word.

30 It makes me think of the Nazis and the Jews. That's not what happened here."

"Isn't it? Kids died. Thousands were abused, exploited. All of them suffered the misery of being separated from their families, losing their heritage, everything that matters to a Koori."

---

16 **Good on you.** (AustrE informal) expression of praise – 22 **to be fired up** to be excited – 24 **to wither away** to become weaker – 28 **genocide** [ˈdʒenəsaɪd] killing of a whole race – 32 **to abuse** to treat in a cruel way – 32 **to exploit** to use to one's advantage

"It wasn't all bad. Some of those kids were desperate. Taking them away saved their lives and gave them opportunities they would never have had. Take the case of that activist who's been in the news lately demanding an apology."

5   I made the connection immediately. "Derek Campbell," I said.

"That's right," Mum continued, surprised that I had remembered. "He wouldn't have started up that organisation of his if he hadn't had a decent education. He's lucky someone had the good sense to get him away from where he was and see that he was educated. So go ahead and protest, by all
10 means, but you have to be fair. There were good things that came out of it all."

"I don't know," I said, just beating Gracey to the punch. "You weren't at that meeting."

Mum gave me a dismissive glare. This was serious! It was easy to see
15 what had prompted Gracey to speak so definitely. Her words had Rhonda Haines stamped all over them. But Tom and Cheryl! Mum in particular. I didn't think she had a political bone in her body yet here she was arguing stubbornly, naming names, as though she was an expert. I was going to challenge her on this but Gracey got in first.

20   "I have to go," she said, standing up suddenly. "I've got some work to hand in tomorrow and it's not finished yet."

There was an uncomfortable aura around the table now and I think we were all relieved to escape it. Gracey kissed Tom lightly on the cheek but for Cheryl there was nothing as my friend swept past like an icy breeze without
25 even meeting her eyes.

The only words she offered on the way back to Taringa came in ones and twos, no matter how hard I tried. All the signs were there, arms folded, mouth tightly set, and when she caught me staring at her doubtfully, a roll of the eyes.

30   Finally I couldn't avoid it any more. "You'd better say something before you burst."

That was all Gracey needed to let her tirade come spilling out. "She doesn't understand, Angela. She was pushing the same ignorant line that gets peddled all the time. You were at that meeting. You heard the stories, that
35 Campbell bloke's as much as anyone elses."

"Look, I'm with you, Gracey. It's just that I don't know enough about it."

---

12 **to beat sb to the punch** (*informal*) to do sth before sb else can – 14 **dismissive glare** unfriendly look

I was saved from the need to say anymore when Gracey let fly again. "Oh shit, it was awful. Tom and Cheryl of all people. I knew they were patronising me. 'Go ahead and protest if you like', she says, like I'm some ten-year-old. How dare she!" And with that she smashed her hand hard against the door, three times, four, again and again. I was too startled to count.

"Does it matter so much what they think?" I asked.

"Of course it does. I'm telling you, Angela, it was only because they've been so good to me that I didn't go absolutely berserk. Can't they see how much pain is tied up in this, what an insult it is to people like Rhonda and her mother who are still suffering?"

I thought maybe this would be enough to let her cool down. After a minute or two of silence I risked speaking again. "I guess you want to give Cheryl a wide berth for a while."

She nodded.

"It's getting hard, Gracey. We've been friends for so long but I can feel you slipping away. Suddenly everything is so ..." I searched for the right words but there only seemed to be one. "So political."

"I'm an Aborigine, Angela. My whole life is political."

Gracey fought her way out of the Corolla as soon as it stopped and slammed the door without a word. Sealed inside the car again, I tried to make sense of what had happened. One thing was certain. I would need to know more about this whole business. All the way home, one question kept at me. How did my mother know so much about Derek Campbell? There seemed only one person who could answer that and I headed straight for her as soon as my car was parked in the driveway.

6

"How's Gracey?" were Mum's first words when I came in.

I laid my hand out flat, twiddling the fingers and rocking the palm from side to side. Worked better than words.

"She looked so tired, like she's under a lot of strain."

There was truth in that. I told Mum of how Gracey had taken a break from athletics, though I kept my mouth shut about the guy who'd turned up in her bed. "She worries me, Mum. She's working three and four nights at that little

---

1 **to let fly** (*informal*) to attack verbally – 2 **to patronise** to treat sb as though they are stupid – 8 **to go berserk** [bə'zɜːk] to get very angry – 13 **to give sb a wide berth** to stay away from sb – 20 **sealed** closed up

coffee shop as well. Her life seems like an endless grind of lectures, working and now all this political stuff."

"She's driving herself into the ground. Something will crack in the end if she's not careful. She'll need you, Ange. You're her best friend."

5 I doubted that now. By the sound of things, Rhonda Haines had become friend, mentor and substitute mother all rolled into one.

"I feel so awful," said Mum. "Did you see the way she cut me dead as she left? And in such a hurry too. She didn't have work to hand in, did she?"

I shook my head. "What's it all about, Mum? She's very touchy at the
10 moment over this stolen generation stuff and suddenly you start telling her she's wrong. How do you know so much about the guy Campbell, anyway. You knew his name before I even went to that meeting."

Mum looked even more stricken. "It's such a fine line and poor Gracey's in no mood to look at the grey areas. A privilege of youth, I suppose."

15 "You're patronising her again," I said, feeling annoyed.

She stared up at me, startled, and began to rub one palm over the other. "Am I?" Then after a pause she seemed to make a decision. "It's to do with Grandad. He knew Derek Campbell as a boy."

"Grandad Malvern, you mean?"

20 "Yes. His first church as a minister was out in western New South Wales. There was an Aboriginal reserve a few kilometres out of town so I suppose you'd say it was part of his parish. Derek Campbell was born on that reserve."

"Grandad remembers him? It must have been a long time ago."

25 "Yes, early sixties. There's a good reason why he remembers. You see, your grandfather was involved in getting this Campbell fellow out of that camp and into a decent home."

"Mum!" I interrupted. "You're not serious. Grandad. But why? You should have heard the man speak about it. People were crying the whole way
30 through. I was crying myself. Mum, people got up and apologised, people who had nothing to do with it."

"That's just the point, Angela. That's why I said those things to Gracey before. I don't know that there's a lot to apologise for in Campbell's case. If

---

1 **grind** *(informal)* dull hard work – 7 **to cut sb dead** to refuse to take notice of sb –
13 **stricken** upset – 20 **minister** priest – 23 **reserve** land set aside for the exclusive use
of Aborigines

you want to understand something, you have to listen to both sides." She stopped to see if I wanted her to continue.

I nodded doubtfully. What could there be to say after I had heard the man himself bring an entire hall of people to tears?

5 "Your grandfather saved that boy's life, if you want to know the truth. He was seriously neglected living where he was and sick all the time. But my father took an interest in him and he saw something special in the boy. Alcohol was causing all sorts of problems on the reserve, there was violence, disease, babies dying. Your grandfather saw that the only chance to save the
10 boy was to get him away from there, so he asked the mother if she would agree to an adoption. After a while she saw the sense of it. She came to my father and asked him to take the boy. He wasn't stolen. He wasn't snatched away, like he said in the newspaper I read last week. I gather he's been saying that in these meetings, too, like the one you went to. He was given
15 the chance of a better life, and when you look at what he's done since, you have to agree that your grandfather did the right thing.

"Do you see my point? Do you see now why I couldn't just sit there and let Gracey go on like they were all monsters grabbing up children willy nilly?"

"But the whole thing, Mum. The people who spoke at that meeting. It was
20 so traumatic. It couldn't all be put on."

"I'm not saying it's all put on. Some terrible things were done and I hope you do go on that march with Gracey. All I want is for you to understand your grandfather's position. He did the right thing by the boy and now this fellow has turned himself into a victim. Just imagine how upset your Grandad is."

25 She seemed to run out of words at this point and sat back in her chair, exhausted, waiting for me to reply. My grandfather was a good man. Mum did not have to remind me of that. As a girl I had snuggled into his lap, like a tiny bird safe inside a nest. There were photographs of us together, my happy little face peeking out between his arms. There were often lollies in
30 that nest as well, I recalled, Minties or caramels that appeared by magic. As Mum explained, her words were fleshed out with these memories and many more until I knew instinctively that she was right.

---

18 **willy nilly** just like that – 21 **put on** false – 29 **lollies** *(AustrE)* sweets – 30 **Minties** brandname for Australian sweets – 31 **to flesh out** to add more details to sth

7

On Wednesday, after I had played an hour of very poor tennis, I told Jarred about dinner the night before. He listened carefully as though I'd invited him
5 to solve a Maths problem. Typical guy! But then, this was one of the things I liked about him.

"Are you sure about your Mum's story?" he asked. "Not that I know anything about it," he put in quickly.

"That's half the problem. I don't know anything about it either. And as
10 soon as anything like this turns up on the tele, I change channels. Shit! Life's too short. You know what I mean?"

He shrugged, giving me a half-smile. "Are you still going on the march? If you don't believe in the cause, maybe you shouldn't go."

"Oh, I still believe in the cause. I just don't believe it was all as bad as they're
15 making out. That's fair enough, isn't it? Trouble is, I feel uncomfortable with the others around. You've been with me when we've run into Gracey and those new friends of hers. Do you feel like that?"

"Not really. That Frank is hilarious."

"Yeah, but don't they keep having a dig at you?"
20 "Maybe they do and I don't notice."

When he saw my face tighten up at this, he laughed and leaned across the table. "You're too sensitive."

I knew he was having his own dig at me. "Don't laugh. Please! This is serious. I'm sick of having all this white oppression stuff hanging in the air
25 like it's still going on and I'm one of the culprits. It's as though they want to build a barrier between me and Gracey, and the busiest little builder of the lot is that Rhonda Haines. I'm sure of it. God, you'd think she was a saint the way Gracey goes on about her, but all the time she's trying to white-ant me, like I don't belong."
30 "Ooh, definitely bad vibes I'm picking up here," Jarred said, mocking me.

I threw the half-empty packet of sugar at him. "Look, all I want is for Gracey and me to go on like we've been for years. I never had to worry about her being Aboriginal at school. We got past that straightaway. The others could never quite forget she was black, but for me it didn't make any difference and I've never said one racist thing to her, not one word, nothing that might hurt her because she was different from the rest. Now I cop it

---

16 **hilarious** [hɪˈleərɪəs] very funny – 17 **to have a dig at sb** to make annoying remarks – 23 **culprit** guilty person – 26 **to white-ant** (*AustrE*) to weaken sb's position – 28 **vibes** (*pl. informal*) feelings

from her friends every time I see them, even from Gracey herself."

Jarred became serious again. "Gracey just looks a bit stirred up to me. When someone gets touchy like that, you have to leave them for a while and it will come good again in the end."

5 "So you think this is just a bad patch for Gracey and me then."

He shrugged. "Hope so. I like her too, you know." Then he kissed me to show who it was he liked the most.

8

On Friday, while I was enjoying my two-hour stretch at The Corner, Gracey surprised me.

10 "How's Cheryl?" she asked.

"Worried you'll hate her forever."

"Oh no," she groaned, slipping into the chair that used to be hers.

"Are you still mad at her?"

She thought about this. "Yes, but maybe not as bad as Tuesday. It's a
15 worry, Angela. I just can't get over the way she thought she knew it all. What did she do? Read an article in the paper and suddenly she's an expert."

I had to tell her but The Corner was not the place. "Do you feel like feeding some ducks?" I asked.

We wandered down through the undulating paths to the lush banks of
20 the lagoon where waterlilies choked every inch of the surface. On a hard and splintery bench I told her about my grandfather and Derek Campbell.

She heard me out calmly before she said, "Doesn't make sense to me. No Aboriginal woman would give her son away like that. It'd be the same as killing him."

25 There was a gaggle of ducks squabbling over the remains of my foccacia. Arguments, everywhere arguments. While this thought was fresh in my mind, Gracey caught me off-guard.

"Do you believe it, Angela? Your grandfather's story?"

She pressed the question on me with such passion, I knew my answer
30 was vital to her. My grandfather and Derek Campbell. What did I believe? The

---

19 **undulating** ['----] rising and falling – 19 **lush** full of plants – 20 **to choke** [tʃəʊk] *here:* to fill – 21 **splintery** broken – 25 **gaggle** group – 25 **to squabble** to fight – 25 **remains** *(pl.)* left overs – 25 **foccacia** type of flat Italian bread

answer came quickly. I believed in my grandfather, of course, but as quickly as I realised this I saw Gracey's face and my certainty faltered.

"No, Gracey. I mean, well … Derek Campbell seemed so sincere."

"So you don't accept what Cheryl told you?"

5 I had never lied to Gracey before, but if I stuck to the truth she would undoubtedly storm off in anger. "No, I don't believe her," I said and immediately she relaxed.

Now I was the one left edgy and confused. "Look, Gracey, this protest march tomorrow," I said tentatively. "Am I still on the team?"

10 She didn't reply and I had my answer. She wanted to go without me, with Shirley and the rest in my place. Rhonda Haines most of all. It didn't have to be like that.

"Look, I'm still coming," I said defiantly.

She thought about this as two pigeons arrived to clean up what the ducks 15 had left behind.

"All right. If you're coming, you may as well give us a lift into town."

How many passengers would I have this time, I wondered, as I pulled up outside the house. In fact, there was only Gracey waiting for me. "Shirley's 20 gone into town already and Wendy's off doing something as well. Barb didn't come home last night. We're meeting them in the Mall and going down together," she explained. "To tell you the truth, I think they're all a bit scared of turning up on their own."

It felt great to be in the Mall with Gracey again, zigzagging our way 25 through the buskers and the milling shoppers. There was always a buzz about the place, so many people, from slobs in thongs and footy shorts to girls who thought they were strutting the catwalk.

I was too busy enjoying the sensation, the vibrancy of the place, to pick up on her mood. I was going to pay for my negligence. Pay more than I could 30 imagine.

"Hey, remember that coffee shop I fell in love with," I called to Gracey.

---

2 **certainty** feeling of being sure about sth – 2 **to falter** to become unsteady – 10 **edgy** nervous – 25 **busker** street musician – 25 **buzz** air of excitement – 26 **slob** fat person – 27 **to strut** to walk proudly – 27 **catwalk** a narrow platform that models walk on – 28 **vibrancy** feeling of excitement – 29 **negligence** ['neglɪdʒənts] carelessness

She didn't respond and I thought maybe she was trying to remember its name.

"Hallowed Grounds," I reminded her. "I used to drag you in there just for the smell. Tell you what. After this is all over, I'll shout you a short black to celebrate."

"Yeah, if you want to," she said listlessly and still I didn't see what was happening, didn't look at her properly and realise how on edge she was.

We arrived at the Information Booth in the middle of the Mall right on time but there was no sign of Shirley or Wendy. The waiting made Gracey even more nervous. I needed to distract her.

"Look, I'm supposed to pick up Mum's watch from a place just a few doors down. She's been at me for a week about it. Come on. We'll do that while we're waiting."

She slouched off after me, hands in the pockets of those same overalls she had worn to the public meeting. It was only a few paces really to the jeweller's door. When she hesitated at the entrance, looking back towards the Information Booth, I said, "You wait here. I won't be long."

And I wasn't. It was a simple matter of fronting up and giving my name. The watch was waiting under the counter and there was nothing to pay, just a receipt slip which I signed. It would not have been more than three minutes before I was on my way, stuffing the tiny parcel into the pocket of my jeans. But it was enough.

As I approached the door, I heard Gracey's voice, her angry voice. "No, I'm not going to move," she said hotly.

Confronting her stood a figure in the same black skirt and frilly cream blouse worn by the girl who had served me at the counter. As I came closer, I could see that this was no girl. The swept-back hair and confident stance spelt manager.

I guessed what was happening immediately. This was an exclusive jewellery store and Gracey didn't exactly look the part.

I hurried to Gracey's shoulder. "It's all right," I said. "She's with me."

A handful of words but I regret them now as much as anything I have ever said.

Suddenly Gracey forgot the manager and turned to me instead.

---

4 **to shout sb to sth** to invite sb to sth – 4 **short black** coffee – 6 **listlessly** without enthusiasm – 7 **on edge** restless and nervous – 12 **to be at sb** to trouble sb with requests – 14 **to slouch off** to move off – 18 **to front up** (AustrE) to turn up – 25 **frilly** having many folds – 27 **stance** way of standing

"What did you say?" she began incredulously. But she didn't give me a chance to reply. It took a few moments for her surprise to boil into fury, so when she started again her voice was still a whisper. But by the end it was pure rage. "I don't need you here so I can stand at the door of a fucking jewellery shop. Who the hell do you think you are? 'She's with me.' And that makes it all right, does it? Doesn't matter if I'm black as long as there's a friendly white girl nearby to vouch for me. Is that the way you see it, Angela? You don't want me to get lumped in with the other blacks around the place, the ones that don't count for anything, the ones that have no right to stand around in the Mall by themselves."

There were people stopping to look now, a little crowd drawn by the strident voice, forming a semicircle as though we were buskers.

"That's not what I meant," I managed to croak when Gracey paused for breath. But she was just warming up.

"Yes it was. You don't even realise it yourself. Just like Tom and Cheryl, like mother like daughter. Generous to a fault as long as it's on your own terms. Come for dinner. Have a coffee, I'm buying. It's all part of your power over me, isn't it?"

That was Rhonda Haines talking, I knew it. I was immediately angry and, as for my parents, dismissed so savagely – it wasn't right.

"That's unfair, Gracey, and you know it. Mum and Dad have always been good to you. So have I," I added, suddenly in tears.

"You're a babe in the wood, aren't you, Angela? Absolutely. Your head's so full of boys and clothes and does he love me and do I look nice, there's no room to see what you were doing to me. You colonised me, Angela. From the day we met, you moved in and started changing me. New hair style, a dress you stole off your mother. They were just the things you could see. What you did inside my head changed me a lot more."

There was no holding back now. I shouted at her, letting go all the frustration and fear I'd bottled up over the weeks. "I don't understand how you can just throw it back in our faces now. Anything we've ever done was because we cared about you."

---

7 **to vouch for** to say that you firmly believe that sb is true or good – 8 **to get lumped in** to be considered a part of – 15 **like mother, like daughter** being the same as one's mother – 16 **generous to a fault** extremely kind and nice – 16 **on sb's terms** the way sb decides to do sth – 20 **to be dismissed** to be forgotten about – 20 **savagely** in a cruel way – 23 **babe in the wood** naive

"Cared about me as long as I was the tame black girl, yes. But as soon as I step out of line, start telling you things you don't want to know, you turn on me quick enough."

I was sick of being on the defensive like this. I had to strike out for myself.
5 "You're on about Derek Campbell now, I suppose. Look, Mum had every right to say what she did. You don't want to know the other side of the story. For all you know, your mate Rhonda wouldn't be here if things had been left as they were. How do you know that what happened wasn't for her own good?"

10 That was it. I should have stuck to Derek Campbell where I was sure of my ground. But I was angry and with Gracey sounding so much like Rhonda Haines I couldn't stop myself. When I'd said this about Rhonda's mother, Gracey's face nearly exploded. "You're out of your depth, Angela. Haven't got a clue what you're saying. You'd better go home to Clayfield, where it's safe
15 and nobody'll bother you with things you don't want to believe."

With that, she stormed away through the little crowd which parted quickly to let her pass. I fell back against the door of the jeweller's as the bemused crowd dispersed. For a few seconds I was exultant, on the edge of laughter even, that I had thrown off such a heavy load. I wouldn't have to creep
20 around anymore, careful of every glance, my antennae seeking out every mood, every word that might have a double meaning. I had struck out heroically and freed myself.

It wasn't until I was on my way home, with the passion cooled to a bitter chill inside me, that I understood what I had done. I didn't feel heroic
25 anymore and as for the things I had said about Rhonda Haines and her mother, I felt sick through every inch of my body. It was the most reprehensible thing I had ever done and I knew Gracey would never forgive me for it. Never.

---

1 **tame** *opp. of* wild – 13 **out of one's depth** unable to understand – 14 **to not have a clue** to not have an idea – 17 **bemused** confused – 18 **exultant** triumphant – 19 **to creep** to move in a careful way – 20 **antenna** (pl. antennae) *Fühler* – 26 **reprehensible** bad

Part two

Sydney

Bankstown

1

That scene in the Mall happened six weeks before the end of the semester. After that, I looked for Gracey whenever I crossed the Great Court or ducked into the library – not to speak with her but to avoid her. Once, when I saw her with Rhonda and Shirley, heading my way along the wide veranda of the
5 Forgan Smith building, I panicked and slipped behind one of the enormous sandstone pillars. Can you believe that? I hid from Gracey!

After they passed, I stood watching her, the trademark overalls now topped with an oversized sweater which had seen better days. It was her hair that upset me though. She'd cut it all off. Must have found a hairdresser
10 somewhere who would do it – zoom zoom with the electric clippers until there was just stubble left.

I wasn't much company for Jarred while all this was going on. Not at first anyway. He listened as I replayed the disaster outside that jewellery store. He kept his cool when Peter and Cathy wiped us six-love because my game
15 had fallen in a heap.

"Hit the ball harder and see how you feel," was his advice.

So I did and I felt a little better after that, even when the ball crashed into the net or whistled over the base line and into the cyclone wire. He offered an endless supply of reassuring hugs, as though he understood the comfort
20 they gave me, and asked nothing for himself in return. In those last weeks of the semester, our farewells in the Corolla became more tender than passionate and I loved him all the more for it.

There was Mum to talk to as well, and Fiona Bennett who was becoming a real friend, and a few of the girls from school had started to call up again.

---

14 **to wipe** to beat – 14 **love** (in tennis) no points – 18 **base line** line marking the end of a court – 18 **cyclone wire** fence with interlocking wire

But most of all there was Jarred. We were heading down to Sydney together after the exams, he to stay with some vague cousin I had heard him mention, and I had a bed waiting at my grandparents'. As the exams approached and I hit the books night after night, I found myself daydreaming. A thousand
5 kilometres was a long way from prying eyes.

"God, I'm looking forward to Sydney," I told him after the last exam. I could feel the strains of the past few weeks blowing away like dark clouds. "I just want to get away from everything, from everyone. I wish we were the only two people in the world."

10 He laughed out loud then whispered in my ear what he would like to do if we were alone, with the planet all to ourselves. Sounded good to me and that dark cloud seemed to lift even higher into the distant sky.

"Did you sort things out with your cousin?" I asked.

"Todd? Yeah, he's fine about it. Says I can stay as long as I like. His flatmate's
15 off to the snow for the second week so I can have his room."

"Does this Todd work during the day?" I asked.

"I know he's with Australia Post," Jarred answered quickly. "Suppose it's during the day ..." Then he saw me staring at him and he went silent. For the next few seconds I watched the little muscles work around his eyes and
20 his mouth, creating a dozen faces laid one on top of the other – surprise, anxiety, desire – until his features shone with a kind of eagerness, the same delicious eagerness that made me ask about his cousin. Three days and we'd be there.

Then out of the blue Gracey called me, the day before we were due to
25 leave. "Are you still going to Sydney?"

"Yes," I said tentatively. There was not a lot of warmth in her voice and no small talk that might open the door a little between us.

"Look, I'd still like to come, if that's all right."

"Of course," I blurted out immediately, and before I'd had time to steady
30 the shock, I was giving her the details.

"I'd better let you have my new address," she said.

New address! She'd moved? I had no idea and felt a sort of pain as I realised how much her life had become invisible to me.

When I had the street name and number written down, neither of us
35 seemed to know what to do next. "Gracey ... what I said in the Mall that day ... I'm sorry. I didn't mean half the things I said."

---

5 **to pry** to look into sb's private affairs – 14 **flatmate** a person you share a flat with – 29 **to blurt out** to say suddenly

"This is probably not the time, Angela. Maybe we can talk on the way to Sydney."

"Sure," I said, relieved, and the call ended.

The journey did not go well. We were an hour late by the time I inched the Corolla along the unfamiliar street and Jarred spotted her on the steps of a house even more ramshackle than the last one.

"I'm sorry, Gracey," was my feeble attempt at a greeting. "Mum insisted on making breakfast even though it was still dark and the time just got away. I think she's a bit worried about me driving all that way."

"Don't worry, Angela," she said. "When you're a Murri, you get used to waiting."

That was how it was going to be then, with the lines drawn from the first words spoken.

We headed out through Ipswich and Warwick then south onto the New England tableland, stopping for petrol at Tenterfield where an icy wind swept in from the hills. Gracey said little, content to stay in the back seat so that Jarred could stretch out in the front. Sometimes when I checked the mirror, she was asleep. I didn't know which was tiring me more, the driving or the effort to build bridges with my friend. Whichever it was, I needed to rest, so we stopped for lunch in Armidale, among the leafless trees, the church spires and the schools with their dark brick walls. When Jarred slipped away to the toilet, I had my first opportunity to speak with Gracey alone. "You're not saying much," I said gently.

"I'm tired, Angela. Dog tired. I've got a lot to think about too."

"About uni. It's not going so well?"

"Yes, there's that but there's other things too." She leaned across the table, her face showing the first cracks in the ice-hard indifference she had shown me all day. "Angela, about Sydney," she said. "I can't stay with you at your grandparents like we planned."

"What do you mean? Where will you stay?"

"I should have explained when I called you yesterday. Things have changed. I haven't even entered for the University Games. I'm really going to Sydney to meet Dougy. He's coming down from Cunningham on the bus, along with a girl I used to know at school. They are already there, to tell you the truth, staying with some relatives."

---

6 **ramshackle** in a bad condition – 12 **with the lines drawn** with everybody knowing where they stand – 15 **tableland** plateau – 21 **spire** church tower

She saw my bewilderment slowly turning to disappointment and was wondering how long it would be before I became downright angry.

"So you just needed a lift."

"I'm broke, Angela. I'm so broke my bones rattle when I walk. I had to put
5 up most of the bond for the new place when we moved. Bastard of a landlord wanted a huge bond but we didn't have any choice. Doesn't matter where you go, if you're black they're afraid you'll trash the place and references don't mean a thing. So I thought, if I could save the bus fare ... Look, it was a lousy thing to do to you." She paused for a moment then murmured, "I'm
10 sorry."

"I would have taken you anyway."

"I think I knew that. But I've been hitching a ride with you for a long time," she said, fixing me with a grim stare.

Our words dried up and in my guts I could feel the half-eaten hamburger
15 turn slowly into a disappointment heavier than lead.

As we drove on, rain began to fall and the further south we went, the heavier it became. Through the windscreen, Tamworth was no more than a watery blur and Muswellbrook the same. The poor visibility unsettled me and kept the Corolla to no more than eighty or ninety Ks. Jarred offered to
20 drive, but I put him off. I'd been looking forward to this journey, determined to do the full stretch myself. But time was getting on and it was clear now we would not reach Sydney until well after dark. Somewhere near Maitland, after the last of the day's light was gone, we stopped to eat.

The diner was like the others we had wandered into during the long day,
25 with its menu chalked on a board behind the counter and a row of tables and chairs bolted to the floor, every surface pock-marked with cigarette burns. Gracey stood gazing into her hand, counting the coins. She looked up at the board and back into her palm, poking the coins with her finger as though this would make them multiply.

30 To the girl behind the counter she said, "Could I have a bucket of chips for one seventy instead of two dollars? Just leave a few chips off the top."

"Sorry," said the girl. "Just what's listed there," and she flicked her head towards the board as though she didn't care one way or the other.

---

4 **broke** without money – 7 **to trash** to ruin – 7 **reference** statement about a person's character – 12 **to hitch** to get a free ride – 13 **to fix sb** to look at sb intensely – 14 **guts** *(pl.)* stomach – 15 **lead** [led] *Blei*

I fingered the ten-dollar note in my pocket. "You want a cheeseburger, Gracey?" It was her favourite takeaway.

"I don't need anything," she said and then added, "getting a bit over my training weight," though it was obvious she was lean as a greyhound. She
5   wandered off towards the tables just as the girl at the counter asked, "What will you have?"

I stared at her, unable to speak as the moments went by, three seconds, four seconds.

"Are you all right?" Jarred asked. He took a step towards me, his arm out
10 as though I was about to fall. "You've gone all white in the face. You'd better sit down."

His words roused me enough to say, "No, I'm OK. I'll have a hamburger, please, with everything and a cup of coffee." I put a ten-dollar note on the counter.

15   "Must be all the driving," Jarred suggested. "Have a feed and a good rest and you'll be right."

He led me to the table where I sat opposite Gracey. I heard a Pepsi fizz open, aware of Jarred's hands twisting the top free. Time seemed to make its own way, separate from the way I imagined it. Suddenly my burger was
20 in front of me and a five-dollar note with a couple of coins weighing down one edge. Jarred was eating something thin and crumbed, a bucket of chips sat steaming on the table at his elbow. "Here, take a chip," he mumbled to Gracey through a half-filled mouth. It was an easy natural movement, pushing the cardboard bucket into the centre of the table, Gracey's hand
25 dipping in, taking a few of the pale yellow chips.

He could do this so easily, but not me, not anymore. My friend was broke and hungry and I wanted to get her a cheeseburger but I just couldn't decide. Should I do it or not? Would she scoff it down happily or would it be another patronising insult that would drive us apart? It wasn't fair that we should be
30 like this. Once there would have been no hesitation, no need to ask, no fear, no risk of offence.

I looked down at the money on the table in front of me. Plenty there for a cheeseburger and plenty of time too. All I needed to do was pick up that crumpled note and walk over to the counter. Should I do it, such a simple
35 thing? Was it the right thing to do? Still I couldn't decide and suddenly I was

---

2 **takeaway** meal you buy but don't eat at a restaurant – 4 **lean** thin – 4 **greyhound** a racing dog – 12 **to rouse** to wake up – 21 **crumbed** [krʌmd] with crumbs on it – 28 **to scoff** (informal) to eat very quickly

angry, burning, screaming, unbearably angry that I should have become like this, unable to buy a simple cheeseburger for the closest, dearest friend I had ever had.

With a flick of my hand I swept the money off the table, the coins scattering
5 across the room until they hit a chair leg and bounced onto the greasy floor. One of them circled noisily, taking an age to lie still in the silence my rage had brought to the diner.

Across the table Gracey stared at me, a chip hovering above the near-empty bucket as the shock of my sudden movement left her frozen. I looked
10 desperately for some sign of the warmth I had once found in her eyes, and for an instant I imagined it was there, melting her just a little. Then her hand moved again and the moment was gone.

After my little tantrum, Jarred insisted he drive the rest of the way. If anything, the rain was worse by the time we reached that intimidating
15 highway through the mountains south of Newcastle. Semitrailers shot past us, their enormous wheels just a metre from the side mirror. Jarred could have this on his own.

"Where are you going to stay?" I asked Gracey as we descended through a deep cutting towards the Hawkesbury River.

20 "In Bankstown."

"Where's that?"

She paused for a moment, still a little guilty, I guessed. "I don't know. Sorry. I thought maybe you had a street directory."

We did, thanks to Dad's foresight. I picked it out of the glove box and
25 began to search the pages under the weak interior light. "Where's your cousin's place?" I asked Jarred.

"Hurstville. Not far from the airport."

That meant nothing to me, but before I could find it on the map, I spotted Bankstown. "Shit, it's way out on the south side of town. My grandparents
30 live in Manly," I told them. "How far is Bankstown from there?"

"Miles and bloody miles," Jarred groaned.

We were exhausted and it was already nine o'clock. I looked back at Gracey and said, "Look. Neither of us has driven in Sydney before, it's dark, it's wet and it's late. Grandma and Grandad will be waiting up for us and
35 worrying. I'm sorry, but we're going straight to Manly and in the morning I'll take you over to Bankstown and Jarred to his cousin's place."

---

13 **tantrum** moment of bad temper and anger – 15 **semitrailer** truck with a mover and a trailer (*Sattelschlepper mit Aufleger*)

Gracey was too tired to fight about it and I was too tired to change my mind anyway.

At last we pulled into the driveway beside a familiar house and through the kitchen window there was my grandfather waving. He was
5 quickly out to us with umbrellas, calling, "Hello, hello, come on in, you must be on your last legs. We expected you hours ago."

"Sorry, Grandad," I said, finding myself in his bear hug. Grandma was there too, fussing about and introducing herself to Jarred. In my tiredness, I had almost forgotten who was waiting for me at the journey's end, how
10 good they were and how much I loved the pair of them.

"This is Jarred Manning," I said, doing the honours. "And, of course, you know Gracey," I added.

"Of course," Grandad crooned. "Good to see you again."

It suddenly dawned on me what could happen here. I had told Gracey
15 about my grandfather and his involvement with Derek Campbell. But when he reached for the heavy Nike bag, she let him take it gladly enough.

"Let's get inside. We've got some soup on the simmer for you."

"Lead me to it," said Gracey, smiling. "I'm frozen right through." And she followed my grandfather into the house, leaving me to breathe a little
20 easier.

They filled us with minestrone, laid out fresh towels warmed over the radiator, and then there was the question of beds. "You girls are in there," Grandma said, nodding towards the second bedroom. "But we were only expecting you and Gracey," she pointed out, "and this is a small house after
25 all."

I explained about the change of plan and pretty soon a makeshift bed was cobbled together for Jarred on the lounge room floor. My grandparents went off to their bedroom and we were happy to do the same. I expected to fall asleep as soon as my head hit the pillow, but an endless stream of cars
30 swept past my eyes accompanied by the slosh and hiss of a wet road and the rhythmic slap of the windscreen wipers. After what seemed like an hour, I went out to the lounge room, careful not to wake up Gracey.

---

6 **on one's last legs** totally exhausted – 11 **to do the honours** to introduce sb – 13 **to croon** to speak in a gentle voice – 14 **It dawned on me.** I realised. – 26 **makeshift** made for temporary use only – 27 **to cobble together** quickly make sth – 30 **slosh** sound made by heavy rain

"What's up?" came Jarred's groggy voice as he stirred and turned on his side to face me.

"Is it warm in there?" I asked, and before he could answer I slipped in beside him. He had to hold on to me so I wouldn't role off the narrow
5 mattress.

"What happened back at the place we stopped for dinner?"

What had happened? I hesitated for a moment, working it out for myself. "I was just a little confused about where I stood with Gracey. It's all right now. We'll take her over to Bankstown tomorrow and that will be the end of
10 it."

"Sad though," Jarred commented.

"It's what she wants."

"No, I didn't mean that," he whispered. "I mean about the University Games. She'd be a show for a medal and the Commonwealth Games trials
15 are next month. Maybe she's not up to that standard just yet, but it would do her good to have a go."

"She brought her track shoes with her," I told him. "In fact, looked to me like she brought everything she owns."

Jarred propped himself up on one elbow. "You know, if she does have her
20 gear, I might talk to her tomorrow. Twist her arm a little. I know a bit about sprints. We could train together this week and maybe she'll have a go at the Games anyway. You wouldn't mind, would you?"

"No! I'd love you to help her. She seems so weighed down. Look, she can borrow you for as long as she likes, as long as I get you back afterwards." I
25 gave him a hint of what I had in mind and slipped away to my own bed.

2

In the morning the rain was gone and I woke to find the sun streaming in through the window, lighting the fine motes of dust that danced above the blankets. Someone was up, judging by the gentle knocks and bangs from the kitchen, and drifting in with the sounds came the most tantalising aroma
30 in the world – bacon and eggs on the fry. I dressed quickly, once again,

---

14 **to be a show for sth** to have the chance to win – 16 **to have a go** to make an attempt – 20 **gear** equipment – 27 **mote** small piece of – 29 **tantalising** tempting, making you want sth

careful not to wake Gracey, and found Grandad by the stove, sporting an apron that claimed "I'm the boss". He wasn't alone. At the table, with his hands cupped around a mug of something, Jarred sat chatting to him as though they'd been mates for years.

5   "Cup of tea?" Grandad asked.

"I'd prefer coffee," I told him and it duly arrived.

We scoffed the bacon and eggs between the three of us and were well into the washing up when Grandma appeared. I was stunned to see her careful, slow-motion movements. "I'm like a lizard these days," she said, 10 when she caught me watching her. "The cold's no good for arthritis, so it takes a little time to get going in the mornings."

We took our time too that morning, with movements as stiff and lethargic as my grandmother's. Gracey emerged and turned down the breakfast Grandad tried to force on her. "Better get going," she said.

15   She didn't get any arguments from Jarred and me. It had just gone ten o'clock, the day was warming up, we were in a different city with its vibrancy enticing us to come and explore, and I for one was eager to take my first adult look at the place.

"Peak hour should have eased off by now," I said seriously, as though I 20 knew Sydney's traffic. "Let's go."

Grandad had been hanging around us, glad of the company I guess. When I said this, he lifted the newspaper to show me the front page. "TRAINS THREATENED" was the headline.

"You might have picked a bad week to be driving in Sydney," he said.

25   "It hasn't happened yet, though," I replied cheerfully. Nothing could kill off my excitement that morning.

Nothing but traffic, maybe. If what we encountered at ten-thirty was off-peak, what was it like at eight o'clock? I've never seen so many cars, kilometre after kilometre. Getting to uni each morning was a trip to the corner shop 30 compared with this.

It didn't help that I got caught in the wrong lane coming off the Harbour Bridge and we ended up shooting along a freeway towards Ryde or somewhere before Jarred, swearing freely as he twisted the street directory this way and that, finally worked out a way back. When a sign welcomed us 35 to Bankstown, we cheered grimly. It was close to midday.

---

1 **to sport** to wear proudly – 9 **like a lizard** very slow – 16 **vibrancy** excitement – 17 **to entice** to attract

By this time he and I were like a rally team, driver and navigator. "Next left, count two on the right, there should be traffic lights," he instructed. I followed without question until at last we found it, a low-set place with little to distinguish it from the houses on either side, a leafless tree on the footpath and the garden, such as it was, dormant for the winter.

No one in the house seemed to have noticed us yet, so we lined up Gracey's bags on the footpath and stood looking at them awkwardly.

"Gracey," Jarred began, "I wondered whether you'd still like to have a crack at these Uni Games. They'll take late entries without any fuss. And by the look of things, you have everything you need." He nodded towards the Nike track bag at her feet.

She wouldn't let him go on, shaking her head before he was halfway through what he had to say. There were no excuses either, no explanation. "Thanks, Jarred. I know you're trying to help. Both of you," she added, glancing at me. "But no thanks."

So this was it then. It would be, "Thanks for the lift. Sorry I tricked you into taking me. See you at uni some time" – which meant never. It had been painful to see her around the campus over the last few weeks. That pain was already withering, until now it was simply awkward and, finally I suppose, I wouldn't feel anything much at all. The memories of a face, a word, a mannerism would simply fade away.

The front door of the house swung open and there was Dougy coming down the few steps from the porch to meet us. It was a year since I had seen him. He was taller now though not as gangly, those long loose limbs more under control. Gracey ran to him, hugging him while they continued out to the footpath where, to my surprise, he put his arm around me briefly. Once I had thought of his willing smile as vacant and foolish. Much as I recognised the gentle goodness in him, I'd used his shyness to ignore him whenever it suited me. But Dougy had found his place in the world, it seemed to me and I wondered what had helped him find it.

The front yard was full of kids now, three boys and a girl ranging from pre-school to maybe ten or eleven. They advanced halfway along the footpath then stopped to form a reception committee, taller ones in front, the younger kids peeking round their backs to take a look. "Are you Gracey?" a voice asked in awe.

---

3 **low-set** house built close to the ground – 5 **dormant** asleep – 8 **to have a crack at** to attempt, to take part – 9 **without a fuss** without a problem – 24 **gangly** moving in a clumsy way – 27 **willing** given freely – 35 **awe** respect

When she nodded, the same brave voice said, "We knew it was you. You're a famous runner, aren't you?"

"Maybe you've got me mixed up with someone on TV," Gracey answered, a little embarrassed.

5 They backed away towards the door ahead of her, with Dougy, Jarred and me tagging along with the bags.

"I'm Muriel," the little girl announced. "And I can run fast too." She sprinted into the house to demonstrate and the youngest boy followed her.

After driving through the bright winter glare, it took a few moments for
10 my eyes to adjust to the sudden dimness of the lounge room. The television blared and a baby was crying weakly in another room and together these distractions put me on edge as a woman emerged from the kitchen to welcome Gracey. She was a little taller than me though thick around the middle. No wonder, I thought, counting the children. As well as the four who
15 had come out to meet us there was an older girl about fourteen watching our arrival from the door of the baby's bedroom. This girl stepped aside and the crying grew louder as another girl about my age brought the little bundle to join the rest of us in the lounge room. I recognised this young mother as Nerida whom I had met in Cunningham last year. At the time she was
20 noticeably pregnant and here she was with the baby in her arms.

Gracey bent over the infant, cooing softly, then turned towards the older woman, who was hanging back as though she was waiting for something. "Gracey, this is Auntie Irene," Nerida announced, standing midway between them.

25 "Where you from?" Auntie Irene asked as she looked Gracey up and down. She seemed a little suspicious of what she saw. Gracey livened up at this. "My mob are from Cunningham now though we didn't always live there. Had to move after the big flood a few years back. My Auntie is Flo Sellars who Dougy lives with and you probably know the Dohertys. My dad's sister is part
30 of the Dohertys – she married Norm and I've got cousins all round their country and plenty in Cunningham."

Talk about overdoing it. Maybe Gracey was nervous because she was here to stay with a family she had never met before, not that Auntie Irene seemed to mind, as she smiled now and asked a question about Norm Doherty which

---

12 **to put sb on edge** to make sb nervous – 26 **to liven** ['laɪvən] **up** to become excited

Gracey couldn't answer. No matter, Gracey had been accepted and the faces turned to me and Jarred. We were greeted with the same question: "Where you from?"

"We're both from Brisbane," I said.

5 There was an awkward pause for a few moments as Auntie Irene checked us over, and though we both offered cheesy smiles, she glanced uncertainly towards Nerida. I thought I had better break the ice so I stepped forward, holding out my hand, and since there was no mention of a surname said, "Pleased to meet you, Irene."

10 Gracey rolled her eyes at this, though I couldn't see why. The woman was not as old as my own mother and I called her Cheryl these days, when it suited. Gracey's disapproving look made me nervous and when I'm nervous I talk too much. "Gracey had quite a welcome out the front. All these kids must keep you busy." I was just trying to make conversation.

15 It didn't work on Auntie Irene, and for my efforts Gracey's eyes did another loop inside their sockets. The crying baby wasn't helping much. The others didn't seem to notice the noise, as the kids were introduced, starting with Bill, about four years old, I guessed, Muriel the sprinter who was missing her front teeth, Kendrick and Trevor, and the teenager who had been lingering
20 near the baby's room. Her name was Carli.

Gracey's bags sat on the floor around us, and after these formalities she bent towards them, ready to take her place in the house.

"Put your stuff in with Nerida's," Auntie Irene told her and the routine of the house, held back by our arrival, seemed ready to flow again. It was a cue
25 for Jarred and me to leave, and he was already drifting towards the door as I sidled across to join him. When Gracey appeared again, it would be time for goodbyes.

Nerida decided she should help Gracey, so she signalled to Dougy who took the baby confidently in his arms. It looked strange. I thought of my own
30 brother David, only a year or so younger. Most boys were terrified of babies, holding them stiffly as though they were made of the finest china and ready to disintegrate at any moment. Not Dougy. He slipped the baby up onto his shoulder, settling its head with a practised shrug and turning himself awkwardly so he could show me the baby's face and watch it himself at the
35 same time. I did a few calculations. This baby would have to be at least eight months old, but she was tiny, with an emaciated face, pasty despite the

---

6 **cheesy** bright – 16 **loop** circular movent – 16 **socket** *Augenhöhle* – 24 **cue** a signal – 31 **china** very fine porcelain – 32 **to disintegrate** [ˈdɪsɪntəgreɪt] to fall to pieces – 36 **emaciated** [ɪˈmeɪsɪeɪtɪd] thin *(ausgemergelt)* – 36 **pasty** pale

brown skin. There was something odd about her lips, not pink-brown as you would expect but darker with a tinge of blue.

"What's the baby's name?" I asked. I couldn't even tell if it was a boy or a girl.

5 "This is Raylene," Dougy replied.

I thought nothing of the name at first, too intent on making a fool of myself with faces and silly sounds to attract her attention. Then it came to me. Raylene. It couldn't be more obvious. Her name, the way Dougy held the baby, the fact that he had travelled down from Cunningham with the child's
10 mother. "This is Raymond's daughter, isn't it?"

Dougy looked up from the baby immediately, staring at me and then uncertainly around the room. "Er, yeah. How'd you know?"

"From the name, of course."

Gracey was back from the room now. "This is your niece," I said. "You're
15 an Auntie!"

She cringed. Once I thought about it I realised what a blunder I had made. Poor Raymond had died before this little one was born. Seemed a pity that such an exciting piece of news had to bring sadness with it.

The moment passed and Dougy, at least, relaxed as he grinned at the
20 baby, a deep happiness glowing in every crease of his face. Nerida took her from his arms. "You'd better get the pram," she said. "We're running late."

"Can I give you a lift somewhere?" I asked. "Jarred and I are just going."

Nerida stared at me as though I had just invented the whole idea of offering someone a ride. "To the train station would be great. We're going
25 to miss the twelve-thirty otherwise."

"Where are you going?"

"The hospital. It's in near the city. St Vincent's."

"Look, if it's in the city, we might as well take you all the way."

"I thought you were driving Jarred over to his cousin's," Gracey cut in.

30 Jarred cleared that one up for her. "Todd won't be home until five and I haven't got a key."

"If you really want to give us a ride, that'd be great," Nerida said, beaming. "On Friday we had to walk for ages once we got off the train."

---

2 **tinge** a little bit – 16 **to cringe** to move away and make os smaller at the same time – 16 **blunder** serious mistake – 21 **pram** baby carriage

"Well, that settles it then. Come on."

The whole family came out to see us off. Dougy folded up the pram and slipped it into the boot while Nerida settled herself into the back seat with the baby on her lap.

Straightaway, I saw the problem. "You haven't got one of those special baby carriers have you?" I asked.

She looked at me as though I'd asked for directions to Mars.

We set off anyway, my eyes on the lookout for police as though I was driving with a flashing sign above the car: "Unrestrained Baby on Board".

"What's the problem with Raylene that you have to go to this hospital?"

"Something with her heart," Nerida said calmly. "She was born with it and the doctor in Cunningham said we had to come down here, to this St Vincent's place, to have it checked out. Might even do an operation."

"That's why you're here then?"

"Yeah, Dougy came with me to help out, eh."

"When will you know about the operation?"

"They've got all sorts of tests to do with these big X-ray machines. Poor Raylene. It scares her, having so many faces around." And though I couldn't see it, I knew Raylene was clutched a little tighter inside her mother's arms.

Jarred was back in his role as navigator and after our earlier disaster, or maybe because of it, he was doing a lot better. "Not far now," he said. "Along Oxford Street and we're almost there."

"This is so much easier," Nerida said from the back seat. "It's a mongrel getting into the hospital from Auntie Irene's. We have to catch a bus to the station, a train into King's Cross and walk from there. Takes over an hour and Raylene gets worn out. Then she's cranky for the doctors, wriggling all over the place. Couldn't do one of their tests on Friday 'cause she was squirming too much."

Jarred's directions were good but the traffic in Oxford Street was not. It still took ten minutes to go the kilometre or so to our turn-off.

"Does it take long at the hospital?"

"Today it will. They said all afternoon."

"How will you get back when they're finished with you?" I asked.

---

3 **boot** space at the back of a car – 9 **unrestrained** not fastened, not tied in – 24 **mongrel** (*informal*) *here:* enraging experience – 27 **cranky** ill-tempered – 27 **to wriggle** to twist one's body – 29 **to squirm** to move around

"Same as last week. Train and then the bus."

I thought of the tiny baby, her quivering lip and those languid, possum eyes. "We'll come back and get you, if you like."

"Gees, Angela, it'd be great, specially for Raylene. But it's a bit tough on you."

I looked across at Jarred who had his eyebrows halfway to the ceiling.

"Your cousin lives out that way, doesn't he?" I said. "Got to take you to his place sometime."

"Yeah, but the plan was to stay in town and have dinner somewhere, then go out to Hurstville."

I didn't want to argue with him in front of Nerida and Dougy, so I used my privilege as owner of the car to settle the matter.

"We don't mind taking you back. I'll give you my mobile number and you ring me when you're ready."

We dropped them outside St Vincent's and headed down into the city where we paid a king's ransom for a spot at a parking station and walked to Circular Quay. There we chose the oldest, quaintest ferry, without a care for where it would take us, and ended up near the mouth of the harbour at a place called Watson's Bay. A short walk through the park brought us to The Gap and there we hammed it up, pretending we were star-crossed lovers ready to leap to a romantic death.

On the way back it was cold on the open deck and we were glad of our jumpers. But we stayed there buffeted by the wind, Jarred behind me, his arms around my waist, my hair whipping back against him until he buried his nose in my neck and I felt his warm breath inside my collar. The sun was out, untroubled by a few wispy clouds, and the harbour shore was dazzling. I saw every detail yet I saw none of it. All I could think of was the pressure of his arms around me and his hands which had slipped under my sweater to keep warm. What did I care for the beauty of Sydney harbour when those hands opened a button on my shirt and I felt his palms against the soft skin of my midriff. When another passenger disturbed us I turned, letting those

---

2 **languid** ['læŋgwɪd] lacking energy, tired looking – 2 **possum** small furry animal which lives in trees – 16 **ransom** money paid to kidnappers for freeing sb – 16 **a king's ransom** *here:* a lot of money – 17 **Circurlar Quay** [ki:] ferry harbour in Sydney – 17 **quaint** attractively old-fashioned – 19 **The Gap** natural entrance to Sydney Harbour, between two high cliffs – 20 **to ham it up** to behave unnaturally – 20 **star-crossed lovers** reference to Romeo and Juliet – 23 **jumper** pullover – 23 **to buffet** ['bʌfɪt] to move forcefully – 31 **midriff** middle part of the body

big arms envelop me again, hugging close, my head deep into the woolly smell of him and wishing there was somewhere private we could go. This is how it happens, I thought. This is how you fall so much in love that nothing else matters.

Afterwards, we wandered round The Rocks and under the Harbour Bridge, bought an ice-cream from a street vendor and settled finally on a bench beside the water. From there we watched the ebb and flow of craft on Circular Quay, the ferries large and small, the hydrofoils and tiny boats, the water taxis, the police. I can't remember a time when I said so little yet felt so much. At about four o'clock the mobile called us from our contented silence and I made arrangements to pick up Nerida and company from St Vincent's.

"How did it go?" I asked when they were safely aboard.

There was a hesitation which sent my eyes quickly to the rear-vision mirror just in time to see Nerida frown and take a heavy breath. "Not so good really. We've got to take her back tomorrow."

After the briefest silence while she came to terms with this, Nerida spoke again. "You couldn't give us a lift again tomorrow, could you?" she asked. For all she knew I was staying just round the corner from the house in Bankstown, not half a world away on the other side of the harbour. Jarred groaned.

"I have to pick you up from Hurstville, don't I," I whispered, though it was pointless in the confined space of the car.

"Depends on what we're doing tomorrow. Todd said it's an easy walk from the train station, so it makes sense for me to meet you in town somewhere. Otherwise ..." He stopped, conscious of the insult he was about to deliver to poor Nerida and Dougy. But I knew what he was going to say. Otherwise, we would spend all day in the car, with bumper to bumper traffic the only scenery!

In the circumstances I squibbed the decision. "Tell you what. I'll give you a ring in the morning, Nerida, and let you know if I can make it."

The traffic was worse than ever now, which hardly brightened the mood inside the Corolla. We found Auntie Irene's house again and helped our passengers onto the footpath.

"You coming in to see Gracey?" Nerida asked.

"We'll keep going. By the time we get to Hurstville, Jarred's cousin will be home."

---

6 **street vendor** person selling goods in the streets – 7 **ebb and flow** coming and going – 8 **hydrofoil** [ˈhaɪdrəʊfɔɪl] fast moving boat with propellers – 29 **to squib** (AustrE) to put off

Not only was he home but he was about to cook dinner, and since it was Jarred's first night as his guest, he insisted we stay and eat with him. That turned into a night in front of the TV which I didn't mind really. We were both still weary from yesterday's driving and Sydney's night life would not be at
5 its best on a Monday in any case. Jarred saw me out to the car and we took our time saying goodnight. At some stage we arranged to meet at Circular Quay and take a ferry across to the zoo.

"I can come across on the ferry from Manly," I said brightly, remembering my first hydrofoil ride years ago.
10 "What about Nerida and the hospital?" Jarred asked.

I'd forgotten about my offer. "Have to put her off, I suppose." When that little baby was not there in front of my eyes, generosity seemed to desert me.

That's what I thought, anyway. I slept late and even Grandma had beaten
15 me to the breakfast table by the time I roused myself. A call to Nerida was the last thing on my mind. But as I started on a pile of toast I couldn't jump over, all buttered and jammed by my fussing grandfather, the distinctive trill of my mobile demanded attention.

"Er, Angela," came Nerida's voice.
20 Oh well, she'd saved me the effort of ringing. "Oh, hi. Listen, about today ..."

I was ready to launch into an excuse when the sound of crying drowned out my voice and Nerida asked me to hang on while she attended to Raylene. Dougy's deep tones mixed in with the general melee. The scene
25 would be the same as yesterday, the little thing with her blue lips starved of oxygen, listless and cranky. And I was consigning her to a lengthy journey, a bus ride, a crowded train and a pram ride through the cold morning air.

Nerida was ready now. "I was wondering, you know, you said you might take us again. It was really great yesterday."
30 "What time do they need you?"

"Early this time."

"OK, I'll leave straightaway."

I rang Jarred, who laughed at me. "You're a soft touch, Angela", but he didn't seem put out. We readjusted our meeting time and I bet he decided
35 to head out for a long run anyway. I knew him. The traffic gods were merciful that morning and by nine-thirty I was in Bankstown. It worried me a little what Gracey would think of all this and I half-expected to find her on the

---

24 **melee** [ˈmeleɪ] confusion – 26 **listless** without energy – 26 **to consign** to send – 34 **soft touch** (*informal*) person easily influenced by emotions – 35 **put out** angry

footpath, waiting for me and demanding an explanation.

She wasn't on the footpath, though, nor anywhere inside either, it seemed at first.

"Gracey's asleep," Dougy told me. "Been asleep since lunch time yesterday."
5 He smiled when he said this because he knew his sister as well as I did. She had gone into hibernation to get over the long journey and, more likely, the long months before that.

We set out to do battle with the congestion along Parramatta Road. Watching Nerida in the mirror I remembered something Gracey had told
10 me. "You've got a little boy as well, haven't you?" I asked.

"That's right. Steven."

"He stayed back in Cunningham, did he?" I was making small talk to keep my mind off the traffic, but Nerida had a surprise for me.

"No, he's in Meewah. My sister's there with her two kids. Stevie lives with
15 them just at the moment."

"While you're down here, you mean?"

"No, he's been there a while now. My grandma's there and my mum sometimes. Whole bunch of them."

A while! How long was a while? She sounded a bit vague about it all. "You
20 must have been down to see him."

"No. Grandma brought him with her when she came to see the new baby. Couldn't get down to Meewah myself though. I was pretty sick the last few months before Raylene was born and then she's been so sick herself 'cause of this heart thing."

25 I waited for her to say more. That her son was all right. That she would go and see him on the way back from Sydney. Anything. But Nerida stayed silent and a few seconds later she was talking to Dougy, asking how many nappies he'd put in the bag. I looked at her in the mirror again and this time I saw her with different eyes. What kind of mother left her kid with someone
30 else, for months at a time – left him for someone else to raise?

By ten-thirty I had dropped my passengers and found a spot in the same parking station. Nerida was sure the tests would take until well into the afternoon, so Jarred and I had plenty of time to see Taronga Park.

---

6 **hibernation** [haɪbə'neɪʃn] a very long sleep (as of animals during winter) –
8 **congestion** traffic jams

The wait at Circular Quay was delightful torture. Every tall, fair-haired man I saw seemed to be Jarred, and my heart would leap, only to fall back with disappointment when the figure came closer with its unfamiliar face. In the end he caught me by surprise, creeping up from behind and leaning into my ear.

"Hi!" he whispered and I nearly jumped out of my skin. He kissed me to make up for the scare. Nice, but it was a public-places kiss and I hoped he'd do better a little later.

3

It was another fabulous day and I decided that not only was Sydney a great place to be in love, it was a place I could fall in love with. Afterwards, Jarred came with me to St Vincent's where my three passengers were waiting patiently.

"How was it today?" I asked Nerida when she and the baby were nestled comfortably in the back seat beside Dougy.

"They never tell you anything," she complained. "Going to be a few days before they get the results from all these tests. At least we don't have to go in tomorrow."

"I can have a day off then," I said laughing. We all laughed. This was better than another "thank you" from Nerida. I was feeling a little uneasy about her after the morning ride and had to be careful I didn't show it.

Gracey was awake when we arrived. She came out to the footpath to greet us, a cheer squad of Kendrick, Muriel and Bill close on her heels.

"You've certainly wheedled your way in here while I was asleep," she said with a light-hearted resignation that took the sting out of her words.

"I wanted to help out."

"Well, you've won Nerida over, anyway. Guess it doesn't do any harm."

Oh thanks, I thought.

Jarred came to my rescue. "I hear you've been sleeping," he said to Gracey.

"Yeah, a real princess, that's me. I haven't slept like that since ..."

"Since Noosa," I finished for her.

---

23 **to wheedle** to persuade others to let you do things

Gracey was embarrassed by the memory and sought out Jarred's face as though I wasn't there. "Are you all set for the Uni Games?"

"Will be when I've had a run on the track. Most of the team's coming down by bus on Thursday but I thought I'd get out to Homebush and do some training before they arrive. Would have been out there already if it wasn't for certain distractions." He pulled me close and we grinned together. "Are you sure you don't want to have a go? You could do with the competition, with the Commonwealth Games trials coming up next month."

"I haven't been invited to the trials," she said.

"Why not? You're a chance for the relay. An outside chance maybe, but they've got to give you a go."

"I haven't posted a decent time since Canberra last year, so I don't qualify."

"That's crap," said Jarred suddenly angry.

Gracey shrugged helplessly. "The rules say six months. Any time clocked before that doesn't count."

"All the more reason to enter the University Games then."

We had been over this just the day before and I expected Gracey to cut off the conversation any second. So it was a surprise to see her hesitate.

"When I asked Angela for the ride it was the last thing on my mind." She stared into my face and I saw a hint of shame. "But, well, I've been thinking about it this afternoon, since I woke up. Trouble is, I haven't been to training for months and I'm ragged as hell."

Jarred charged in, taking control, and I worried for a second that he would scare her off. "No problem," he declared. "Come out to Homebush with me. I know enough about sprints to see what's wrong. We've got three days to sort you out."

She looked unsure. "What about you, Angela? It's your holiday too."

"Oh, he's not going to be any use until after his race anyway. Go for it."

Jarred tried to settle the matter. "You've come all this way. Why not have a go for the hell of it."

"How many runners will have their own private coach and a chauffeur-driven car," I put in, not sure whether this would help or not.

---

10 **relay** race between teams in which each runner runs part of the distance (*Staffel*)
– 14 **crap** nonsense – 23 **ragged** ['rægɪd]exhausted

But my words brought a smile to her face. "You're on," she said, adding cheekily, "Bloody white slavedrivers. I suppose you'll want your name on the medals if I win." She darted away towards the gate, daring us to grab her. She was too fast for me. I never caught her when she played this game. But Jarred did. For such a big guy he was quick on his feet. His arm looped out and caught her by the waist, dragging her back and holding her there while I joined them, all of us laughing. For a few seconds we were three together, Jarred with an arm round Gracey on one side and me on the other. Oh, where had this Gracey been hiding?

"When will we start, coach?" she asked.

"There's no hospital run tomorrow, is there?"

From my comfortable position nestled under Jarred's arm, I shook my head.

"Tomorrow morning then."

4

For dinner, Jarred and I found a cute little Italian restaurant in Leichhardt, all booths down one side and candles in red glass. To us, coming in from the cold, its heavy warmth was like a hand reaching out to draw us inside, a hand steeped in garlic and basil and espresso. We ordered and began to make plans for the next day when Jarred would take Gracey for her first training run.

"You don't mind helping Gracey out, do you? I mean, it's not exactly what we came to Sydney for."

"No, I'm pleased about it," he said with real enthusiasm. "This is the sort of thing I want to do when I graduate. Gracey has so much talent, it's a challenge to get the best out of her. I didn't think she'd do it," he added. "Not after she was so adamant yesterday."

I had been thinking much the same thing myself. The long sleep had refreshed her – but to change her mind so quickly."Things are different for her down here. There's no Rhonda Haines for a start," I said bitterly. "Maybe she'll be a different person away from Brisbane."

"You don't sound very happy about it."

I was confused more than relieved and I told him so. "There's Gracey this afternoon, smiling, wanting to play, yet she and I haven't spoken to each

---

1 **You're on.** Agreed, OK – 3 **to dart away** to move away very quickly – 26 **adamant** [ˈædəmənt] impossible to persuade

other for weeks. We haven't really talked, talked like we used to since she moved out. When she rang asking for a lift, I thought, wow, an olive branch. But we're still in a kind of stand-off. We said some pretty awful things to each other in the Mall that day."

5 "Friends have bust-ups all the time. I've seen it with Clare. In the end they sort things out between them."

"Gracey and I had more than a fight that day. We were getting down to what we really believe, the kind of things you can't throw over quite so easily."

10 "You mean the Derek Campbell business?"

I nodded my head reluctantly. "I don't know quite what to believe. When I first told Gracey about it, she looked like she'd eat me. I backed right off, pretending my grandfather must have it wrong. But it didn't work and Gracey knew it. The things I said in the Mall…she knows what I think."

15 Our meals came, two steaming bowls of pasta, and we dropped everything to enjoy them. Mine had a creamy sauce with pine nuts and avocado. A dream. Jarred attacked his fettuccine ravenously, looking up once and smiling at himself. "Sorry. I was starving."

It was so cosy in the booth together. We should have been talking about 20 our time at the zoo and on the harbour yesterday or where we would go next week when the Uni Games were over. I tried to steer the conversation that way but Jarred was a problem-solver and I had a problem.

"Can't you both just ignore this Aboriginal stuff?" he said. "It never got in the way before. Just don't talk about it, make it a sort of no-go area. I mean, 25 what's Gracey expect? Is this some kind of test you have to pass before you can be mates?"

"It feels like that. So you think if we just don't mention it, the whole thing will blow over?"

He immediately lost confidence in his own suggestion and we were left 30 to stare at one another, sharing the same doubts. Before I knew it, a spark of anger ignited me and I slammed my hand down too hard on the table. Why did this Derek Campbell story have to hang between Gracey and me?

It was still early when we tumbled out of the restaurant, so we found our way to King's Cross and wandered around the gaudy main street, rolling our 35 eyes with embarrassment when the hard-faced touts urged us into the strip shows.

---

3 **stand-off** unfriendly state – 5 **bust-up** quarrel – 17 **fettuccine** pasta made in ribbons – 17 **ravenously** ['rævənəslɪ] extremely hungrily – 31 **to ignite** to set fire to – 34 **gaudy** showy – 35 **tout** person who repeatedly tries to persuade you to visit a bar or show

Jarred wouldn't let me drive him home afterwards. "You've done nothing but drive since you left Brisbane," he reminded me and took the train back to Hurstville. I was in Manly before ten o'clock. My grandparents were surprised to see me back so early.

5 "A coffee, Angela?" Grandma asked, hauling herself painfully out of the chair.

I was awash with the stuff, but when she said, "I bought some grounds especially," I could hardly say no. I had been with them for a couple of days now but there had been little chance to talk. With the coffee cups on the low
10 table between Grandma and me, my grandfather put down his book and turned to join us. He left the gossip to Grandma, but when I managed to refuse a second coffee and made a show of yawning, he was suddenly ready to talk.

"Cheryl tells me you went to hear Derek Campbell speak when he was up
15 your way."

"Yes. With Gracey and a few of her friends."

"And what did you think?"

"It was pretty sad," I said lamely. "Had me in tears some of it." I had suspected we would get around to this conversation during my visit but I
20 was caught off guard all the same.

"He's an impressive speaker, isn't he?" Grandad said, and I was shocked at the pride in his voice, the pride of a father for his successful son.

"You've heard him?"

"Oh yes," Grandad assured me. "When he spoke at the town hall."

25 "But Mum said he was lying."

"No, no, no. Not lying. Not Derek. He's just mistaken and it's not surprising really. He was a little boy when his mother gave him up and he's had to rely on the memory of others, people who might not know the truth themselves."

30 "Mum said you saved his life."

Grandad was embarrassed by this. "Who can tell?" he asked, opening his hands for a moment. "Certainly I was concerned for his well-being because his mother was neglecting him. Poor thing, she had two other little ones, one just a few weeks old. Whenever I saw him he was with some aunt or old
35 woman from around the camp. And what a squalid pest hole it was, a death

---

5 **to haul** to lift up with great effort – 7 **to be awash with** to be full of, to have had enough – 7 **grounds** *(pl.)* coffee beans – 20 **off guard** unprepared – 35 **squalid** [ˈskwɒlɪd] filthy, extremely dirty

trap for babies, children sick all the time. It wasn't right that anyone be left there to an early death, let alone a boy with so much potential."

"Potential?"

"Yes. It was the teacher at the local school who pointed him out to me. He
5 was teachable, she told me. He came to school with the other children, though he didn't have to. Knew his alphabet. I wanted to do something for him."

"So you arranged an adoption?"

"No. I suggested a few things to the mother, things we could do to give
10 her boy a chance. Once she'd thought about it, she came to me, eager for him to go."

"That's not what he said in the meeting."

"Yes, I realise that. But I was there and that is what happened. The couple I placed him with were wonderful people I'd known for years and they put
15 Derek through school, gave him his Christian faith and loved him like their own. Even he says as much. And look at him now, a fine man, a leader, and that health unit he set up does valiant work."

The pride was back in his voice and a conviction too that said he would do it all again tomorrow if he had to.

20 "Mum's pretty upset about the whole thing, the way people like you are being called criminals. Don't you feel bitter?"

He shook his head ruefully.

"What about you, Grandma?" I asked, turning towards her chair. But it was empty and I realised she had not come back from the kitchen after gathering
25 the dirty cups. When I went looking for her, I found the cups rinsed and left to drain on the rack but Grandma had taken herself off to bed.

5

Rather than have me drive all the way to Hurstville then across to where Gracey was staying, Jarred caught the train to Wynyard Station where I could pick him up without going too far out of my way. At Bankstown we collected
30 Gracey.

"Where to?" I asked like the taxi driver I had become.

---

17 **valiant** brave – 22 **ruefully** showing that you are sorry

"Homebush. The Olympic site," said Jarred. "All the events are being held out there, on the warm-up track. Competitors can use the facilities for training all week."

I looked at him sceptically. "They're letting you use the Olympic track?"

5 "Just the warm-up track." When I still didn't look convinced, he laughed. "I rang up about it. Trust me!"

Olympic site! It looked more like a bomb site. They left me in the small stand beside the track while they warmed up. Jarred was taking his new position as Gracey's coach very seriously. He put her through a series of

10 short explosive sprints, then they stood together, heads down, as Jarred explained some point or other and she had another go over a short distance. Later he worked her hard until she flopped on to the grass inside the track. Slavedriver. Athletes must have some weird code that says it's no fun unless it hurts. What a sport. I went back to my car and listened to Triple J, then

15 when they still weren't finished I drove around looking for a newsagent and grabbed a couple of magazines.

At last Jarred was satisfied with Gracey's exhaustion and called off the torture. "That was great," she sighed, stretching herself across the Corolla's back seat. "Best training I've done for ages."

20 "You deserve a coffee," I said. I was desperate. If I didn't smell properly brewed coffee soon, I'd pass out.

"You can have your coffee at Auntie Irene's," said Gracey, killing off my plan to find a cafe close by.

The house was quiet when we returned. Raylene was asleep and the

25 younger kids seemed to have disappeared. There was a new face though, a young guy about our age.

"This is Kaz," said Nerida introducing us. From the nonchalant way he greeted us, he seemed to be another son of Auntie Irene's. I wondered if he was an athlete; he had the same lithe muscular body that gave Gracey her

30 easy balance. But it wasn't raw speed he used it for.

"Kaz is a dancer," Auntie Irene told us proudly. "Scored a spot in the Aboriginal dance school. Doing real well, too."

Kaz looked mortified and I got the impression his family was a frequent source of embarrassment. Watching him near Dougy, the difference was

35 painfully obvious, the slow bushy next to the ambitious boy from the city. It

---

1 **site** area, ground – 27 **nonchalant** behaving in calm manner, often seeming uninterested – 29 **lithe** [laɪð] moving easily and gracefully – 31 **to score a spot** to win a place – 33 **mortified** embarrassed

set me thinking. What had Gracey said back in Noosa? It came to me suddenly and I headed for him, whispering, "Dougy, have you been to the beach?"

"The beach!" He shook his head, bewildered.

"Gracey tells me you haven't been."

5 "Never got the chance," he said. "I seen it on TV though."

"Believe me, it's not the same thing," I assured him. "How 'bout we go this arvo?"

He looked a little worried and I thought, oh no, I've insulted him, but when I glanced behind me and found the whole room eavesdropping, I
10 understood.

"Would you like to go?" I asked again.

"Sure. Be great, I reckon. You going to take us in your car?" Being Dougy, he could not imagine that I would take him alone. He looked to Gracey, wanting her to come as well.

15 "Where will you go, Angela?" she asked.

I hadn't thought that far ahead. What were the beaches in Sydney? It was obvious. Embracing the whole room I said, "For Dougy's first time on a beach it has to be *the* beach. Bondi. Who's coming?"

"You're crazy. It's winter," said Jarred with a laugh.

20 "Beaches are just as much fun in winter."

"Can I come?" Nerida asked. "I haven't been on a beach since Stevie was born."

Before I could answer she was talking to Auntie Irene, railroading her. "Raylene's asleep. Probably stay like that for hours. You can watch her, eh!"

25 Auntie Irene didn't need much convincing, it seemed to me. Six kids of her own and she was happy to take on another one, even if it was just for the afternoon. The woman was a saint.

Nerida wasn't the only one. Kaz, who had quietly slipped from the room, reappeared zipping on a jacket.

30 "Where are you going?" Auntie Irene demanded.

"With this mob. They're going to Bondi, aren't they?"

"They are. You're not. Dad'll be here soon. You've got to help with the afternoon deliveries."

"That's Trevor's job and Carli's."

35 There was a full-blown argument on the way, I could see, so Jarred and I just kept walking out to the Corolla. Minutes later, with the shouting still at

---

7 **arvo** *(AustrE)* afternoon – 35 **full-blown** fully developed

full volume, Dougy, Gracey and Nerida joined us. "What's all that about?" I asked.

"Uncle Dennis is a milkman," said Gracey, grinning. "You can work out the rest."

5   Jarred tried to find us a cross-country route to Bondi. In the back seat, there was no doubt who was the most excited about this little outing. Nerida was busting out of her skin. "I've only ever heard about Bondi," she was saying to Gracey. Whether Jarred's short cuts saved us any time, we'll never know. We made it eventually, slipping down through the eastern suburbs
10 until we found the ocean stretching away to the horizon. On the beach Dougy was hilarious. It was the noise that got him in at first. "It's roaring," he said, smiling from ear to ear. "Like a lion." He stayed behind the rest of us as we walked straight towards the waves, poking his head between Gracey and me, over our shoulders, desperate to see it all but in need of protection just
15 the same. Where dry sand met wet he stepped forward, determined to show a little bravery, and followed a wave as it swept back into the ocean. Suddenly he was charging up the beach as a new surge licked his heels. It was difficult to know whether he screamed with delight or fear.

    This set us all off. Seconds later I was looking at an upside-down view of
20 this famous beach as Jarred threw me over his shoulder like a rag doll. He marched off towards the water with me dangling there squealing. "Can't come to Bondi without getting wet," he threatened, and I felt myself launched towards New Zealand. He caught me though, just as a wave scooted in, soaking his jeans up to the knee. I felt the sudden cold of water
25 on my backside.

    We were all wet soon enough, as Nerida kicked a spray of salty water at each of us until we ganged up on her. I was back on my feet now and watching Nerida as she fought like a wildcat to keep the others at bay. My earlier misgivings rose again. This girl was the same age as me, yet she was
30 the mother of two children, one of them ill with a heart complaint, the other she hadn't seen for months. What was she doing here on the sand of Bondi beach, laughing and playing as though she didn't have a care in the world?

    I looked for Gracey to see if she was staring at her old school friend and perhaps thinking the same thing. But she had split away from the rest of us

---

7 **to bust out of one's skin** *(informal)* to be very excited – 17 **to charge** to run – 17 **surge** wave – 19 **to set sb off** to make sb start doing sth – 24 **to scoot in** *(informal)* to arrive – 29 **misgivings** *(pl.)* feeling of doubt

and was heading along the beach, hands in her pockets. I wanted to go to her, walk beside her and let her say what was wrong. But I didn't follow her. I couldn't. Not yet. Things had barely begun to improve between us.

It was Jarred who went after her. He reached her in a few long strides and
5 they continued away together, as I had seen them on the training track that morning. They were talking, Gracey mostly. Jarred was listening as I longed to do, hearing the troubles pour out and taking them into himself. Nothing stood between them, no ocean as wide as the Pacific that seemed to separate Gracey and me still.

10 Eventually they turned and Jarred put his arm over Gracey's shoulder, the action of a friend, given with warmth and accepted freely.

I headed away from the water's edge feeling the cool dry sand on my feet, frozen from paddling. Halfway to the concrete wall that hemmed in the beach, I dropped cross-legged to look back at the ocean. Jarred and Gracey
15 had stopped now, both with their hands up against the afternoon sun to find where I had gone. Gracey left him and was moving closer, coming towards me until she tossed her training shoes on the sand and shuffled her backside in beside them.

"It's been a while since we sat like this," I said.
20 "It was Noosa, wasn't it? Seems like a long time ago."

"We were happy together at Noosa."

"Yeah, seemed that way. But it wasn't real, Angela," she said in a strident voice I barely recognised. "In the real world, Murris have to fight every inch of the way."
25 "Does it have to be that way?"

She sighed and as instantly as it appeared the harshness was gone, as though she'd said to herself, to hell with that. "It can seem that way sometimes. It was fun at first, being with all the other Murri kids, but once I met Rhonda ... well, Rhonda opened my eyes to what was going on, what I
30 was doing, what the world was doing to me."

She swept her arms wide to take in the beach, the ocean, the sky. "The things she said to me, the stuff she gave me to read. I couldn't get enough of it. I started to see my life in a different way. I started to see *you* in a different way, Angela. Suddenly my best friend was my biggest problem."
35 "I didn't understand."

---

13 **to hem** *säumen* – 14 **to drop cross-legged** to sit down with your ankles crossed –
22 **strident** [ˈstraɪdənt] harsh and aggressive

"No, and neither did I really. I still wanted you close. Rhonda told me to ditch you. I kept saying to her, what does it matter if she's not a Murri? But it did matter, Angela, and pretty soon just looking at you made me angry. I needed space but you wouldn't let me have it. What did I say to you? That
5 you colonised me. Shit, where did I read that? My hair. I did that to spite you."

"I sort of guessed that."

"Your mum's dress. The blue one you pinched from her the first time I stayed at your house. I tore that into rags to use round the house. It was why
10 you gave it to me that hurt. You were trying to make me less like a Murri."

"No, it was because I liked you. I never said anything that hurt you, did I?"

"No, of course you didn't. You just forgot I was a Murri at all and after a while so did I. Rhonda Haines changed all that. Crash course in being black,
15 it was." She stopped and laughed at herself, scooping up a handful of sand and tipping it slowly back to earth. "I'm so conscious of being a Murri now that it hurts to think of the way I was."

Now she smoothed out a patch of sand in front of her and began poking her finger into it at regular intervals. "You know what the lowest point of my
20 life was? Coming to you at Noosa, the way I cried all over you in that coffee shop. Remember what you told me? You and Cheryl and Tom, you were my family now. But you can't be a Murri and belong to some other family, it doesn't make sense."

She explained all this without bitterness, it seemed to me, but with those
25 last words she stopped and abruptly swept away the pattern she had created. Her face was serious and hinted at a pain she was still struggling with.

"Do you want me to go?" I asked.

She threw her head back, checking me over until the corners of her mouth
30 curled up a fraction. "And give me some space?" she said with a smirk.

"Something like that. Apparently I'm not very good at knowing when you need it?"

She smiled again. "No, don't go. Six weeks was plenty of space. Do you know why I'm here with you now?"
35 "I thought maybe Jarred talked you into it."

"No, I'm here because I missed you."

---

2 **to ditch sb** to get rid of sb – 5 **to spite** to upset on purpose – 30 **smirk** unpleasant smile

How did I feel, to hear her say that? Tugged in a dozen different directions is the only way to describe it. One of them, or maybe it was all of them, squeezed tears into my eyes.

Gracey saw them. "Don't get carried away," she warned quickly. "I'm
5 still working out how I feel about you, but I do miss you. The girls in the house … it's not the same. I like them but I can't talk to them for hours about absolutely nothing like I talk to you."

"I thought Rhonda was the one."

"Rhonda. She's important to me for other things. I ask her questions and
10 she gives me straight answers. Everything is clear-cut – no compromises, no back-downs. You have no idea what she's been through, Angela – so much more than that Derek Campbell. They took her away from her mother too, you know, just as her mother was taken away in the first place. Finding her again was the only bit of luck she ever had. Poor Rhonda. She was shunted
15 around from family to family, and then when she was eleven, one of her foster fathers … well you can guess. All her life she was abused, taught she was useless. She's the one who's had to fight every inch of the way, and if she's bitter and spits in your face every time you go near her, I can't blame her."

20 She paused again, then looked at me for the first time since she sat down. "Tell me the truth, Angela. Do you like blacks?"

It was so abrupt, so unexpected. We had come so far in just a few minutes, she had admitted that she missed me, yet here she was, testing me again. "Yes, Gracey. Of course I do."

25 She continued to stare at me as though my answer had been a disappointment. How many ways were there to convince her? Did I have to shout it up and down the beach?

Then she stunned me again. "I don't know if I do much, sometimes."

"What! But …" How could I follow the girl?

30 "Maybe Hamilton spoiled me and I'll never be able to get it out of my system. You know, I went to that first meeting at the Support Unit expecting to hate it. But Shirley and the others, they were so friendly, so funny. I'd forgotten that about my own people. Then when I met Rhonda I started hating everything white and I fell into the trap, you see, that if everything
35 white was wrong and bad then everything black must be good and right. Shit, was I naive. It was the guys that caught me out."

---

11 **back-down** excuses – 14 **to shunt** to move – 16 **to abuse** to treat violently – 36 **to catch sb out** to show that sb is naive

"Guys. You mean that one in my car, the one who got into your bed?"

"Him, no, he never showed his face again. But at least he was up-front about it." She stared across at me, deciding whether to go on, and there was a sadness in her, the look of someone who has been let down, betrayed. I
5 knew what she was going to tell me even before the words came.

"I was such a fool," she began bitterly. "So naive, so fucking stupid. There's this tutor." She peeked at me sheepishly and relaxed a little now that she had made up her mind. "I met him when he sat in on one of my tutes. He was so much like Rhonda, so sure of himself, so proud."

10 "You slept with him?"

She hesitated a second, then slowly blinked her eyes. "I was so stupid. After the first time, he just expected me to turn up at his place, kept hassling me like I owed it to him, 'cause he was such a freedom fighter. When I told Rhonda she went for him, tore strips off him in public, but I wasn't the first
15 and I won't be the last. I found out later the Support Unit won't even let him in the door. I wish all guys were like Frank ... and Jarred," she said, turning her head to watch the others who were wrestling playfully close to the water.

"You're so lucky," she said more than once in those few minutes.

20 Her story stunned me, and though I tried a few responses in my head, they all sounded trite, so I changed tack a little and said what I felt. "Gracey, if I could take back what I said, about Rhonda, about your friends, I would. I'd like to erase them, like a video tape. Gone." Watching her face closely, I asked, "Are you still angry?"

25 "I was trying to be when we left Brisbane. But it's a funny thing, the further we went the less I felt like I was holding up the world all by myself. I've been so sick of Brisbane lately; just had to escape from uni, from Carlo's, from everyone. Even Rhonda. She's so full-on all the time. Just being with her winds me up. So I thought I'd ring you and get a free ride down here, see
30 Dougy and Raylene. Then when you swept that money off the table in that cafe outside Newcastle, I realised what a bitch I was being and started to feel ashamed."

---

2 **up-front** open – 8 **to sit in on** to attend – 8 **tute** tutorial – 12 **to hassle** *(informal)* to keep on asking sb to do sth – 14 **to tear strips off sb** *(informal)* to speak angrily to sb – 21 **trite** dull and boring – 21 **to change tack** to change one's strategy – 28 **to be full-on** *(informal)* to be direct – 29 **to wind sb up** *(informal)* to annoy

"Don't be ashamed. I've cornered the market on that one since our day in the Mall."

"Maybe. Look, if I'm angry with anyone still, it's Cheryl – for the way she talked about Derek Campbell that day I came for dinner, as though he should
5 be grateful for what happened to him."

My mouth was suddenly dry and I looked away before she could see my face.

"I tell you, Angela, that story Cheryl told you doesn't make sense. For Murris, giving up your kid is like killing him. It's no different from plucking a
10 leaf off a tree. We're only alive while we're connected to our own people."

She stood up, brushing the sand from her bottom and reaching for her shoes. Then she held out a hand for me and taking hold, I let her wrench me to my feet. Jarred and Dougy were already heading up the beach towards us, carrying Nerida between them while she bucked and writhed like a huge
15 fish dragged from the sea.

6

At the house we found a station wagon parked outside and pandemonium inside. Not only were the kids back, Trevor, Kendrick, Muriel and Bill, but they seemed to have sprung clones, not just doubling the noise but multiplying it by ten. Raylene was letting everyone know what she thought of this.
20 Nerida took the howling baby from Carli's arms as Auntie Irene appeared from the kitchen.

"Arrh, you're back are you," she called, as though there had been some doubt. "You lot staying for tea?"

This obviously referred to Jarred and me. I looked at him, then at the
25 television still blaring in the corner, which some of the kids were watching while desperately trying to shush the others who wanted to wrestle instead.

"Let's go for a pizza," he suggested. "What about you, Gracey?" He swivelled from face to face. "Dougy?"
30 "I can't go," Nerida cut in, the quietening baby on her shoulder.

"My shout if you like," I whispered to Gracey.

She smiled. "It's OK. My Abstudy went into the bank on Monday. But thanks," and she touched my forearm lightly.

---

1 **to corner the market** to be the market leader *here:* to be the most guilty –
16 **pandemonium** noise and confusion

The four of us drove to a Pizza Hut which Jarred had spotted on the main road. All the talk was of Saturday's race and Gracey's prospects. "If you get away fast enough, you could do it. It's a matter of keeping your form right through to the line."

5 Athletics-speak maybe but it was fun to be part of it. I reached for Jarred's hand under the table and without looking at me he took it and squeezed. I might have had a grip on his hand but it was Gracey who held his attention, the old Gracey, the lively, attractive Gracey who drew glances in the street for more than her athletic prowess. I was glad to have them both.

10 "What are your chances now that you've done a bit of training?" I asked. "Are you going to win?"

"It's not a question of winning," Jarred explained. "Doesn't really matter if she finishes first or third, whatever. It's her time that counts. She has to post a qualifying time to get into the trials next month."

15 "What happens then?" I asked.

This time Gracey answered. "If I qualify, I'll go back to Brisbane and prepare properly at the Academy."

"And if you don't make it this time, do you get another chance?"

She shook her head. "There's no other event before the trials." The waiter 20 arrived with a basket of garlic bread and we each took a piece. Then Gracey was speaking again, her eyes locked on the melting butter as it soaked into the bread. "If I don't post a time, I think I'll go home to Cunningham for a while."

"Cunningham!" I said. "But what about uni, your job?"

25 "Stuff the job," she said bitterly. "And uni for that matter. It's too hard, Angela. I don't mean the study. I could probably handle that, but it's being broke all the time and the hours at Carlo's and trying to fit in the training. That's the reason I gave it a rest. One of the reasons anyway," she corrected herself. "I've got no time for anything else, for a life."

30 "But Brisbane's your home, where you belong," I insisted.

"Is it, Angela? I don't know anymore. I've been thinking about it since I came down here, to Bankstown, to Auntie Irene's house. She reminds me a lot of Auntie Flo back in Cunningham and Mum's buried there and Raymond too. Rhonda reckons it would be good for me to spend some time with my 35 relations." She turned to Dougy who was smiling, not some faint smirk but a radiant, full-faced grin of joy. She leaned across and pecked him affectionately on the cheek.

---

9 **prowess** [ˈpraʊɛs] skill – 13 **to post** to finish with – 25 **stuff sth** *here:* forget

"You come home to *Mingenah*," he said. That last word I had never heard before, an Aboriginal word, I guessed.

"What's that, a nickname for the place, is it, Dougy?"

Brother and sister exchanged a glance before Gracey replied. "That's one
5 of Dougy's names, Angela."

"What, his tribal name?"

She winced. "No. Look, don't make a big thing out of this. Tribal name's not the right way to put it. More what you'd call a middle name, really."

"What is it again?" I asked.

10 Dougy shrugged, smiling lamely. He didn't want to repeat it so I didn't persist. Another thought was already taking over. "You must have a name like that too, Gracey."

She nodded.

I waited. "You're not going to tell me, are you?"

15 "No, Angela. Not now. Not like this."

The pizzas came and we went back to discussions of tactics and what Gracey was doing wrong with her arms over the final twenty metres. Poor Dougy, he barely said a word, but he seemed content, as always. I knew why too. He missed Gracey, had missed her since the day she left Cunningham
20 for Hamilton College, three and a half years ago. Now she was talking of a return. Talking. But that was a long way from doing it and, really, she couldn't be serious.

Jarred volunteered to take the wheel afterwards for the trip across to Hurstville and I let him have it. I was sick of driving, so sick of it a little plan
25 was growing in my mind.

"Tomorrow, would you mind if I didn't come to Homebush with you?"

"I'm sorry if it's a bit tedious for you, Ange, but Gracey has to train and how are we going to get out there?"

"Relax," I told him bluntly. "I've got it all worked out. You get the train into
30 Wynyard, same as this morning, and I'll bring the car from Manly. But this time, I'll get out and you can take the car. How does that sound?"

"But what are you going to do?"

"Don't worry about it. I'm going to shop."

He laughed at that, as I knew he would. "You didn't steal Cheryl's credit
35 card, did you?"

---

6 **tribal** *here:* Aboriginal – 7 **to wince** to change the expression of your face because of sth unpleasant – 27 **tedious** tiring

"Of course not. I probably won't buy a thing, but anything is better than half the day stuck in that windy stadium."

"What will we do if there *is* a train strike?" he asked seriously. "Todd says it's looking bad."

5 "Worry about that when it happens," I said dismissively.

We had pulled up outside Todd's unit by this time. The lights were on and the telltale flicker of television was visible through the curtains. It took half an hour to say goodnight, even though it was damned cold in the Corolla. I drove back to Manly with the taste of him on my lips and wondering vaguely
10 about a name that had remained hidden from me for more than three years.

The next morning, there he was again, waiting in the same spot outside Wynyard Station. A quick switch of driver and I was on my own on the footpath, ready to hit the shops. It was dreams mostly but I did find a
15 fabulous little dress; perfect fit as well. It cost way too much and I walked out into the busy street empty-handed, consoling myself that this was an informal holiday and there would be no chance to wear a dress like that. There was an interesting little boutique across the road so I joined the crowd on the corner, but when the lights switched to green, I turned around, went
20 back into the shop and bought the dress.

The plastic bag hung tantalisingly from my hand when Jarred returned with the Corolla. There were no extra dints that I could see.

"How'd it go?" I asked.

"She's making progress," was all he would commit himself to.

25 "What about you?" I asked.

He made a face. "Gracey's the one. I'd love to see her do well."

He wasn't alone there. We went to the movies that evening, then I left Jarred outside the train station and went home to hang up my new dress in the wardrobe. Next week I'd find some place to wear it.

7

30 I woke on Friday to the news which had threatened all week. "TRAINS OUT" roared the *Sydney Morning Herald*. Jarred was soon on the phone. "What do you want to do?" It was his male problem-solving voice that came down the phone at me, wanting to know all the options before a decision was made.

---

21 **tantalisingly** *here:* promisingly – 22 **dint** damage to a car, dent

"Don't suppose you'd consider cancelling the session with Miss Champion?" I asked. But I guessed the answer before he spoke. Bloody athletes.

"She needs the work. Could make all the difference."

I couldn't argue with that. "I suppose I'll have to come out to Hurstville and get you."

"No, listen, Todd has to get into town anyway. He works near the mail exchange in Redfern." There was a pause and I could hear a muffled discussion in the background. "He says he'll get me as far as the Town Hall and you should pick me up outside the Queen Victoria Building. Got that?"

I had a bad feeling about this from the start. After battling the congestion I found the Queen Victoria Building without too much trouble, but there was no sign of Jarred, nor any place to wait either and I had to keep circling the block, three times, four. Where the hell was he?

Finally, my mobile phone rang. "Angela. I'm so sorry. I'm still down in Redfern. Just arrived. You won't believe the traffic."

Oh yes I would, I thought grimly.

"Look, can you come and get me?"

He gave me the address and said something about the railway line. Had to go over the tracks. I was too busy reaching for the street directory to listen carefully. Oh God, I hated this sort of thing. My sense of direction doesn't seem to work, left and right always turn out to be the opposite. I set off along George Street, looking for railway lines. They appeared soon enough, a mass of them on my right, no, my left. Oh shit!

I had already crossed one lot of lines. Should I turn now? I had to wait forever to get through one enormous intersection and the train lines were on the opposite side now. Did this mean I had crossed them? Damn, I should have kept Jarred on the phone and he could have talked me through it. The traffic was moving just enough to stop me checking the street directory. I had already passed a dozen signs naming the Redfern this or the Redfern that. I must have to turn over the train lines soon. Coming up was a street on my right that led over a rail bridge. That must be it!

I turned right and met a sign telling me I had just entered Darlington. I'd gone the wrong way! The cars behind me sat right on my bumper bar, giving

---

1 **to cancel** to call off – 6 **mail exchange** post office building – 7 **muffled** not heard clearly – 25 **intersection** street crossing

me no time to think. At the next side street I turned right again, just so I could find a place to stop and get my bearings. With the Corolla pulled into the kerb, I reached for the directory and began to trace my finger along the route I should have taken.

5 "You're a bit lost, sweetheart," a voice called.

I looked up and found three young Aboriginal men smiling at me from further along the footpath. One of them waved, a mocking, teasing wave which I was in no mood to return. The Corolla had a central locking switch and I pressed it, making the car jump as the four locks shot downwards at 10 once. The men made no movement towards me but I was uncomfortable under their gaze so I moved the car on another forty metres. The street was lined with terrace houses. Not many like them in Brisbane. These were particularly rundown and despondent, a gate hanging from one hinge, junk piled up on the tiny veranda, broken windows on the first floor. The street 15 looked more like an American crime drama on the tele than Australia. The few people I saw on the street or in doorways were all black, the kids that kicked a can around in the street, the men who had called to me. I looked back and saw that they were still there, ignoring me since I had moved on. An old woman was walking along the footpath towards me, her 20 arms straining under a load of four plastic supermarket bags. She was moving slowly, her face impassive, the little of it I could see, because she kept it bowed towards the pavement as she came on. When she drew level with my car, I saw that she was not so old really, just tired, as though, along with the Coles bags, she carried the worries of the world on her stooped 25 shoulders.

She reminded me of someone and it came to me quickly. Gracey's mother. When I saw her in Cunningham, she was ill, more ill than anyone realised, and within a matter of weeks she was dead. Maybe that was why she had the same weary step as this woman, the same hint of a struggle that had 30 gone on too long and become too hard.

I couldn't concentrate with all this around me, crowding in with memories of that visit to Cunningham, memories that seemed to collide and intertwine with scenes of Gracey among her new friends at uni. I guided the Corolla through a few more turns and although the terraces seemed just as rundown 35 I was seeing students on the streets, and no wonder, for in the distance I spotted a collection of buildings that could only be a university. The street directory seemed to make sense now and I did what I should have done in

---

2 **to get one's bearings** to make os familiar with one's surroundings – 13 **despondent** sad – 32 **to intertwine** to be closely connected with

the first place, turned the stupid book in the direction I wanted to go. With a route planned and map open on the passenger seat next to me, I set off again. This time I managed to drive straight to where Jarred was waiting. He wasn't so much impatient as frantic.

5 "What happened?"

"I needed my navigator," I said simply.

It was not an easy journey out to collect Gracey. There were two Sydneys, I decided: the Sydney of Bondi Beach and Kings Cross, of the harbour with its yachts and its ferries and Taronga Park, of the Opera House and the
10 Bridge. Then there was the Sydney of Parramatta Road, of Bankstown and Hurstville and Homebush. I was already in love with one but quickly learning to dislike the other.

By the time we reached Auntie Irene's, I was ready to explode, and Jarred must have read the signs. "Look, if you trust me with the car ..."

15 Now there was an idea. "Do you mind going without me again?"

They dismissed this worry immediately. "You're lucky though, Angela," Gracey said dryly. "If he drove your car the way he drives me, you'd end up with a wreck."

So it was settled. They were buckled up and gone before I realised this left
20 me in the wilds of Bankstown with not a lot to do for a few hours. But anything was better than wrestling that traffic with deadly boredom my only reward.

"Where's Dougy?" I asked.

"Working with Uncle Dennis," Nerida replied. She was wandering the
25 room with Raylene, a little nervous it appeared to me. The phone had rung once already since Jarred and I arrived, and she had jumped, surprising the baby who took a while to settle again on her shoulder. When the other two left for Homebush, she glanced at me. "You want to help me with this one? Better give her a bath before we feed her."

30 "So I get to play mother," I said under my breath.

Under Nerida's instructions, I gathered the towel and a special bar of soap the doctors had given her and joined them in the bathroom. "We'll do it here in the sink," she told me. "Ray's so small she almost fits in."

The baby's tiny dress came off and the nappy, then Nerida lifted her
35 carefully, naked now, into the warm water. The body was so frail, bones with little flesh, not enough strength to splash at the water. Her pale brown skin

---

4 **frantic** extremely nervous, nearly panicking – 19 **to be buckled up** to be strapped in – 20 **wilds** *(pl.)* area where there's nothing to do

showed the lines of the blood vessels under the surface. I felt myself grab an inrush of breath.

"You all right?" Nerida said, noticing.

"Fine," I said, recovering quickly.

5 Nerida slipped one hand behind the baby's shoulders, wriggling expertly to a position lower on the back. There was so little baby to wash it was over in seconds and she was held dripping over the sink for a moment. I saw the large, almost hairless head, the huge dimples curving into the side of her bottom and those tiny legs dangling in midair. She looked like a little African 10 baby in a Save the Children advertisement.

"Hand me the towel," Nerida was saying. I moved quickly to help wrap the child securely then to my surprise I found myself holding her while Nerida cleaned up around the sink. Clutching her close to my chest, I was ludicrously afraid that I would drop her, until slowly the bundle seemed to rest more 15 comfortably in my arms. The little face looked up at me curiously as though she was thinking, you're not my mother. Where's my mother? It was my first real look at that face. Before, I had simply acted like you were supposed to act around a young baby, and if I made noises about who she took after, it was all a sham really. Well, here was my chance and I searched for signsof 20 her father, the Raymond I remembered and the Dougy and Gracey I knew. Couldn't see anything there to be honest, but knowing the connection seemed enough. My fears were gone now and it was only reluctantly that I gave Raylene up to her mother to be dressed again.

Carli appeared at the right moment, just as the last button was fastened. 25 She scooped the baby into her arms. "Bottle's warming up," she told us sagely, as though she had ten of her own. What was she, fourteen?

Fourteen or not, Carli seemed practised at this feeding business, so much so that Nerida went off into the kitchen, leaving her to it. The girl saw me watching. "You want to have a go?"

30 I'd never done this before and Carli must have guessed. "You have to keep the bottle up, like this," she said, tilting it high and making my hand follow. "Don't want her sucking on air. Fills her up with nothing, eh!"

---

2 **inrush** sudden flow inside – 8 **dimple** *Grübchen* – 13 **ludicrously** [ˈluːdɪkrəslɪ] ridiculously– 19 **sham** untruth – 22 **reluctantly** [rɪˈlʌktəntlɪ] unwillingly – 26 **sagely** wisely

Raylene was so light, and her head flopped around weakly even as she sucked on the teat. The new-baby smell filled my nostrils, a combination of milk and soap and gentle warmth. When she pushed the bottle out of her mouth, Carli reached for her again, but I wouldn't surrender her.

5 "She's got to burp," Carli explained. "Hold her up on your shoulder, quick."

I did as I was told and first heard then felt a dollop of milk shoot from her mouth onto my jumper. Didn't matter. It would wash off. Carli put a cloth over my shoulder in time to catch the next few explosions, but after that the baby settled and I stayed there, enjoying the weight of her against me. I

10 must have impressed my tutor enough to earn a solo run, because Carli disappeared into the kitchen. Nerida came out then. "You OK with her?" she asked.

"Great," I answered.

"Well, I might have a shower then."

15 What would I do if Raylene started to cry? Plenty of help in the kitchen, I told myself. After a few minutes I wanted to see her face again, take another close look at those features. I lowered her from my shoulder and found her little blue lip quivering but she decided against crying. Too much effort maybe. She jumped though when Kendrick roared in from the yard with

20 Trevor on his tail, and a half-fun, half-serious battle raged around the sofa until Auntie Irene sailed out from the kitchen and cuffed both of them around the ears. She made more noise stopping the fight than the two boys combined. "You whack 'em if they start up again, Angela," she told me bluntly, as though I had been ignoring an obvious duty. The two boys were laughing

25 together by this time.

Nerida was taking her time over the shower and might have stayed there longer if the call hadn't come from the hospital. Auntie Irene stood listening, then banged on the door. "Nerida, doctor wants to talk to you." The poor girl had to stand in the lounge room with towel around her, dripping steamy

30 water onto the carpet.

"Tomorrow morning," I heard her say. She looked up at Auntie Irene. "They want to operate tomorrow." She was shaking now with nerves.

---

2 **teat** rubber part of a baby's bottle – 5 **to burp** *(informal)* to let out air from the stomach through the mouth – 6 **dollop** *(informal)* amount of – 21 **to cuff** to hit – 23 **to whack** *(informal)* to hit hard

Dressed again after her shower, Nerida took her daughter from me and hugged her forlornly while I went off to wash my milky shoulder. So the operation was set down for tomorrow. I had known it was coming, due any day, but suddenly it meant more to me than it had on those rides to St
5 Vincent's. I realised I was afraid for Nerida and most of all for Raylene.

I expected to find a rather sombre atmosphere when I returned to the lounge room, but no, a visitor had arrived and the anxiety of the earlier phone call was pushed aside. The new face belonged to Gail, who turned out to be yet another of Auntie Irene's children. God, how big was this family?
10 Gail looked to be in her early twenties, strong and confident in a pair of old jeans and a grubby tracksuit top.

"You watch," Nerida whispered in my ear gleefully after a few minutes. "I heard Auntie Irene moaning on about Gail all week. Going to be a fight, for sure."

15 She was joking, I thought. Gail was chatting happily to her mother in the doorway of the kitchen. Bill appeared from the back of the house and went straight to her, leaning against her leg and sucking his index finger contentedly. Without looking at the boy, Gail's hand found its way down and brushed the side of his face, then after a few strokes he was hauled up and
20 hugged, the two women talking the whole time, not missing a beat of the gossip that passed between them. Still I didn't twig to what I was seeing.

"Not exactly a fight," I teased Nerida, but she was proved right soon enough.

"You don't need it," Gail was saying, her voice suddenly a little louder.

25 "Of course I do," Auntie Irene countered indignantly. "He's been with me now for two months, nearly. You've got to help out with a bit."

"But we're just getting some money together. I thought you didn't mind."

"He can stay as long as you want, but you're earning a bit of money and a
30 few dollars always helps."

"But Dad's making heaps with the milk, isn't he?"

"If the bastards would pay their bills, maybe."

Auntie Irene's anger was building, not just towards customers who didn't pay for their milk either. Gail's own crime wasn't clear as yet, but she was
35 fighting back with a voice that cut like a siren.

---

2 **forlornly** alone, lost and unhappy – 6 **sombre** ['sɒmbə] sad and serious – 11 **grubby** rather dirty

"Not my fault if people don't pay up," she shouted.

"If you paid up, it would help." Auntie Irene was standing belligerently, hands on hips, daring the young woman to keep on at her.

"Ah, Jesus. Look, if we have to fork out to you all the time, Len and me will
5 never have any money." She put Bill down and started walking around the room, throwing her arms about and crying.

"What's going on?" I whispered to Nerida.

"Auntie Irene wants some money from Gail for looking after Bill."

That was when the penny dropped. "Bill's her son?"

10 "Yeah, Auntie Irene's been taking care of him while Gail was working. She and her bloke cook for a gang of shearers. Go away for weeks at a time."

The battle raged back and forth for a few minutes, but in the end Gail handed over a couple of notes and her mother looked satisfied. So did Gail, for that matter, judging by the look on her face as she slipped away into the
15 kitchen. Bill followed, the finger still in his mouth, and I caught a glimpse of him climbing into his mother's lap as she sat at the kitchen table, chatting quietly again.

Nerida followed my gaze. "Auntie Irene knows everyone from the family who's down here in Sydney. Takes care of them too. You watch how many
20 show up here today 'cause it's Friday. Bet there's half a dozen extra kids sleeping here tonight. She's a top woman. I couldn't believe it the first day you came and you called her Irene."

"Oh God. Was that wrong?"

"You should have called her Auntie, sort of respect, you know what I mean.
25 She was waiting to see if you were one of us, even though you don't look much like it. She asked you where you were from, eh."

"And I told her. Brisbane."

Nerida laughed. "Yeah, well, so what? She was really asking who you were. Once you just left it at that, Brisbane, she knew you were no Murri." She
30 seemed to find this very funny. "You didn't even notice what Gracey did, I bet."

I thought back. "She rattled off a whole lot of names, family names."

Nerida nodded slowly, smiling. "She was letting Auntie Irene know who she was and where she was from and how she fitted in, so Auntie Irene
35 could recognise her."

---

2 **belligerently** [-'----] aggressively – 3 **to keep on at sb** to continue to speak in an annoying way – 4 **to fork out** to spend a lot of money – 11 **shearer** person who cuts the wool off sheep

A hoot of laughter shot from the kitchen, Auntie Irene's overpowering cackle, drawing Carli who had somehow ended up with the baby through all of this. She delivered Raylene into my arms, a tick of approval if ever there was one, and went off to join the fun.

5 I wasn't complaining.

8

Auntie Irene had to take Muriel to the doctor's just before eleven, and soon after, Kaz emerged from one of the bedrooms, still wearing the loose tracksuit he had slept in.

"What are you doing here?" Gail demanded.

10 "I live here, don't I?" he snapped back.

"No, I mean, what about the dance school?"

"Can't get into town, can I? Trains are on strike."

This was news to Gail apparently but she accepted the explanation.

He wandered into the kitchen for something to eat, then sat next to me
15 on the sofa. I quickly discovered there was one topic of conversation he enjoyed more than any other.

"I was one of the youngest to get in, you know. Ever. They reckon I'll be the best dancer going round in a couple of years."

"That's great," I said lamely. I couldn't very well walk away. But it wasn't as
20 bad as it might have been. He reminded me of Gracey, the way he was so keen to do well. She spoke like this about her running sometimes, without the cocksure vanity, thank God, but with just as much confidence.

"Once I'm finished my course here, I'm going overseas," he continued. "Big audience for indigenous dance in America and France and places like that."
25 He had me convinced.

Kaz eased himself from the sofa into a series of graceful exercises, deep knee bends, slow turns with hands in just the right place. It was all for my benefit, I realised, so I watched, liking him. As far as I could tell, he looked pretty good.
30 At about one, Auntie Irene returned, not just with Muriel but with a car load of kids and their parents who had apparently given her a lift. There were bags of groceries to carry in. Trevor, Kendrick and even little Bill did the

---

1 **hoot** loud noise – 2 **cackle** laugh in a loud, high voice – 22 **cocksure** *(informal)* confident in a way that is annoying to others – 22 **vanity** too much pride in os

honours, looking like the porters on an African safari as they tramped through the lounge room one behind the other. Soon after, the sound of a second car brought me to the door, not Jarred and Gracey as I expected, but another bunch of visitors who piled into the house. The kitchen table was
5 brought into the lounge room and before long, every adult was sitting round it with cards in hand, taking the game light-heartedly considering the amount of money that changed hands. I looked for Nerida to see if she was going to play and maybe I could join in as well, but she had disappeared into the bedroom with Raylene. I could understand why.
10 When a large man appeared at the door, grinning at what he found inside, I thought he was another visitor. "Hey, Dennis," a voice called, and a place was found for him. This was the father of all these kids I'd come to know. Dougy slipped into the house soon after and went straight into the bedroom where Nerida had taken Raylene.
15 "You want a beer, Den?" the same voice called from the scrum around the table.

"No, got to finish me round later. Any of you mob want a carton of milk?"

They all laughed. It seemed that milk was a recurring joke among the players. There was a loud cheer mixed with deep moans and groans when
20 one pot was settled.

"Someone's going to pay their electricity bill this week," a woman teased the winner.

"Bugger that. Pay your milk bill first," Uncle Dennis cut in and again the players broke up with laughter.
25 The game went on oblivious to the noise around it. The television was on again though I couldn't spot anyone who was actually watching it. The kids were all over each other, chasing, tackling, giggling and screeching until one of the parents would turn and shout, "Shut up, you lot."

I looked for Kaz but he had disappeared. A little later I saw him in the
30 backyard, ignoring the bitter wind, absorbed in his movements, so determined and controlled. By this time I was starting to worry about Jarred and Gracey. I expected them back by early afternoon but it was nearly three o'clock. Surely Gracey couldn't train for that long. She'd be too exhausted to run tomorrow. I was beginning to imagine car accidents or worse when
35 finally they turned up just before five.

---

15 **scrum** disorderly group of people – 20 **pot** amount of money bet in a card game –
23 **bugger** (*informal*) swear word – 25 **oblivious to** not paying attention to

"You must be frozen right through," I said as they scuttled in from the cold, but they didn't look too bad as they stood around apologising. "You won't believe the traffic," were Jarred's first words.

Oh yes, I would believe, but it wasn't traffic which had kept them this 5 long.

"No," Jarred explained. "The place was crawling with people. All the teams are here now, ready for tomorrow."

"We were side-tracked, talking," Gracey said. "Time got away a bit. Sorry."

Oh well, I thought. If Gracey was talking to her old mates, the kids she 10 used to train with, I was pleased to hear it.

Meals seemed to be a scratch affair with whatever was available. Gracey opened a can of soup and Dougy started with the toaster. I made the drinks, three instant coffees and a cup of tea for Dougy. "Where's the sugar?" I asked.

15 Gracey brought the bowl to the bench. With the table in use for the card game, we had to eat standing up. "Watch out you don't spill that," Jarred called.

It was such an odd thing to say, delivered in a jokey, affectionate voice. I stared at him quizzically.

20 Gracey saw my face and laughed. "Jarred doesn't like to waste sugar," she said.

I was left out of the joke here, it seemed to me, but when I continued to look at her, expecting an explanation, she suddenly flushed with embarrassment and glanced briefly at Jarred. The smile fell from both their 25 faces and they each turned back to their tasks, Gracey stirring the soup and Jarred buttering the toast. It was a strange moment that left me uneasy though I didn't want to think about why.

After the soup, I drove Jarred back to his cousin's. "How did the training go?" I asked. Hadn't I said the same thing yesterday? I was starting to sound 30 like a CD stuck on the same spot.

"Well, it's up to her now."

"She won't really go back to Cunningham, will she?"

He shrugged and shifted restlessly in the passenger seat beside me. "She's had a lot of pressure on her, Angela. I think she's lonely for 35 something."

There it was again. Lonely. If she came back to Brisbane, she didn't need to be lonely.

---

8 **side-tracked** distracted, not concentrating – 11 **scratch** put together in a hurry – 19 **quizzically** [ˈkwɪsɪklɪ] in a puzzled way

"It would be such a waste, going back there," I said. I wanted him to understand, to help me convince her if it should ever come to that. "We can't let her rot away, let her get eaten up by all these aunts and uncles and cousins she's supposed to have out there."

5 "That's a bit rough, Angela. What's wrong with that family in Bankstown? Looked OK to me."

"Yes, but ..." I couldn't find words for what I felt. This whole business of Gracey back in Cunningham had me worried. I didn't know why it had me stirred up. Somehow it was wrong for her.

10 Jarred was out of the car at his cousin's place as soon as the car came to a halt.

"Hey," I called. "Haven't you forgotten something?"

He pushed his head and shoulders back into the car, straining across to kiss me. "Sorry. My mind's on the race tomorrow."

15 I knew that. Should have realised what it meant to him. Should have been more careful with the tone in my voice when I called him back to say goodnight properly. There was not just his own race tomorrow but Gracey's and so much was riding on her success. Yet, for all that I knew these things, I found myself fighting a new and unwelcome anxiety during the drive back

20 to Manly. Sure, I wanted this athletics meeting over and done with. But more than that, I wanted to know how Jarred and Gracey could have spent all afternoon out in that blustery stadium, talking to a bunch of runners who were hardly close friends. Most of all, I wanted to know what spilled sugar really meant to them.

---

22 **blustery** very windy

The Race

1

Jarred was waiting outside the station on the corner which had become our rendezvous point, a tall figure in his tracksuit, his bag slung easily over his shoulder. At the sight of him I knew how lucky I was, and I realised too that I had driven all the way from Manly looking forward to the moment when
5   he would climb awkwardly into my too-small Corolla and lean across to kiss me.

The driver behind us jabbed at his horn but I ignored it and lingered with our faces close.

"Are you nervous?" I asked when we were moving again.
10   "Would be if I was much of a show," he laughed.

"You've been building Gracey's hopes all week. Why not yours?"

"The difference is that Gracey at least has a chance."

More than a chance, I hoped. She was alone on the footpath when we arrived. "The rest have gone up to the hospital. Everyone." She looked at her
15   watch. "The operation has already started."

"How was Nerida?" I asked.

"Out of her tree. Dougy's just as bad. He'll be pacing up and down like a bloke outside the labour ward in one of those old comedies."

"How long ... before there's news."
20   "Mid-morning, they said. Dougy's got your mobile number so he's going to let us know."

"She'll be OK, won't she?"

"Christ, I hope so."

With this niggling worry in our minds, the journey to Homebush was the
25   quietest of the week. By the time we arrived, the carpark was almost full and there was a crowd all ready in the stand, not just a scattered collection of bystanders as there had been on my last visit. We made a base for ourselves in one of the last rows, high above the track.

"We should get you warmed up," Jarred said to Gracey, who was already
30   bouncing around on the spot in a nervous dance. They set off for the far side of the track and I watched them, so easy together now. For the past few days

---

17 **to pace** to walk steadily – 18 **labour ward** part of hospital for childbirth – 24 **niggling** continuing – 27 **bystander** onlooker

it seemed like my own life had been on hold, and though I'd been close to both of them at times, it was not as close as I wanted.

It was an age before the heats of the 100 metres were called and the runners came from all corners of the track to mill about anxiously behind the starting line. Jarred had told me a hundred times already that it was not a question of winning the race. All that mattered was the time. Just the same, I couldn't contain my excitement when Gracey blasted away in her heat, leading clearly after a dozen strides, and though the others seemed to close the gap a little, she was five metres ahead at the finish line. She'd won the race. Surely the time would be good enough.

It took an age for the result to come through over the loudspeaker, first her name and the other place-getters and finally, "The winning time, eleven point eight three seconds." It was not enough. Jarred had told me earlier, "She has to go under eleven point six."

We made a dejected party when Jarred and Gracey climbed into the stand to sit with me. "So close," Jarred moaned. Gracey said nothing as she watched the rest of the heats. Then, as the final race stormed up the track, she sat up suddenly. "Look at that."

One girl was ten metres ahead at the halfway mark and doubled the margin by the finish.

"Jodie Kelso from Monash," Jarred told us. "She was relay reserve at the last Olympics. Can't see you taking home the title today, Gracey."

"Got enough medals already," she whispered. "What I need is the time." There was determination in her words but a hint of defeat as well.

This unhappy mood was broken when my mobile phone started to ring.

"Angela?" asked a timid voice.

"Yes," I said abruptly then realised who it must be. "Dougy! How did it go? Is Raylene all right?"

The other two stopped talking and leaned closer as I waited for the reply.

"Yeah, she's OK. They brought her out of the operating room a little while ago. Only Nerida can see her though."

I relayed the good news to the others, but on the phone Dougy seemed hesitant and I wondered if there was something he hadn't dared tell us. But this hesitation wasn't about Raylene. "How did Gracey go?" he asked.

---

1 **on hold** in standstill – 3 **heat** race whose winner competes in the next race *(Vorlauf)* – 15 **dejected** disappointed – 33 **to relay** [riːˈleɪ] to repeat sth you have heard

"She's had one race already. Won by a mile."

I could almost feel him smiling through the phone. "I knew she would."

"She has to run again, Dougy."

"She'll win that one too."

5 He hadn't seen the girl from Monash but I bit my tongue and ended the call.

In the meantime, Jarred had his chance on the track. We left him at the runners' entrance and made our way back into the stand. There was activity everywhere now – jumpers, throwers, hurdlers high stepping on the in-
10 field.

"You're lucky to have him, Angela," Gracey said gently as she watched Jarred warming up – stretching out on the back straight, slowing, turning round, accelerating again. There was real affection in her voice and I grinned happily.

15 "You said I'd do better with a sprinter."

"Yeah, well. A lot I'd know. He's been so good to me these last few days. Both of you." Suddenly her head drooped forward, as though she couldn't hold my gaze. That wasn't like Gracey. What was going on here?

I glanced up to see runners stripping out of their tracksuits, Jarred's
20 pony-tailed head above the rest. A bunch of guys was forming round him; suddenly they all shuffled to a line on the track and the gun sent a puff of smoke into the air.

Each time I had seen him race, Jarred went straight to the front, though always the others caught him before the finish. This time he could not even
25 do that. He settled into a spot halfway through the field and seemed content to stay there. A pack of a dozen or so broke away from the rest, and after five laps, Jarred was a hundred metres from the lead. Gradually, inevitably, he slipped back with the other runners around him and as the winners sprinted desperately to the line he still had half a lap to go. He
30 wasn't last by any means, but it seemed such an anonymous way to end, unnoticed as the winners bent over one another, puffing and already shaking hands.

"We'd better console him," I suggested.

Gracey followed me along the row, then down the steps to ground level.
35 There were signs at each gate – "Officials and Competitors Only" – and I hesitated. Should I wait here until he came from the track?

---

17 **to droop** to move downwards – 33 **to console** *trösten*

Gracey showed no such fears. She breezed through the gate, leaving me well behind, and reached Jarred while he was still bent over, hands on his knees. Perhaps she called to him – I was too far away to hear – but he straightened up as she drew nearer, a grim smile forcing its way between
5 his gasps for air. Then Gracey was with him, arms around him, laughing with him until that smile widened into real joy, and she reached up on her toes, holding his head steady in her hands while she kissed him on the cheek. I felt as though a horse had kicked me in the ribs.

When Jarred came through the gate, I took my turn at consoling him,
10 held myself against his sweating body and felt his arm around me. How close was he squeezing me? Was there real affection? Did he greet me as openly as Gracey? He chatted freely, making light of his performance in the race, as though it didn't matter. I thought again of the ferry from Watson's Bay and reaching for his hand I extended that long arm like a rope and
15 wrapped myself in it until I was snuggled against him. For a moment, I stopped measuring his every gesture, his every word, content to enjoy the feeling.

2

There was a two-hour break before the final. None of us could settle for more than a few minutes in those moulded plastic seats. Jarred kept Gracey
20 moving, all the time talking gently into her ear about what she had to do. There seemed so much to remember for a race that was over in a matter of seconds.

At two-thirty, the runners were called down to the track and it was time for a final "good luck". I decided to stay up in the stand where I
25 could see the race more easily, but not Jarred. He had to be there, as close as possible, whispering encouragement to the last second.

The girls took their places along the starting line, the gun was raised like an executioner's sword and the race began. At her first stride Gracey stubbed the tip of a spike into the track, bringing the slightest stumble. She
30 recovered quickly, but she had lost the advantage of her explosive start. With a third of the race gone, the Olympian was well ahead and Gracey was struggling to do any better than the line of girls roughly level across the track. Then she seemed to straighten, running higher on her toes, with her

---

1 **to breeze** *here:* to move confidently – 16 **gesture** [ˈdʒestʃə] *Geste–* 19 **to mould** to shape into a particular form – 29 **to stub** to accidentally hit

knees, elbows, arms working together instead of against one another, and soon she had broken free of the field. She was gaining on the leader now, too far behind to catch her but cutting down the margin with each surge of those powerful legs. At the finish line she was no more than five metres
5 behind, with another ten at least to third place.

I looked towards Jarred and knew there was still hope as Gracey joined him anxiously at the fence. They went off together, one on each side of the barrier to ask for her time. Already they were talking to an official who pointed them on to another. There was no time to reach them and I would
10 know soon enough from their reactions. Now they were talking to the second man who conferred with his walkie-talkie and, after an unbearable pause, he spoke a few words to them. Jarred sprang off his toes, an impressive sight considering the size of him, and even though the chain-wire fence stood between them still, he grabbed Gracey and hugged her tightly. Then
15 he turned towards the stand and raised his fist triumphantly to leave no doubt at all.

"Eleven point five nine!" he was shouting as he pulled an embarrassed Gracey up the aisle amid a sea of inquisitive faces. "Eleven point five nine. One hundredth of a second to spare." Jarred repeated this over and over as
20 we gathered in a group hug. If he was jubilant I was light-headed – more with relief than anything else.

"Now for the trials," I said, hugging Gracey all over again. "You never know, my best friend might end up at the Commonwealth Games. With a month back in Brisbane to get ready, all you can do is improve."
25 She flinched when I said this, giving the first hint of what was to come.

"Gracey," I said cautiously. "You'll go on to the trials, won't you?"

When she didn't answer immediately, our celebrations were cut short. I expected Jarred to question her as well, but he seemed to hold back, watching.
30 "I'm not coming down again for the trials, Angela. To tell you the truth, I'm not even going back to Brisbane with you. Cunningham's my home now, for the time being anyway."

"But that's not what you said. You had it all planned out. If you qualified for the trials, then you'd come back to Brisbane. Well, you got the time you
35 needed, now you're trying to renege on the deal."

---

18 **aisle** [aɪl] path between rows of seats – 20 **light-headed** overwhelmed – 25 **to flinch** to move back suddenly – 35 **to renege** [rɪ'neɪɡ] **on sth** to not do sth you agreed to do

"Angela! What are you taking about? There was no deal. You're making this up. I told you at that pizza place I was thinking about Cunningham. The bit about going back to Brisbane...I was forgetting what it's been like the last few months."

5 "But why go back to Cunningham?"

"It's been in my mind for a while, long before I left Brisbane. You saw how much gear I brought with me. It's everything I own. Then, staying with Auntie Irene, having so many people around and watching them together ... I was part of a family like that once, not just Dougy and Raymond and me but

10 Auntie Flo and her kids, the cousins. Last Christmas I couldn't stand being around them all, but I'm a different person now, thanks to Rhonda, thanks to the kids at the Unit. I'm ashamed of the way I acted at Christmas, running off to you at Noosa. It's time I went back, really went back."

"So why did you go through with the race?"

15 "For Jarred mostly." She turned to him, smiling. "It was a challenge, wasn't it, Coach? And we did it." She touched his arm for a moment and they shared the glow of their achievement. "Look, a race is one thing, but we're talking about my life here, my future. Can't let a single race decide that for me, can I?"

20 "But there's so much more for you in Brisbane – uni, the job at Carlo's, Frank and all those black friends you made."

"I'm finished with Brisbane, Angela. I've got no time for myself there, no life. I can't go on like that month after month and next year wouldn't be any different."

25 "What about the Institute of Sport then? You can transfer your course. You said yourself you won't have to work if you have a scholarship and the coaches are the best in the country."

"I've thought of all that. A guy from the Institute came to see me yesterday while we were training. He said because I'm only eighteen I'd still be a show,

30 even if I left it a year, so long as I stay fit and fast. Maybe I will, but I'm going to Cunningham first and I've got to go now."

"Gracey! The place is a dump and the only stretch of grass you could train on is the football field. Even that's a cow paddock. How will you keep up with your running there? And that's only part of it. What about uni? It's goodbye

35 Law, goodbye to any kind of a degree. No jobs in Cunningham either, I'll bet, not even waiting on tables. What are you going to do all day? You'll be bored out of your mind in a fortnight."

---

33 **paddock** small field – 36 **to wait on tables** to serve food in a restaurant

This pulled Gracey up and I thought for a moment I might be getting through to her. "There's more to life than medals,' she said vaguely. "Or a career in Law. There's more than one Law," she added defiantly.

I had no idea what she was talking about, but the words made her more
5 stubborn and it was plain I was getting nowhere. "Jarred," I called desperately. "You can see what I'm trying to say. I'm right, aren't I? Going back to live in Cunningham will throw away everything Gracey's worked for."

He looked at her while he shuffled his trainers on the smooth cement, until finally he faced me. "I think I can understand Gracey ... what she wants
10 to do, what she needs right now. We talked about Cunningham yesterday when you stayed with Nerida. It's up to her really, Angela, and maybe we should be helping her instead of trying to change her mind."

"You talked about it?" I said. "Gracey, why didn't you talk to me?"

She didn't answer but instead tried to stare me down. It was not one of
15 her iron-hard glares. In fact, she seemed as vulnerable as that last morning in the boarding school.

"I always talked to you, Gracey. No secrets, remember." I knew it sounded childish, but I was hurt, and there were things stirring in me that wanted to hit back. "And all the time you had another name you never told me about,"
20 I said harshly.

"That wasn't a secret, Angela. You don't understand. I didn't tell you at school because ... I didn't want anyone to know. What if the girls like Lisa Fenwick had used it as a nickname to put me down. Besides, I didn't want them to think of me as a Murri and after a while I don't think I wanted to be
25 one either. That's changed now. That's one of the reasons I have to go back to Cunningham. To make sure I never forget I'm black, ever again."

There it was again. Cunningham. I had to make her see what a mistake it would be. "You've worked hard to get away from the bush and there might not be another chance. Your mother wanted you at Hamilton, she would
30 have wanted you at uni. It's such a waste if you give up now and go sneaking away just because things got tough."

---

3 **defiantly** proudly refusing to obey authority – 8 **trainer** type of sports shoe – 14 **to stare sb down** to look at sb for so long that they look away

"I'm not sneaking away. I'm choosing to go," she said coldly. "Angela, for all that's happened this year, you haven't really moved from that coffee shop in Noosa. You still think it's about becoming a lawyer and saving my people. But without a family that I feel part of, I'm not a Murri at all. That's where
5 everything starts and finishes for me."

When I could make no reply, she pressed on. "You remember what I said about that Derek Campbell, about a leaf pulled off a tree? Well, I'm the leaf and I want to get back on the tree."

"But what will you do?"
10 "It's not what I'll do, it's what I'll feel. There's stuff I never took any notice of, things about my people and where my land is. You can't see it maybe, but those things are more precious than a job or money or some achievement you can point to and say, hey, aren't I clever, I built that, I changed that."

"How long then? Will you apply to the Institute of Sport for next year?"
15 "No time limits, Angela. If I go there with a deadline then all I'll think about is when I'll be leaving. I wouldn't settle. It would be as bad as last Christmas. I wouldn't let myself be part of the place."

No plans, no time limit. So much could happen so quickly. Look at how much she had changed in just six months. She might never get away from
20 the place. "You'll end up like Nerida," I said.

Gracey sat back for the first time, breaking the intimacy of our huddle. "Nerida's happier than me right now," she said sharply. "You've got no right to judge her. Even with Raylene at the hospital, she's at peace inside herself. Got her family, her friends, and she's happy with what she does each day.
25 Doesn't matter what you do, as long as it means something to you. Whether I'm in Cunningham or Brisbane or Canberra, that's not going to change."

"I didn't mean it to come out like that."

"What did you mean then?" she said hotly.

Oh God, I was floundering here. My mind snatched at the raw fears that
30 swirled in vivid images behind my eyes. I had to make her see them too. "Look, I've been out to Cunningham, remember. I've seen the mesh on the shop windows and the drunks sleeping it off in the park, the kids roaming around with nothing to do." I moved closer, keeping my voice down as I

---

15 **deadline** time by which you must have completed sth – 21 **huddle** sitting closely together – 29 **to flounder** to be unable to decide what to say – 31 **mesh** wire

added: "There's the men, too. You said so yourself. They kind of expect you to …"

"Those guys I told you about, it happened in Brisbane, Angela. And I don't really think it's for you to say, anyway. Plenty of white blokes act the same."

5 "But you know it's a risk you're taking."

She stayed silent, still intent on stubbing her toes at the seat in front.

"Yes, it's a risk," she muttered. "But Auntie Flo'll be there and she's a strong woman, like Auntie Irene, and no bloke, black or white, is ever going to waltz straight into my bed like he owns me." This was the defiant Gracey and her
10 fiery eyes locked onto my face again. "You and Rhonda are as bad as each other, you know. She wouldn't see anything good that was white and you don't want to see anything good that's black. You've got some kind of TV blackfella in your head, that's your trouble."

I was afraid she would storm away again as she had done in the Mall. She
15 seemed tensed for it, the same anger rising. Then as quickly as it flushed the skin of her face, it receded again and she surprised me by placing her hand gently on my forearm.

"I'm afraid, Angela. There's a life out there for me and I want to live it. But well, some of the things you've said … they frighten me too. That's why I'll
20 need you, more than ever."

"But I'll be a thousand kilometres away. What good will I be?"

"I'll need you on the phone. And writing to me, to tell me I'm doing the right thing and to stick it out if things get ugly. I need you to see this is the right thing for me and to say you'll help me."

25 But it wasn't the right thing. Couldn't she see that? She was asking me to help her go the wrong way and I wouldn't do it. I couldn't.

I looked into the face of my best friend, knowing that as the seconds ticked by my head was shaking, just enough for her to see. There had never been such pain in my life. I closed my eyes, hoping it would go away, and
30 kept them closed when I felt her hand slip from my arm and they were still closed when I heard her walk away.

Watching, listening nearby, Jarred couldn't stop himself. "Angela," he called. "What are you doing? You can't cut Gracey loose like this."

My eyes were open now and I saw that he had Gracey by the arm, stopping
35 her from walking away altogether. She turned and leaned in against him, for support, for comfort, I couldn't tell. He put his arm around her and the lean

---

8 **to waltz in** to walk into a room without care – 15 **tensed** *(informal)* nervous and worried – 23 **to stick sth out** to continue to do sth that is difficult

became an embrace. It was not the first time he had held her close like this. That was plain. "Angela!" he called again, a sharp edge in his appeal. It seemed to me that he was defending her. Defending Gracey from me.

Before I knew what I meant by it, I said, "You always take the tall ones, Gracey."

Jarred didn't have a clue what I was talking about but Gracey did. "It's not like that, Angela," she said, her voice cool.

"What do you mean?" Jarred asked suspiciously, his eyes darting between the two of us.

"She means that I'm getting too close to you," Gracey answered.

I searched their faces for a hint of guilt and found the faintest tremor there. My knees went weak, almost ready to buckle, as I asked bluntly, "Well, how close are you?"

"Angela! Don't go on like this," said Jarred. "There's nothing between Gracey and me."

I eyed them sceptically and saw again the uneasiness in Gracey's face.

"You're being silly," he assured me, his arm reaching out, touching my elbow.

I was a statue.

"Jarred," Gracey urged.

He looked down at her and I couldn't see what passed between them but I was certain now that something had happened. My legs simply would not hold me any longer and I found myself sitting oddly in the moulded seat, looking up at them both. I gave way to fear now, the nameless suspicions I had fought back since yesterday but had refused to let take hold. But I was overrun now. Helpless against them. "You did more than talk yesterday," I said too loudly. "For that matter, you had enough time to go over to your cousin's place."

"What are you saying?" Jarred demanded. But he knew already. "You think the two of us ... that we ... Angela!" He looked down at Gracey, cradled still in the crook of his shoulder. She broke away from him and ran along the empty row of the grandstand. He watched her go, then turned back to me. But only for a second. Without a word he backed away after her, swivelled his body to face along the row and began to chase her. I watched as first Gracey and then Jarred reached the distant aisle and hurried down the stairs

---

8 **suspiciously** [səˈspɪʃəlɪ] in a way not trusting the other person – 12 **to buckle** to become weak and bend – 30 **to cradle** to hold gently – 31 **crook** part of the shoulder where it bends – 33 **to swivel** [ˈswɪvl] to turn

to ground level until finally, just before they disappeared around the corner, he caught her and pulled her to him.

The cold wind swept through the stand, an arctic breath that turned my head away. I saw that in either direction I was alone in the long row of seats. For all I cared at that moment, I might have been alone on the entire planet.

3

I drove back to Manly and spent the afternoon in my room.

Grandma called me for dinner but I was poor company at the table and they were soon exchanging silent glances of concern.

"Gracey's going back to Cunningham," I said.

"Oh," was Grandma's reply, though I realised that neither of them had a clue what that meant.

"Did she win the big race?" Grandad asked trying to liven the mood with his sprightly enthusiasm.

I was suddenly annoyed. It wasn't whether she won or not but the time she ran. Couldn't people get that through their skulls? What did it matter now anyway? If I tried to explain it would all have to come out. "Came second," I said and excused myself from the table.

While they watched television, I lay on the bed in my room and must have drifted off eventually because I woke freezing about midnight, hauled the heavy blankets over me and slept the rest of the night in my clothes.

There was movement in the kitchen before dawn but I rolled over and slept again. By the time I went in search of breakfast, Grandma was up and about. "Richard's gone to a service out past Parramatta somewhere. He left very early."

He obviously knew what the traffic was like, I thought, and even that brief memory hurt.

"He'll be away most of the day," she said brightly, as though she wouldn't miss him in the least. I suppose that's what happens when you've had fifty years together. I wondered if I would speak to Jarred today and that hurt even more.

"Are you going over to Bankstown again today?" she asked.

I shook my head as she poured the first cup of coffee from the plunger.

"I thought you might have a rest today. After breakfast, could you take me for a walk along the foreshore, under all those pines. Richard doesn't like the cold wind off the ocean so he never wants to go. But I love it. We'll rug up warm and have a good stroll."

5   If she insisted. My day did not look very full otherwise.

    It was overcast and windy when we parked the car one street back from the beach. Grandma looked like a blimp with two heavy jumpers under her jacket, gloves, beanie and scarf, all odd patterns and colours. She'd never cared much what she looked like.

10   There was a wide concrete path above the beach, skirting the famous pines which stretched further than Grandma could possibly walk. She was right, though. There was a freshness and energy to struggling against a bitter wind. We hadn't gone very far when Grandma started in on me. "You've had a falling out with your friend, I take it."

15   "Both of them," I said miserably.

    "The tall boy as well. I'm sorry to hear that."

    "I said some stupid things."

    "Did you mean what you said?"

    She was a devil, my grandmother, the way she could sneak up on you with 20 a question that shot an arrow straight into your heart.

    "I've only been thinking about that every minute since it happened," I told her meekly.

    "And?"

    My hands were already well inside the pockets of the spray jacket. This 25 made it easier to hunch my shoulders and look down at the cracked cement. "To Gracey, yes," I muttered. When Grandma stopped on the path, waiting for more, there was no choice but to explain. Despite the wind I took one hand out of the cosy warmth to make some kind of gesture, something solid, something I could see. "Out of the blue, she gives up everything," I said, 30 frowning. "Wants to go back to that little town in the bush. I told her what a mistake it was but she wouldn't listen." I was crying by then, as I knew I would. "Probably never see her again."

---

2 **pine** tree with needle-like leaves – 3 **to rug up** *(AustrE informal)* to put on thick clothes – 4 **stroll** [strəʊl] walk – 7 **blimp** small air ship – 8 **beanie** small hat – 13 **to start in on** to approach a topic – 14 **falling out** quarrel – 19 **to sneak up on sb** to get at you without your noticing – 22 **meekly** gently, without complaining – 24 **spray jacket** rain jacket – 25 **to hunch one's shoulders** to raise them in a round way – 29 **out of the blue** just like that

"That's rather melodramatic," Grandma responded.

I cried a bit more then found myself laughing. "You never were the sentimental one," I said, unable to decide between more tears and more laughter.

5 "No, I leave that to Richard. He's the sympathetic partner in our marriage."

I took my grandmother's arm as we walked on at her pace, huddled safely inside the cocoons of our sturdy coats.

"Oh Grandma," I began, "I thought all the things between us had been
10 cleared away. We had this talk on Bondi Beach, Gracey and me, sitting in the sand. We've always been honest with one another about what was bugging us, what we were thinking. I even told her about Grandad and Derek Campbell, that Aboriginal man he rescued as a boy."

Grandma said nothing, just kept walking, staring straight ahead, waiting
15 for me to go on. As we walked, I turned that afternoon at Bondi over in my mind. Honesty. There was one thing I had said that day which niggled at me. "Gracey asked me if I liked Aborigines. I said yes, of course, because – well, it would sound awful if I didn't. I was a bit annoyed too that she was testing me out all over again, looking for an excuse to push me away. I meant what
20 I said, or I thought I did. Now I'm not so sure."

"But you like Gracey, don't you?"

"Of course, and her brother Dougy and this guy named Frank back in Brisbane and Nerida and Auntie Irene and that whole bunch out in Bankstown. But there are blacks I don't like too, a woman named Rhonda
25 Haines for a start and there's a couple that turn up on the news now and again whingeing about things. I don't like them."

"You can't expect to like every black you meet, Angela. It's too much. Are you sure she was expecting you to?"

"No, that's just it. I think I know what she was asking me now and that
30 makes it worse."

My grandmother stopped to look at me more closely while I explained, and I had to turn away while I spoke. "She wasn't talking about one or two people, she was talking about...all blacks. Everything, their way of life."

---

5 **sympathetic** showing understanding for sb else's problem – 8 **cocoon** sth wrapped around you to give you protection – 8 **sturdy** strong – 16 **to niggle at** to irritate – 26 **to whinge** [wɪndʒ] to complain in an annoying way

I looked out at the Pacific Ocean, the biggest thing on Earth, and I was suddenly aware of how insignificant I was there on its edge. It made my shame even worse. "Grandma, I don't think I do like them. They ... well, it repels me. I don't know why. I can't put my finger on it."

5   "And that's why you don't want Gracey to live out there in this little town. What's it called?"

  "Cunningham. There's nothing there, Grandma. I've seen it. A couple of thousand people, not much work and even less if you're black. She got her chance to leave, to go to uni, maybe the Olympic Games one day, and she's
10 giving it all away."

  It was my grandmother's turn now to look out at the ocean. I wondered if she felt small and ineffectual as I did. She laughed to herself grimly. "You're so much like your grandfather, Angela. You love so intensely and you have to give those you love all the things you want for them. You'd move
15 heaven and earth to do it, the both of you."

  "I'd do anything to change Gracey's mind," I said.

  She looked at me sharply, a piercing gaze that seemed to search deep behind my eyes. "Would you?" she asked.

  "Yes, I'd do anything to stop her."

20   Without warning she seemed to give up against the wind saying, "This is far enough. We'll head back now," and I had to hurry a step or two to take her arm once more. I tried a few times to fire up our conversation again on the way back to the car but she offered only a word here and there in reply and my attempts sputtered out in the wind.

25   There was no call from Jarred on my message bank. No call through the rest of the day or evening. I wondered how little Raylene was doing but couldn't muster the courage to ring the house in Bankstown. Grandad returned by mid-afternoon and surprised Grandma who was bent over the phone book. "Who are you looking up?" I heard him ask as he moved through
30 to the lounge room.

  Grandma didn't answer at first, as though she had been caught out. "Oh, no one," she said lamely, closing the book. "Angela," she called, "will you be home for dinner tomorrow night?"

  She had never asked me this before, content to let me ring late in the day
35 to tell her my plans. Plans. I had none now. "Yes, Grandma," I said. "Most likely."

---

4 **to repel** to feel dislike – 12 **ineffectual** *here:* unimportant – 24 **to sputter out** *here:* to be lost in – 25 **message bank** mail box of a mobile phone – 27 **to muster** to try to find

4

On Monday morning I woke to a dark and silent house. When I flicked on the bedside lamp, grandma's old-fashioned alarm clock showed five minutes to six. Too early to be awake, but I knew there was no chance of sleep, even as I rolled over under the heavy blankets, so different from my lightweight
5　doona at home. After a minute or two of pretending, I rolled onto my back again to stare into the blackness, folding my hands under my head and ignoring the cold.

There was no rush to get out of bed, to dress and hurry over to Bankstown as there had been for nearly a week now. I could lie here all day if I wanted.
10　Wasn't this a sensation I loved, snuggled inside a warm bed on a cold morning, knowing I could stay as long as I liked and dream delicious dreams undisturbed?

That morning there was no delight, just a dull ache filled with a smiling Jarred which quickly dissolved into pictures of him side by side with Gracey
15　as she turned to embrace him.

When the first rays of sunlight brightened the edge of the curtains, I pushed the blankets aside and lowered my feet onto the threadbare carpet. Perhaps I would walk down to the Manly foreshore and look at that enormous ocean again with the sun rising steadily above it. Even the largest things
20　could be put in their place. In jeans, a windcheater and spray jacket I entered the kitchen and found my grandfather making a pot of tea.

"Will you have a cup?" Just like him. I'd been there a week and he still didn't know I was a caffeine addict.

"Yes," I said gratefully. I was learning to like his tea.
25　"I hear you're having trouble with your friend," he said, offering a cup balanced precariously on its saucer as a little of the brown, steaming liquid sloshed over the lip. "Boyfriend too?"

I nodded, failing with an attempted smile.

He pursed his lips. "Abandoned on all sides." From someone
30　else, this might have been an insensitive put-down but not Grandad. He patted my hand and kissed the side of my head awkwardly. Suddenly I longed for home, my mother and my own room and familiar things. "I'll probably head back to Brisbane soon," I told him. I wondered whether I would have a passenger. Jarred had to get home somehow.

---

17 **threadbare** thin, worn out – 18 **foreshore** *Vorland* – 26 **precariously** likely to fall –
30 **put-down** *here:* remark

"Whatever you want. Keep talking. I'll make us bacon and eggs. Jean's never about till it's too late. Could do with some company over a good fry up."

So while he fired up the pan, I told him of the mistake Gracey was making
5 and I produced enough toast for ten people.

Afterwards he insisted I take him grocery shopping. "Has to be early on a Monday. The crowds are terrible."

Crowds! A dozen cars in the carpark beside the store and hardly a customer in sight. "Last time I went shopping with you, you sat in the basket,"
10 he said, laughing.

"Bit big for that now, Grandad." I followed him round the supermarket, stopping now and then to be introduced to a mate. "Cheryl's girl," he would say. "Isn't she a pretty one?" It was embarrassing but it was fun and I loved him for the distraction it brought. I had no doubt he was hamming it up with
15 just that in mind.

In the end though we returned to the little brick house and my dilemma. If Jarred didn't ring me then I would have to ring him. I picked up the phone three times but lost courage before dialling the last number. I tried the house in Bankstown, simply for news of Raylene, but there was no answer
20 there, though I kept calling right through the morning.

"Why don't you ring the hospital," Grandad suggested when he saw the studied look on my face.

When I got through to St Vincent's, a bored voice asked, "Are you a relative? Well, I'm afraid patient information is confidential."
25 "You can tell me how she's doing, at least," I pleaded.

She thought about this for a second, asking me the name again. I could hear her stab at a keyboard then a hesitation. "What is it?" I demanded.

"The patient's condition is listed as critical."

As soon as I heard those words I knew something had gone wrong and I
30 had to be there. "I'm going to St Vincent's," I called to Grandad, grabbing my coat.

My grandmother emerged from the bedroom. "You will be home for tea though, Angela, won't you?"

Tea. I wasn't looking that far ahead. "Yes, Grandma," I answered halfway
35 through the door. I have never spun the wheels in reverse before but I did

---

2 **fry up** (informal) here: bacon and eggs – 14 **to ham it up** (informal) to exaggerate deliberately – 35 **to spin** to make very fast turning movements – 35 **in reverse** going backwards

that day. Spun them again when I slammed the car into first and headed for the main road.

5

At the enquiries desk where I stopped for directions, I didn't dare ask if there was any improvement in Raylene's condition. I was so crammed full of worry
5 that it came as a shock to realise the waiting room was full of people. The whole family was there, it seemed, Trevor in the corridor looking bored and miserable. Through the plate glass I could see Auntie Irene's head with Bill slouched on her knee, half in, half out of sleep. But the face I looked for was Gracey's.
10 I approached cautiously until I was sure she wasn't there. Dougy saw me first.

"Angela," he called wearily.

"Can I come in?"

"Of course, love," Auntie Irene said from her chair nearby. She switched
15 Bill from one knee to the other and he fell back against her, barely roused. I might have been welcome but there was no room, not unless I wanted to step carefully over Kendrick who was playing on the floor with Muriel stretched out beside him fast asleep. Even then, the only space on offer was a spot in the corner where I would have to stand. At the doorway still, I
20 asked, "How's Raylene?"

"No news for a while now," Auntie Irene told me. "Going to be quite a wait. That's why we're all here."

"What happened? They wouldn't give out any information on the phone."

"Got an infection after the operation. Affecting her heart, according to the
25 doctors. They pumped her full of drugs and stuff and now all we can do is wait."

Dougy saw me stranded and unsure of what to do. "You want this chair?" he offered, standing up and making his way carefully into the corridor. Did I belong inside that room, especially if it was Dougy who had to make a place
30 for me? Shaking my head I backed away and he followed me along the passage a few paces.

"I only heard an hour ago. How long have you been here?"

---

1 **to slam** to push forcefully – 1 **into first** into the first gear – 7 **plate glass** *here:* glass door – 15 **barely** hardly – 15 **roused** woken up – 27 **stranded** left in a place with no chance of leaving

It was a silly question to ask Dougy. He didn't bother with a watch. "We got the call after Gracey left for the bus station."

"She's gone? Already!"

He nodded. "Didn't want to stay any longer in case she changed her mind. That's what she said yesterday when she booked the ticket. Used up the last of the study money she was keeping by and Jarred gave her the rest. He came round this morning in his cousin's car and took her to the bus station. By the time we heard about Raylene, she was gone."

I wanted to ask him whether Jarred and Gracey had spent their time together since Saturday afternoon. But it was unfair to question Dougy. He was taken up completely by his concern for the baby. And I wasn't sure that I really wanted to know anyway.

"Dougy," I said softly. "You'll take care of Gracey when you get back there yourself?"

He looked at me as though I'd spat on the ground beside his foot. "She's me sister" was all he said.

"Make sure she keeps thinking about uni, won't you? She'll do great things if she gets the chance. You know that, don't you?"

"Gracey's already done great things. To me, she's the greatest person in the world." He turned towards me, the smile I usually found on his face wiped away this time. "She told me what you said yesterday, out at the running. Angela, you think everything about you is better than everything about me. And Nerida. And Gracey. You think that, don't you?"

I was stunned by the tone of his words, a sharp edge I didn't expect from him. He was always such a gentle boy. *Boy?* I was conscious for the first time that he towered over me now, not as tall as Jarred but well on the way.

Nerida appeared from behind the door which prohibited entry into Intensive Care. She looked haggard, her face marked by the tears that had dried under her red-rimmed eyes. Suddenly the whole family were on their feet, talking at once, gathering round her firing questions.

"Ray's still pretty bad," said Nerida. "They say she's going to be that way until the morning most likely. Unless she dies before then," she added, and the weight of this pushed her into a chair with Auntie Irene crowding round.

"Your baby's going to be all right, girl. Don't you start giving up now."

---

24 **stunned** amazed – 28 **haggard** *here:* worried

After ten minutes with the family Nerida shuffled away again through the forbidden doors which flapped noisily back into place after her. They all settled down to waiting again, Dougy back inside, the kids wandering in and out, chasing one another from time to time, bringing a nurse to quieten them. I stayed propped against the wall until my legs ached then sat with them stretched out into the corridor, careful that Kendrick and Muriel or Trevor didn't trample on them when the games started again. About two, Uncle Dennis arrived.

"No milk going to be delivered in a few streets today," he told Auntie Irene, and though there had been no room for me in the waiting room, space was found for him. I heard a gentle weeping and realised it was Auntie Irene herself, the rock of the family, a woman I thought must never cry. She was nestled into Uncle Dennis' shoulder, letting go of the burden a little. Perhaps she was making room for what might come. Later, Gail turned up and Dougy gave her his seat, slipping into the corridor and coming to sit beside me without a word.

The afternoon wore on, with little news, my only distraction the sight of this family waiting. It sent my mind back to the Manly foreshore, to my walk with Grandma under her beloved pines, buffeted by the ocean wind and my own admissions. It was true what I had told her. I liked every person in that waiting room but I was as alien amongst them as they seemed alien in this claustrophobic hospital with their noise amid the silence, their determination to stay, the whole mob, sharing their fears for Raylene.

The little girl had to live. I couldn't bear it otherwise. Gracey gone from my life and now this baby was on the edge as well. The dreadful weight of what I had done threatened to drag away what little peace I had found here in the corridor and I had to reach deep within myself to push it back. "Not now," I whispered, bringing Dougy's eyes to bear on me. "Not now," I repeated soundlessly. There's only room for so much misery.

Time had ceased to mean anything in that corridor. When my mobile rang, disturbing the silence, I didn't even bother to glance at the clock at the end of the passageway. "Angela?" asked a tentative voice.

"Grandma! I didn't think you knew my number."

"I rang Cheryl in Brisbane," she answered as though she tracked down people on their mobiles every day. "Angela, it's quarter past six. You said you would be home for dinner."

---

20 **admission** saying that sth is true – 26 **to drag away** to pull away – 32 **passageway** corridor – 34 **to track down** to find after searching

"I'm sorry, Grandma. There's been a crisis. The baby's …" It was all I could do to hold back the tears. "I'm still at the hospital."

"Oh," she said, the annoyance in her voice suddenly fading. I could hear a conversation in the background. Grandad was joking loudly with another
5 man.

"Is there any chance of you coming home soon?" she asked.

"No, I can't, Grandma. There's still no word." Again I fought the urge to sob into the phone and seek her sympathy and her comfort.

The silence that followed put me on edge and I didn't need that just at
10 the moment. "I'm sorry, Grandma. It's just that I can't leave right now. We're all in this together. The whole family is here."

"Yes, yes. I can appreciate that. But when you seemed so sure you would be home, I went ahead with …" She seemed to decide halfway through this explanation that it was not the way to persuade me. Her voice changed,
15 hinting at the authority I had heard her use at times with my own mother and on the telephone talking to her friends. "Angela, I've never asked you to be home with us, to eat with us. I have let you do pretty much as you pleased while you've been staying here. But just this once, I must insist."

Insist! Who did she think she was? Miss Glencross? I deserved
20 a better explanation than that. Why didn't she come out and say what was so important? With this in my mind and the words formed for an indignant no, the background chatter turned to laughter and it suddenly occurred to me that Grandma couldn't say anymore. The guests were right there beside her, listening with half an ear at least.

25 "Please do this for me," was Grandma's final appeal.

What could I do? Though I wanted to stay with the drowsy, restless family until we had the news, one way or the other, the truth was they didn't need me.

"OK," I sighed reluctantly. "I'll be there. Fast as I can," then punched the
30 "end" key on the mobile.

---

19 **to insist** to demand, to ask with force – 19 **Miss Glencross** title of a beauty queen – 21 **indignant** expressing surprised anger – 26 **drowsy** tired and almost asleep

The Gubba Man

1

If Jean Malvern wanted her granddaughter home simply to show off to friends, they were hardly going to be impressed when I walked in. The face in the rear-view mirror was long and weary, with unwashed hair straggling down either side, eyelashes a mess, lips pale and cracked. The waiting had
5 sapped my spirit and my energy and instead of playing the vivacious student at the dinner table, what I craved most was a shower and that narrow bed at the back of the house. I scooped the untidy strands quickly between thumb and forefinger and worked them back into a hair-tie, and then went inside to meet the guests.
10 There was only one guest, I discovered; a big man, or so he seemed. Not as tall as Grandad, but he was heavy-framed and rather overweight. I guessed him to be about the same age as my grandparents, though I soon realised that all those wrinkles on his face were caused as much from laughter as from long years in the sun.
15 "Hello, hello," he said, jolly as a Santa Claus when we were introduced. His name was Harry Falkirk and he wouldn't let me call him Mister. "Harry will do," he said, holding onto my hand for too long. "Should always be on first-name terms with a pretty young lady, eh," he added, showing me his smoker's teeth.
20 This was meant to be a compliment but I had to hide the shudder that crawled up my spine like an icy spider. What was going on? Grandma had pulled rank on me for this old guy?

They'd been waiting for me for over an hour and Harry Falkirk had not wasted the time. He must have known the Malverns were non-drinkers
25 because he'd brought plenty of his own. I saw it in the fridge when I went into the kitchen to help Grandma serve the meal. There was only one stubby left in the plastic wrapping of a six-pack.

"Who is this guy?" I asked in a whisper.

"Richard and I have known him for years. Since our days in the west."
30 The two men were sitting at the dining room table when Grandma and I brought out the plates. Grandad took his usual position at the end, Mr

---

5 **to sap** *here:* to take away – 6 **to crave** to long for – 21 **spine** back (of the body) – 22 **to pull rank** to take unfair advantage of one's position – 26 **stubby** *(AustrE informal)* bottle of beer

Falkirk sat to his right opposite Grandma and I sat next to her. This left me out of the conversation somewhat but I didn't care. I was suddenly very hungry and attacked the roast beef with relish, barely listening to what was said. Even so, it was not long before I picked up another puzzling piece of
5 information.

"Must be nearly four years," Harry was saying.

"No, it couldn't be that long," Grandad protested.

Harry thought for a moment. "Yes, I think I'm right, Richard. You had me around for dinner not long after Marie died. I was so grateful, the way
10 friends rallied round in those first months. But that would be the last time I was here. And Marie's been gone nearly four years."

So we were all making history here. Richard and Jean Malvern had chosen tonight to mend a neglected friendship and I was privileged to watch it happen. Give me a break! What was going on here? There had to be a
15 catch.

"What do you do, Harry?" I asked, hunting for a clue.

"Oh, I'm retired. A few years now. I was in the Public Service. Finished up in Parks and Wildlife, though I swapped around a bit."

Grandad began to say something about work in the national parks, but
20 Grandma cut him off. "Harry was with the Aboriginal Welfare Board when we first met," she said calmly, then followed this quickly by asking, "Will you have a little more beef, Harry? There's plenty left."

Harry thought he would have some more and my grandmother slipped away to oblige.

25 "The Welfare Board. So you were," said my grandfather leaning back in his chair and tilting his head so he could inspect his old friend through the narrow frames of his glasses. "You used to visit the reserve, checking on the little ones."

"That's right."

30 I couldn't believe it. He was a gubba man.

"Well now. You can help us out here, Harry. Angela's been getting me to tell her about one of the Aboriginal boys we had there with us, Derek Campbell. You see that name in the paper every week now. It's the same fellow, right enough. Do you remember him as a youngster?"

35 "Derek Campbell. Yes, I remember him. Little half-caste he was."

---

10 **to rally** to come together as support −14 **to give sb a break** *(informal)* to stop annoying sb − 15 **catch** hidden disadvantage − 18 **to swap around** *here:* to do many different things − 35 **half-caste** [kɑːst] child of racially mixed parents

Half-caste. The word grated in my ears, as though Harry Falkirk had scraped his fingers down a blackboard. If Gracey was here she would go for him with all guns blazing. Me, I sat back piecing things together. Grandad hadn't caught on, not yet anyway, but I certainly had.

5 "Of course, he's grown up to be a real chest-beater these days, I notice," Harry added, reaching for his knife. "That's the white coming out in him. Sort of vindicates you, Richard. As I recall, you were pretty keen he get a chance in life. You saw something in him, didn't you?"

My grandfather beamed. "Potential. That's what I saw in him. Only four
10 years old but you could see the intelligence shining in his eyes." He placed his hand palm upwards on the table and let his fingers curl in as he said, "Left where he was, it would be slow death, like a flame starved of oxygen."

"Yes, well, he's burning pretty brightly at the moment and he doesn't sound too thankful for what you did for him, Richard."

15 My grandfather dismissed this lightly, shrugging his shoulders and looking pensively down at his hand.

"Well, you might take it in your stride, Richard, but to tell you the truth, I've had a gutful of all the stuff coming out in the papers about the Welfare Board. Where would half of them be today if blokes like you and me hadn't
20 stepped in? Dead, most likely. Look at them now. Leaders of their people, lawyers, educated, confident. And they've got the hide to spit in our faces. It sticks in my craw, I have to say. You'd think they'd have the grace to thank us for the good that was done. Back then, they didn't have a clue what was good for them and it was up to us to make sure it happened."

25 "Not entirely, Harry. Some of them saw what was best. Derek Campbell had his mother to thank."

This sounded familiar. The story of Derek Campbell's adoption was going to be trotted out again. "She came to me, you know, once I'd explained what I had in mind. She wasn't keen at first but she saw the sense of it in the
30 end."

Harry Falkirk listened, shifting in his seat, while I watched him. The blood vessels on his temples were standing out, courtesy of the five stubbies and

---

1 **to grate** to have an irritating effect – 3 **to blaze** to fire continuously – 5 **chest-beater** person taking advantage of the finances of an institution – 7 **to vindicate** to prove right – 17 **to take it in one's stride** to deal with an unpleasant situation without difficulty – 18 **to have a gutful** *(informal)* to have as much as one can take – 21 **hide** *(AustrE informal)* impertinence, cheek – 22 **to stick in one's craw** to be unacceptable – 28 **to trot out** to produce – 31 **blood vessels** *Blutgefäße* – 32 **temple** side of the forehead

the anger he had stirred up in himself. He dived in again. "You're being a bit generous there, Richard. She still didn't see the sense of what you were offering, even after you kept at her. I remember when you came out to the reserve, wanting me to have a special look at him. You were desperate to get
5 that boy away to a decent home. Already had a white family picked out for him. But oh, no, she wasn't giving up her kids. Not that one. She was going to drag them down with her. Now that's what I mean about it being up to us in the AWB. It was our job to see that half-caste kids like him could make the break, even if we had to twist a few arms to do it."

10 My grandfather's face, when I looked, had lost its patient resignation as he stared wide-eyed at Harry Falkirk.

If he wasn't going to ask, I would. "What do you mean, twist a few arms?" A queasiness grew in my stomach. What was this horrible man about to do to Grandad? To me?

15 "Campbell's mother," he said, tossing his head with an air of exasperation. "She was never going to let you have the boy, Richard. No amount of reasoning with her would change her mind. I could see how much you wanted to do something for the poor kid and he was half-white after all, so I went to see her, didn't I. She'd just had a third one. The other two looked to
20 be full-blood, probably fathered by the blackfella she was living with, but Derek must have had a white father, a shearer most likely, and they were the kids the Board was interested in. I told her she had to let you have the oldest one or else we'd take away all three."

"No, Harry. That's not so. You can't be serious."

25 "I am. That was the policy from high up, you see. Leave the full-bloods 'cause they wouldn't survive anyway but separate the half-castes and the quadroons and give them a chance. If the mothers were stubborn, that's the way we had to do it. Mostly they'd come good in the end."

"You've got your cases mixed up, Harry. Understandable really, the Board
30 took quite a few away from the reserve over the years. You've mistaken this Campbell case for another boy, I'm sure of it. The mother came to me specially."

---

1 **to dive in again** to approach a topic again– 3 **to keep at sb** to continue to criticize sb – 8 **AWB** Aboriginal Welfare Board – 8 **to make the break** to be able to get out of a situation – 9 **to twist a few arms** to use pressure – 13 **queasiness** [ˈkwiːzɪnəs] feeling of sickness – 15 **exasperation** [ɪgzæspəˈreɪʃn] intense irritation – 25 **policy** rule, order – 27 **quadroon** [kwəˈdruːn] person of one-quarter Aboriginal origin

"Have it your own way, Richard. Memory plays funny tricks, I must admit. Maybe there was a similar case and I've got the two muddled ..."

"No," came a voice from beside me. It was uttered softly but there was no doubting the firmness behind it. "There's nothing wrong with your memory, Harry," my grandmother assured her guest. "You're right about the Campbell boy." She said this with such certainty that neither man questioned her. Grandad sat at the end of the table, staring at his wife without a word.

Harry seemed surprised by all this and when the silence ticked on uncomfortably, he tried to put our minds at ease. "What we did, you and me, Richard ... Well, it's obvious for all to see. It helped Campbell and it's helped all Aboriginal people to have someone like him to lead them. I'm not taking any backward steps here. Doesn't really matter how we went about it, as long as you can see the benefits."

My grandmother watched Harry give his explanation, while Grandad, the horror slowly growing on his face, let his eyes drift out of focus and wander aimlessly along the edge of the table. Neither of them seemed likely to say anything.

"Mr Falkirk," I said, finding my voice a little more than a whisper. I couldn't call him Harry. There was too much intimacy, too much recognition in a first name. "Mr Falkirk, did you ever feel bad about what you were doing?"

"Of course I did. It wasn't all kids like that Campbell boy. Some of them I couldn't see the point. They were happy enough where they were, treated all right, nothing wrong with them. Their name just ended up on a list because they had a white father maybe. There was one time ... sweet Jesus, I still have nightmares. It wasn't anywhere near the reserve we're talking about here. Was years before, way out on the edge of the desert somewhere. We went looking for this kid but every woman in the district knew we were coming and they all took off, trying to hide from us. We tracked this mob for two days and when we found them, there wasn't a child in sight. Must have split up, sent the kids off with one bunch and tricked us into following this crowd on some wild goose chase. That's what we thought anyway. So we loaded them all into the truck and took them back to their camp so we could work out what was going on. But, ah, the women, they started wailing and carrying on, the further we went. They wouldn't tell us what was upsetting them. If only they'd told us."

---

2 **to muddle** to confuse – 13 **benefit** ['benɪfɪt] positive result – 31 **wild goose chase** hopeless undertaking – 34 **to wail** to make loud cries of pain

"Why?" I asked, my own distress mounting.

He seemed reluctant to go on.

"What happened," I demanded. The dread which had begun to grow in me earlier when my grandfather fell silent was spiralling now, swinging me
5   round uncontrollably. "What didn't they tell you?"

"It was the babies," he said. "They hadn't given them to another mob at all. They'd known we were close so they hid the little things in a hollow log. Only we didn't know that and they wouldn't tell us. S'pose they thought we'd take the babies, but we didn't want those babies. They were mostly
10 full-blood anyway. We were after a different kid altogether."

"What happened to the babies?"

"It was days before they could go back, you see, and no one else knew ..."

He tried to stop there but I wouldn't let him. I couldn't. "What
15 happened?"

"It was forty degrees out there in the daytime."

"You still haven't said," I demanded. "What happened to those babies?"

Harry Falkirk looked around the table, first at my grandfather, then my grandmother and finally at me. "Dead," he answered. "Every one of them."
20   "No," I cried and then it came over me, as though someone had reached into me and turned everything upside down. The meal I had devoured so ravenously would not stay inside me. I stood up suddenly, the chair toppling backwards as I dashed from the room. My stomach was already heaving and it took all the willpower I had left to hold it back until I kicked open the
25 toilet door and fell to my knees. Out it all came, the brown mess of my dinner. But what I was really trying to purge lay in my mind – the image of those babies, their tiny bodies hidden inside a log, crying for their mothers who could not come for them. One by one they must have stopped crying, stopped moving, stopped breathing, until the bush around them was silent.
30 I could hear those bewildered, desperate women filling that same bush with their wailing as the lifeless bodies were finally dragged into the light

---

1 **distress** great mental or physical sadness – 2 **reluctant** hesitant – 7 **hollow** empty – 7 **log** thick branch of a tree – 21 **to devour** [dɪ'vaʊə] to eat fast and greedily – 26 **to purge** to get rid of

and cradled in their mothers' arms. What I saw were tiny babies, frail, with rib bones visible, legs hanging limp from fleshless bottoms and the terror of this image kept me retching.

At last my body seemed to surrender. By then my clothes were soaked
5 with perspiration, my hair as well, and the palms of my hands were too slippery to grip the toilet bowl. That same smooth porcelain was shockingly cold and helped to clear my head a little when I heard Grandma in the hall behind me. "Angela," she called pushing at the door until it jammed against my feet.

10 She forced her way further into the space, reaching for me. "Come out, darling. Let me help you."

"The babies," I whimpered.

"It's all right, dear. Harry's leaving now. You won't have to see him."

I wiped my mouth and tried to stand up. Too fast. I swayed a little but
15 Grandma could open the door now and she steadied me as much as her arthritis would allow, then guided me along the hall to my room where I sat on the end of the bed shivering.

"I can't bear it," I said.

"There's nothing you can do, Angela. It happened decades ago, before you
20 were born, probably before your mother and father were born."

"It's not that. It wasn't just that awful story." I was starting to realise this now. As I pictured that scene, the tiny figures being hauled from their hiding place, I had seen Raylene's emaciated face. Everyone of those babies was Raylene. Harry Falkirk had not said how many. Somehow, the number had
25 become endless, filling the bush, every fallen tree giving up its tiny dead body. I tried to tell Grandma. "The baby in hospital. Gracey's niece. She can't die too," I moaned, "I couldn't take that."

I fell across the bed, exhausted.

"Why don't you go off to sleep?" Grandma suggested. "In the morning we
30 can …"

"No, I'm all right," I said vehemently, sitting up again. My stomach muscles ached with the movement. "I have to talk to Grandad."

She made no effort to talk me out of this demand. I felt a blanket placed around my shoulders which helped the shivering subside enough for me to
35 speak more easily. "You knew what would happen tonight," I said. "You invited that man so it would happen this way."

---

3 **to retch** *würgen* – 4 **to surrender** to give up – 34 **to subside** to go away

"Yes, I did," she answered without hesitation. "But I had no idea about that other business, the babies in the log. I'm sorry it has hurt you so much."

"But why did you bring him here?"

"Because I couldn't bear to hear Richard tell the story of Derek Campbell
5 anymore. Not when I've known Harry Falkirk's part in it all these years."

"How did you ..." I couldn't finish my question because Grandad spoke from the doorway. "Harry's gone," he said.

Grandma eased herself painfully from the edge of my bed where she had comforted me. "We'll be in the lounge room when you've cleaned yourself
10 up."

2

I washed out my mouth, threw cold water into my face then returned to the bedroom for a change of clothes. When I joined them in the lounge room, Grandad stood up and taking my arm guided me to the sofa. The room seemed cold even though the electric heater glowed in the fireplace; I
15 realised that they had not spoken since leaving me in the hallway.

"Are you feeling better?" he asked, desperate to hear a voice in the room at last.

"I'm fine, really," I assured him though I hardly convinced myself. "I guess it was the shock, about the babies on top of everything else. I've been at the
20 hospital all day worried about Raylene."

Grandma stirred next to me and squeezed my arm gently, but she didn't speak.

Grandad seemed uncomfortable with the awkward silence that followed. "Harry said he was sorry if he upset you. He wants you to know he still
25 blames himself for what happened with those babies. It's something he's had to live with for forty years."

He didn't seem to be suffering, I thought cruelly, though I didn't say it. My mind was on the first story Harry Falkirk had told. "Grandad," I began, "Derek Campbell wasn't given up by his mother. She was forced into it."

30 "So it would seem," he admitted timidly. He looked at me briefly then down at his hands, sliding one across the other while his elbows rested on the heavy arms of his chair.

I ignored him and turned instead to my grandmother. "I started to ask you before, how you knew."

"Derek's mother came to see me, a year after he was adopted. She wanted to get him back. I tried to put her off at first, because as far as I was concerned,
5 she had agreed to the adoption in the first place. It was all tied up in legal papers and those things were notoriously difficult to reverse. It was an official adoption, you see. Richard made sure of that."

My grandfather listened, nodding his head to confirm this last piece of information.

10 Grandma went on, looking at her husband who would not return her gaze. "That was when she told me about Harry, that he had been to see her. She was terrified of him. Living in fear that he would come back and take her other two. I thought maybe the best thing to do was talk to the couple who had the boy, explain what had happened so that they would
15 perhaps ..."

Grandad looked up suddenly when she said this. He had no idea she had taken such a step and now, so many years later, he was confronted with it.

"Wouldn't they listen to you?" I prompted her.

She took a few moments to look away from Grandad's stricken face. Even
20 then, it was a while longer before she could continue. "It wasn't that they wouldn't listen, Angela. I discovered something else. They were hundreds of miles away so I had to telephone them, and with a delicate matter like this I couldn't just come out with it. I got chatting to them, about how Derek was doing. They were a decent pair, there was no doubt of that. It was the wife I
25 was speaking to and something she said struck me as rather odd, about the boy being an orphan. I drew her out as carefully as I could until it dawned on me. They thought the child had no parents at all, that his mother had died giving birth to another baby."

"That's right," I interrupted. "I heard him say so in Brisbane."

30 My grandmother was glaring at her husband now, the anger visible in her unyielding gaze. "I'm right, aren't I, Richard? They were told the boy's mother died in childbirth."

He nodded faintly as he whispered, "Yes."

"And of course they told the boy the same story."

35 "Yes," he said again, even more softly.

---

6 **notoriously** famous for sth bad – 6 **to reverse** to change back into the former state
– 26 **to draw sb out** to help sb to express his / her thoughts

"So Derek Campbell grew up thinking his mother was dead," Grandma continued, offering no quarter.

"Yes," my grandfather said a third time, but here he interrupted. "It had to be that way. I'd seen it happen before that if the children knew where their parents were, they would try to make contact and all the good that had been achieved was put at risk."

"It wasn't the Welfare Board who told them, was it, Richard?"

Grandad had sunk back into the seat, his elbow resting on the overstuffed arm of the chair, a hand cradling his chin. He sent a breath noisily down his nostrils. "I … it was … you see …" He couldn't find the words to start a sentence, until finally he closed those bewildered eyes and said, "No, not the Board. I told them."

This time when he opened his eyes he saw our stern faces and it was too much for him. He stood up suddenly, fast enough to make himself dizzy so when he walked behind his chair he was forced to grasp the headrest for support. "The mother couldn't care for him, not the way he needed. She would always have a baby on her hip and one on the way. She had no time for the boy." He switched from Grandma's face to mine, urging us to agree. "Who would have cared for him, given him the attention every kid deserves?"

He did not expect an answer, and a week before, when I first walked into the house in Bankstown with Jarred and Gracey, I would have had no answer either. But I did now.

"His family, Grandad. The whole mob of them, grandmas, aunts and uncles, all of them would have cared for him with hugs and backhanders and games and tears and tender words and loud angry chases around the place. That's who was looking after him. When you went out to that camp, you were just looking through the keyhole. I've only had a peek through that same keyhole, maybe, but I've seen that much. He wouldn't have wanted for love, Grandad. I've seen enough to know that."

"You don't understand. The boy had real ability. That's what counts in all of this. Left where he was, he would have become just like his mother."

He seemed frustrated that I would not concede and started up again in another direction. "The real measure here is Campbell's life now. Look at him. A spokesman for his people, a man who has been trained to know the real world and how to deal with it. He is far more useful to his

---

9 **to cradle** *here:* to hold – 13 **stern** grim – 15 **headrest** support for the head on a chair – 25 **backhander** slap with the back of the hand – 28 **peek** quick, secret look – 29 **to want for** to lack – 33 **to concede** to admit you have lost

people this way than he could ever have been if I'd left him languishing there, halfway to nowhere."

My face had hardened to stone and my grandfather, a man I'd loved all my life, was breaking himself against it.

5 "This business in the paper, it's offensive to me. I cared for that boy and now they're lumping me in with the rest, as though I was no different from the farmers who went out shooting them like vermin. What a twisting of history, to speak like that. For heaven's sake, Derek Campbell isn't dead. What killing was there?"

10 There was a rage building in him and I was suddenly afraid. Amid all the other fears that weighed on me, it seemed too much to bear. How could I answer him when it was a struggle just to stay in the room. Then a voice broke in beside me.

"I'll tell you what the killing was, Richard," said my grandmother. "You 15 were determined to kill off the black man in that Campbell boy, and to do it, you knew you had to cut him off from his family and his kind. Harry knew it too and his bosses. They used you, Richard, to help them do it. That's where the killing was, leaving all those half-dead people with their grief, longing to know what the other half of them meant. You only cared for half the boy 20 because you couldn't see the rest of him."

With Grandma so powerful beside me and my grandfather shrivelling into himself at her attack, I found my own courage returning and with it an anger.

"I believed you, Grandad, everything you told me about Derek Campbell. 25 That story has hung between Gracey and me for months, pushing us further and further apart. All because I believed in you. I trusted you and now she's gone."

My grandfather straightened to his full height behind the chair. "I listened to you this morning, Angela, about how you want the best for this girl you 30 care so much about. Are you any different from me?" He took his hand from the chair which had steadied him then turned his back on me indignantly and walked into the hall. A few moments later I heard the click of the bedroom door echo through the silent house.

"That's it?" I demanded of my grandmother. "He walks away. How can he 35 compare me and Gracey with what he did? All the pain he brought on that family, the mother most of all."

---

1 **to languish** to grow up without strength and support – 6 **to lump in** to throw together – 7 **vermin** small animals which are harmful, e.g. rats, grasshoppers – 21 **to shrivel into** to loose energy and turn small

"Angela …" Grandma said softly, and though I sensed she wanted to say more, she stopped.

There was plenty more I wanted to say. "You were right, what you said," I told her. "Grandad couldn't see the life those people were living. He still can't
5 see it."

"Sometimes it is harder to admit you are wrong inside yourself than it is to say so out loud."

It was the way she looked at me and the appeal in her voice that alerted me. What was she saying? I twisted round to face her on the sofa beside me
10 and the hesitation must have turned my face into a question.

"Be as hard on him as you like, Angela. He did a terrible thing, making that boy believe his mother was dead. Just remember, though, you'll have to answer for yourself one day."

"I don't understand."

15 Grandma shifted restlessly against the cushions, reluctant to go on but steeling herself all the same. "Have you been listening to yourself, girl? You told me down on the foreshore you'd do anything to stop Gracey going off to the bush."

"But everything in Cunningham is wrong for her. Everything here is …
20 Everything …" I said again leaving the word to hang in the air. The sound of it on my tongue began to dig out a memory and I relaxed a little, sitting back to stare at the electric glow of the heater in the fireplace. "Everything about …" I muttered once more, letting the words come with the memory, "everything is better." No, that wasn't how he had said it. The memory was
25 with me now, of Dougy, sweet Dougy, sitting next to me in the corridor, taking me to task with the first hint of anger I had ever seen in him. He had spoken those words, vague mutterings, I thought at the time, but delivered with all the power of his gentle presence. *You think everything about you is better than everything about me.* Dougy had seen into me deeply, in a way I
30 could not see for myself.

"You are so like your grandfather. So sure you are right and so eager to save the ones you love, no matter what damage is done."

I pleaded with her. "I just can't bear to think of her there, living that life …" The truth of it began to overwhelm me, robbing my tongue of words.
35 I looked to my grandmother, begging her to make sense of what I felt.

---

8 **to alert** to warn – 34 **to overwhelm** to grow stronger

"The poor blacks," she said. "They have no idea how much we despise them. I doubt we have much of an inkling ourselves."

"How can you say that? I love Gracey."

"Yes, you say that, but you despise what she comes from. We despise any
5 view of the world that's not our own, we demand change, and when it doesn't come, we force it. The pity is that we can't see ourselves doing it and for people like Richard the time is long past when he ever could. The things you learn on your mother's knee are the most difficult to set aside. But it's not too late for you, girl. What did you say to me yesterday – blackness repels
10 you? When I heard you say that, I thought, yes, if you're aware of this in yourself, perhaps there's a chance."

"Harry Falkirk. That's why …"

She nodded. "Of course. I never thought to see that man again in my life. Do you think I wanted to hurt my own husband like that? No, I brought Harry
15 here tonight for you."

Harry Falkirk. He had stepped into this house for just a few hours but he had brought with him the devastation of a hand grenade and all of us, even my grandmother, were left dazed and bleeding.

"Grandma, if you knew about Harry Falkirk and how he threatened that
20 poor woman, why didn't you follow it through? Didn't you try to get the boy back for his mother?"

"It was too late, Angela. You don't realise what she was up against. The Welfare Board, the adoption people. This was before Aborigines even had citizenship rights. It was hopeless." She paused for a second to compose
25 herself, swallowing hard as though she too was holding down things that threatened to burst from her throat.

"As for me, it was cowardice, Angela. I faced the same obstacles and one more besides. My own husband. I told myself the boy was happy. Best to leave him where he was. So I did nothing. I regret that now more than
30 anything else in my life."

She stood up gingerly, looking towards the hallway where her husband had disappeared, then left me there on the sofa, pulling the bedroom door closed behind her with the same sharp click.

Sleep was out of the question and there seemed no point in retreating to
35 my bedroom. I stayed there on the sofa, thinking yet afraid to think. There was so much pain in what had happened in this house since my return from

---

1 **to despise** to look down on sb as inferior – 2 **inkling** little idea – 17 **devastation** damage – 18 **dazed** bewildered, confused – 27 **cowardice** [ˈkaʊədɪs] lack of courage – 31 **gingerly** [ˈdʒɪndʒəlɪ] carefully

the hospital. In the main bedroom just off the hall, I could hear voices murmuring. After a time, I had no idea how long, a sound drifted through the house that I had never heard before, though I recognised it at once. The sound of a man crying. It was a deeply disturbing noise and then I heard in
5 my mind the wailing Harry Falkirk had spoken of, the wailing of those mothers as they dragged the limp bodies from their false refuge and began their grieving.

Grieving. Derek Campbell had spoken of it. And Gracey. Grieving for the ones who had been lost, those barely known yet longed for. My life was free
10 of such grieving, as though my parents had done a deal with the fairies when I was born. Maybe they didn't need to. Maybe it was part of who I was and the life that had been mapped out for me. Gracey was right. I had never lost anyone close to me, never felt helpless in the face of death.

Until now.
15 Raylene's weary face drifted back into my eyes, and I could almost feel the weight of her in my arms, smell her milky warmth. She was not one of the babies in the hollow logs. She was still struggling for life, with her family around her. Suddenly I couldn't stay in the house another minute. I grabbed the spray jacket from my room, slapped at the pocket of my jeans to be sure
20 the car keys were there and slipped quietly out the back door. As it closed, I realised the house was quiet again, no distant crying, no voices. The same abrupt click echoed though the house as I hurried away in the darkness to unlock the Corolla.

3

At the tollgate on the Harbour Bridge I discovered I had left my purse behind.
25 Loose coins from the ashtray paid the toll and I hurried on, but I was left feeling absurdly penniless and exposed. A dread was closing round me, made worse by the haphazard struts and girders which hemmed me in, trapping me between the pylons at each end which themselves became prison towers brooding over me. The traffic was still heavy, even in the

---

7 **to grieve** to feel sorrow – 10 **fairy** magical power – 15 **weary** ['wɪərɪ] tired – 25 **toll** money you have to pay to use a road – 26 **exposed** not protected – 26 **dread** fear – 27 **haphazard** [hæp'hæzəd] having no particular order – 27 **strut** long pieces of metal used to support the bridge – 27 **girder** strong piece of metal supporting a bridge – 28 **pylon** tall metal structure that supports the wires of a suspension bridge – 29 **brooding** threatening

middle of the night, though I was glad in a way of the delays which kept me from the hospital. What news would be waiting for me there? I tried to block Raylene out of my mind altogether, focusing only on the car in front and the street signs and red lights. This got me to the car park, but after I had locked
5 the car, the fear drove into me like a blow from some invisible madman and I fell against the door. By the time I reached the corridors, it was an effort to make my legs move.

Hospitals are not part of the real world, the world of traffic noise and shouting and laughing, a place where you can see the sky and feel alive
10 because the sun is shining. Once you are inside those heavy glass doors, there is no telling night from day. It was nearing one in the morning when I followed the corridors to the waiting room, just as I had done half a day before. Was that all it was? Twelve hours. My journey was punctuated by the same murmur of distant voices, the same occasional glimpse of a nurse
15 scurrying by, until I entered the long corridor that led to the waiting room outside Intensive Care. There was no one in the passageway or milling around the door as there had been throughout the afternoon. I hurried closer, afraid that the room would be empty and even more afraid of what it would mean.

20 But the room wasn't empty. On the floor lay Uncle Dennis, next to him Trevor and Kendrick and lying crossways beyond their feet was Carli. They were all asleep and so was Auntie Irene, lying awkwardly at one end of the sofa, a cushion wedged under her ear. She gave out a deep resonant purr with each slow breath. Dougy was there too, his long legs laid out like poles
25 that seemed to wedge him into his seat, his head slumped forward onto his chest, nodding slightly as though he was fighting sleep. As I watched the fitful peace of the room from the doorway, unable to enter, he turned to me dreamily.

"Angela." A shudder passed through him, bringing him quickly awake. "I
30 must have dozed off." He stood up and, careful not to disturb the others, stepped his way between the bodies and into the corridor.

"I had to come back. Is there any news?"

He shook his head. "Nerida came out a few hours ago, after Gail took the little kids home with her. Raylene's still the same. Won't know if the drugs
35 are working until the morning."

---

25 **to wedge** to squeeze – 27 **fitful** *opp. of* calm

"It's morning now," I murmured, though he didn't hear me. "She won't die," I said and made sure he heard it this time. "Too much has been taken away already."

I was talking for myself now and despaired that I brought my own pain
to this waiting. "Oh Dougy, I heard a story tonight, about some little babies, black babies so like Raylene. I don't want her to die like them."

The wall of the corridor was suddenly hard against my back and I felt Dougy's hand under my elbow, ready to catch me. He didn't say a word but the touch of another human being was enough to steady me.
"I'm all right now," I said at last, leaning back a little to look at his face. The same smile was there still and even through his weary eyes the hope shone more brightly than his fear. I stretched up on my toes and kissed him on the cheek, leaving him startled. "You're a wiser man than any of us, Dougy," I told him. "The best person I've ever met."

He blushed under his dark brown skin and I regretted all over again how much I had discounted his part in Gracey's life.

"I met a gubba man, Dougy, and he told me the truth, at last. Truth's always the last thing to come kicking and screaming out of the past. We bury it deeper than the dead. Inside us."

Exhausted and already leaning against the wall, I let my back slide slowly towards the floor until I was sitting with my legs sticking out into the corridor. The cold surfaces fed on the warmth of my body and I shuddered, drawing the jacket closely around my waist and shoulders. "I'll stay here," I said without looking up. "You go back and get some sleep."

I was aware of his stove-pipe legs beside me still and then his hand in front of my face, opened in offering. "Too cold out here. Come on. There's room inside for you now."

He lead me gingerly through the tangle of legs to the sofa, nodding towards it silently as he took up his own position in the chair, stretching his
legs into the same position and folding his arms. There among the family I settled in to share the waiting and the fears. Dougy's head started to bob again and finally my own eyelids drooped, my head slipped closer and closer to the inviting pillow of the armrest until it touched and I fell deeply asleep.

---

4 **to despair** to lose hope or confidence – 16 **to discount** to regard as unimportant –
25 **stove-pipe** tall and black – 31 **to bob** to move up and down

4

The rattle of a trolley stirred us all as it passed the door of the waiting room, leaving behind it the tantalising suggestion of breakfast. My stomach growled and from the way the others looked longingly towards the corridor where the trolley had passed, I realised we were all starving.

5 They noticed me then. "Hello, Angela," said Auntie Irene as she rummaged in her bag. "Didn't think you'd come back so early."

Her hand reappeared holding a heavy purse and I was forgotten as she told Carli to fetch us all some breakfast from the canteen.

"Trevor, you and Kendrick go with her, eh."

10 I reached for my own purse then remembered I had left it behind. My pockets yielded three silver coins, not even enough for a cup of coffee. Auntie Irene offered me a toasted sandwich when the kids returned, but she had asked for only two cups of tea so I had to be content with cold water from the water cooler.

15 Through it all, we waited. It was seven o'clock and there was no sign of Nerida or any news from behind the heavy swinging doors at the end of the passageway. Trevor and Kendrick took to the corridors, returning every ten minutes or so. When Dougy joined them to calm his own restlessness, a half-sleep began to claim me, drifting in and out of my head as I fought it off.

20 Dougy and the boys returned then Uncle Dennis took a wander along the passageways, and through all the comings and goings I dozed and came awake and drifted away again without a sense of time. I dreamt of coffee and running shoes squeaking on polished lino until the squeaking stopped and the aroma of coffee seemed alive in my head, irresistible, and I was

25 diving into pools of it, splashing, tasting, drinking it up. I knew it was a dream, even though I slept, and I let myself enjoy it until Dougy appeared, calling me to get out of the water. "Angela, Angela," he called, and reluctantly I started my way upwards, gliding to consciousness.

"Angela." Dougy's insistent voice spoke again and this time he was
30 kneeling in front of me.

I let my head roll back and opened my eyes. Behind him, towering over both of us, a tray balanced between his hands, stood Jarred Manning. In the middle of the tray sat two Styrofoam cups each with a wisp of steam hanging above it in the morning air.

---

19 **to claim** *here:* to come over – 28 **to glide** to move

"Hi," he said softly. "Thought you might need one of these." He tried a smile that didn't work as he placed the tray on the little table beside the sofa. I could see croissants in an open bag and pastries.

"How did you know I was here?" I asked, still groggy.

5 "I rang your grandparents. Mrs Malvern told me you'd gone off in the middle of the night. She guessed where you were though and told me to bring you breakfast. Said you must be starving by now."

"Dinner didn't agree with me," I said darkly.

As I spoke, Kendrick stood by eyeing off the pastries. "Share them out," I 10 told him. "Just leave me one of the coffees." A cheap instant brand but, it went down my throat like nectar.

"I didn't have the nerve to call you. I was worried you'd already found another way back to Brisbane."

"Let's go for a walk," he said, and I let him pull my lethargic body out of 15 the sofa and into the corridor.

"Gracey's gone, you know," he said once we were parted from the others. "I put her on the bus at Oxford Street yesterday morning. She's been travelling ever since." He stared down at his watch, calculating the hours. "If those timetables mean anything, she's still going. Gets into Cunningham 20 about half past eight."

"Dougy told me she was gone," I managed to reply. "Look, about the things I said out at Homebush. I'm sorry. I was upset about Gracey and, I don't know, my mind went berserk."

"I know, I know. And I'm sorry too. Sorry that we took so long to come back 25 on Friday. Things got a bit complicated. We didn't go to my cousin's flat, you know that, don't you."

I nodded.

"She didn't want to come back to Bankstown. Said she wanted to talk, so we went to a coffee shop. Funny really. Just the kind of place you'd choose. 30 All I did was listen, didn't say a word. She already knew what she was going to do but she had to talk it through, over and over. It was getting late and I must have looked like I wanted to get back to you. She asked me, straight out, did I love you. I said that I did and these great big tears came up in her eyes and she said something, it was hard to hear, her voice was so soft, 35 something like "Where is the tenderness in my life?" She was fiddling with this little packet of sugar without even noticing and suddenly it spilled out on the table. I looked down at it for a second but she didn't. She stayed

---

8 **darkly** moodily – 35 **to fiddle with sth** to keep touching sth because you are nervous

looking at me and leaning across the table. I knew what she wanted. Just a little tenderness. So I leaned across and kissed her, for maybe ten seconds, with a dozen people in the coffee shop watching us out of the corner of their eyes. I'm sorry, Ange. It was just something she needed. She had to have someone on her side. It had always been you before, but there's something between you, I don't know, something in the way."

My head fell forward, suddenly packed full of shame and as heavy as a cannon ball. "There was," I whispered. "There was."

"She needed a friend and she still does. That was why I had to go with her out at the track on Saturday. She's got a tough time ahead of her and she knows it. She was asking for your help and you wouldn't listen."

I wanted to shout at him, about my grandfather and Harry Falkirk, of how I had been betrayed, scream it out down the corridors, send the shame away with my anger, but I knew as the words gathered in my throat that it would all be lies.

"I didn't understand the need in her. I do now, but I didn't on Saturday, not even yesterday. Oh Jarred, why didn't she stay just one more day so I could tell her face to face."

"You'll see her again, don't worry. You're inside her head just as much as she's inside yours. She knew better than I did that you didn't mean a word of what you were saying there in the stand. She was the one who calmed me down. When I saw her onto the bus yesterday, she was still thinking about you, because she sent me off to find a piece of paper, even though the bus was ready to leave." He reached into his pocket and brought out something bright green, a sheet which had been folded many times. "All I could find was this flyer from a backpacker's hostel. She begged a pen from one of the other passengers and wrote something for you. Had to pass it down to me through the window," he said, holding the note towards me.

I took it. My hands trembled as I opened it first one way then the other. One side listed the facilities of somewhere called *The Traveller's Haven* but there was nothing written by hand on that side, so I turned the paper over and there it was, scribbled quickly as the paper rested on her knee. A single word.

Janderil.

---

13 **to betray** to be unfaithful to

For a few seconds I let the word burn an image on the back of my eyes then I passed the piece of paper to Jarred.

"You know what it is?" he asked.

I nodded, fighting tears again.

5 "What are you going to do?"

"I don't know. Her Auntie Flo doesn't have a phone. I can write to her maybe but I don't know whether she'll trust me, not after the way I held back from her."

"Seems to me you're not holding back any more, Angela. If that piece of 10 paper is anything to go by, she still trusts you."

It was too much. I launched myself onto Jarred, clinging desperately and forcing him backwards a pace or two until he locked his arms around me. I felt his finger run along the side of my cheek collecting untidy strands of hair as it went, until he hooked them all behind my ear. "I missed you," he 15 said. "What made me realise it most was standing in that cafeteria this morning. I've missed the smell of coffee that hangs around you."

I crushed my face into the wool of his sweater and cried all over again, with relief this time. I don't know how long we stood like that but eventually I let him go and we returned to wait among the others with my head 20 slumped against him, completely drained in spirit as much as in body.

I did not notice the figure in the doorway. Dougy turned first, a low cry escaping his lips, sending a warning to the rest. The family began to tumble out of the waiting room and into the passageway where the voices began.

That was Nerida's voice, I told myself, and there was an older man. A 25 doctor, surely. I was on my feet and out to join them. They were smiling, embracing one another and weeping openly, especially Dougy who stood by Nerida, his arm over her shoulder, listening to the doctor. They saw me and called out, "She's getting better, Angela. Going to be OK."

Then the doctor was speaking. "Off the critical list now. Blood pressure's 30 stabilised, heart is beating regularly. She should be out of intensive care by the end of the week." He was hugged by Auntie Irene, even Uncle Dennis, and was finally surrounded by the kids who started to whoop loudly, letting everyone in the hospital know that the waiting was over and we had all come through.

---

7 **to hold back** to be unwilling to do sth – 10 **to go by** to judge by – 32 **to whoop** to make a loud sound – 34 **to come through** to live after a dangerous situation

We stood in the corridor, a huddle of people rejoicing, reluctant to let go of one another, pulling more tightly together until we staggered drunkenly and our relief turned to laughing. Raylene was going to live, to grow up with her mother and her Uncle Dougy and her Auntie Gracey as well. We had a
5 life to celebrate.

My eye caught the clock face at the end of the passageway. It was eight-thirty and I remembered what Jarred had said about the trip to Cunningham. Two thousand kilometres away a girl was stepping down from a bus into the town where she wanted to be, where her brother and her little niece and the
10 baby's mother would soon join her, where she would live among dozens of others I would never know.

I realised too that I was glad of it, that I wanted her to be there, that I would write to her and she would write back and she would call me and reverse the charges and Dad's company would pay the bills as we talked and
15 talked and she cried to me down the line of the hard things and we laughed when she was happy. A relief swept through me so complete I felt I would surely float into the air and only Jarred's long arm would tug me down again.

Gracey was home and I was glad.

---

2 **to stagger** to move unsteadily

Additional texts

Facts about the Stolen Generation

Records show that the Australian Government created a policy of removing Aboriginal and part-Aboriginal children from their families between the 1930s and the 1970s.

But in parts of the continent the removal of Aboriginal children started
5 very much earlier. The earliest records state that in 1864 the governor of Victoria gave permission to take any Aboriginal children from their families and place them in reformatory schools in order to teach them the skills necessary to work for European settlers. In New South Wales children were taken away from their families as early as 1883. Western Australia followed
10 this policy in 1905. In 1937 the first Commonwealth-State Conference on assimilation as a national policy was held. The policy aimed to integrate indigenous Aboriginal Australians into "white society" in order to give them more chances in a white community. Several acts were amended under different names from then until the early 1970s, all with the aim of controlling
15 and assimilating children of Aboriginal descent. In 1967 Aborigines were included in the National Census for the first time. Only after the Commonwealth Racial Discrimination Act was passed in 1975 were the removals finally ended.

Because the country is so big and records have often been destroyed,
20 there can only be estimates as to how many children were actually taken away. The National Inquiry "Bringing them Home", published in 1997, concluded that from approximately 1910 to 1970 as many as 10 to 30% of the Aboriginal children were taken away to live with white people. The figures vary in certain regions and times. Generally it can be said that most
25 Aboriginal families were affected by this policy of forced assimilation in the course of the 20th century.

---

12 **indigenous** [ɪnˈdɪdʒɪnəs] native to a land – 13 **to amend** to change in order to improve – 15 **descent** *Abstammung* – 16 **Census** official counting of people – 17 **to pass** to agree on sth

Pip Masson-Naake

Angela

by James Moloney

Angela by James Moloney is the third in a series which includes award-winning novels *Dougy* and *Gracey*. Like those novels, Angela explores the relationship between Aborigines and Anglo-Saxons in contemporary Australian society. Powerful issues such as the Stolen Generation are woven
5 into this tale of two friends, one black, one white, as they embark on their new lives. The safe environment of their school, Hamilton College in Brisbane, shelters Angela and Gracey, letting them embrace their equality as they see it. They work together as a team overcoming the fierce racism that surrounds Gracey at the all-girl school, which results in Gracey's acceptance. University
10 challenges this carefully built up friendship as the two girls undertake two very different tasks. Angela chooses love in the form of Jarred Manning, a third-year student at the university, while Gracey becomes more and more involved in black politics. Up until now Angela's heritage has never been an issue, but when Angela discovers her family's secret, her friendship with
15 Gracey becomes a disaster area.

As the year wears on Angela is torn between her loyalty to her family and Gracey who has become more and more involved with a woman named Rhonda Haines, an Aboriginal postgraduate student who has made it her campaign in life to better any white. Her dislike of Angela is evident and
20 Gracey's views on whites, and Angela particularly, become influenced by Rhonda's own views.

Moloney's poignant tale is told well, with emotions and political issues coming head to head in a massive battle. Aspects of the story will chill to the bone and leave you with an uncomfortable feeling. The racial and
25 psychological conflict chosen by many of the young Aborigines in this story is devastatingly sad and when several efforts are made to apologise, the cool brush-off is distressing. Moloney favours no side of the struggle and both viewpoints are plainly and clearly given. I found myself constantly wanting to take both sides in the conflict, but eventually reason dawned on
30 me: it is not possible. This seems uncomfortably identical to reality, showing Moloney frowns on escapism.

---

1 **award-winning** having won a prize – 8 **fierce** angry and aggressive – 22 **poignant** ['pɔɪnjənt] having a great effect – 27 **brush-off** (*informal*) rude indifference – 31 **to frown on** to disapprove of – 31 **escapism** refusal to face reality

I commend Moloney on his brilliant attempt to try to bring the issue of the Stolen Generation into the Australian youth's vision but some parts of this intricate story don't seem to fit. For example, would Gracey get so quickly involved in politics at such a young age? And could a stranger such as Rhonda Haines drag Gracey away from her best mate so fast? My personal experience of living in a community with a large Aboriginal population, and having a close friend who is Aboriginal, doesn't tie in with the extreme racial tension in this novel. Occasionally race-based fights occur, but aspects such as the Stolen Generation never even trigger these fights, in fact young Aborigines never talk about these deeply moving issues, only about what parties are on, who's with who, schoolwork and other petty things which seem to fill conversations that occur in the school yard. The political issue Aboriginal youth concern themselves with, is the Pauline Hanson factor. The abuse hurled at her is extreme and I must admit it's quite satisfying to hear it. Many of us non-Aborigines also join in with great gusto in the campaign of cutting her down to size, even if she can't hear it. The Stolen Generation is merely a murmur on the lips of the older Armidale community not an issue that youths bother themselves with. In a way Moloney's novel will be able to show these youths the problems that did occur with the 'gubba-men', but the story won't totally tie in with the attitude of young Aborigines today. It seems much more suited to a slightly older white readership, which defeats the purpose sadly.

As a story, *Angela* is brilliant, written with superb clarity and deep penetration of human emotions, but I feel that as an exploration of a social issue, the novel needed to have Gracey older so that her attitude would've been more realistic. One recent literary critic stated characters walk in and out of this novel as fully realised as one's own family. This definitely hits the nail on the head but does the reality of the issues have the same effect?

Viewpoint 6 summer 1998, p.19.

---

3 **intricate** having many details – 7 **to tie in** to help to prove – 11 **petty** minor, unimportant – 13 **Pauline Hanson** leader of the right-wing political party *One Nation* – 13 **to hurl abuse at sb** to shout angrily and rudely at sb – 15 **gusto** enthusiasm – 15 **to cut sb down to size** to show sb that he is not as important as he thinks – 17 **Armidale** city on the inner east coast, between Sydney and Brisbane

The Redfern Park speech

The speech below, on indigenous issues, was given by the then Prime Minister of Australia, Paul Keating, at Redfern Park in Sydney on 10 December 1992 (Redfern is an inner city suburb of Sydney with an historically large Aboriginal population).

Ladies and gentlemen,
I am very pleased to be here today at the launch of Australia's celebration of the 1993 International Year of the World's Indigenous People. It will be a year of great significance for Australia.

5   It comes at a time when we have committed ourselves to succeeding in the test which so far we have always failed. Because, in truth, we cannot confidently say that we have succeeded as we would like to have succeeded if we have not managed to extend opportunity and care, dignity and hope to the indigenous people of Australia – the Aboriginal and Torres Strait
10 Island people.

This is a fundamental test of our social goals and our national will: our ability to say to ourselves and the rest of the world that Australia is a first-rate social democracy, that we are what we should be – truly the land of the fair go and the better chance. [...]

15 Redfern is a good place to contemplate these things: Just a mile or two from the place where the first European settlers landed, in too many ways it tells us that their failure to bring much more than devastation and demoralisation to Aboriginal Australia continues to be our failure.

More, I think, than most Australians recognise, the plight of Aboriginal
20 Australians affects us all. In Redfern it might be tempting to think that the reality Aboriginal Australians face is somehow contained here, and that the rest of us are insulated from it. But of course, while all the dilemmas may exist here, they are far from contained. We know the same dilemmas and more are faced all over Australia.

25 This is perhaps the point of this Year of the World's Indigenous People: to bring the dispossessed out of the shadows, to recognise that they are part of us, and that we cannot give indigenous Australians up without

---

2 **launch** start – 8 **to extend** to reach – 8 **dignity** *Würde* – 9 **Torres Strait Islands** group of 70 islands between Papua New Guinea and Australia – 14 **fair go** fair chance – 17 **devastation** suffering – 18 **failure** sth that has gone wrong – 19 **plight** unfortunate condition – 20 **tempting** desirable, attractive – 21 **to contain** to hold, to include

giving up many of our own most deeply held values, much of our own identity – and our own humanity. Nowhere in the world, I would venture, is the message more stark than in Australia.

We simply cannot sweep injustice aside. Even if our own conscience
5 allowed us to, I am sure that in due course, the world and the people of our region would not. There should be no mistake about this – our success in resolving these issues will have a significant bearing on our standing in the world. However intractable the problems may seem, we cannot resign ourselves to failure – any more than we can hide behind the contemporary
10 version of Social Darwinism which says that to reach back for the poor and dispossessed is to risk being dragged down.

That seems to me not only morally indefensible, but bad history. We non-Aboriginal Australians should perhaps remind ourselves that Australia once reached out for us. Didn't Australia provide opportunity and care for the
15 dispossessed Irish? The poor of Britain? The refugees from war and famine and persecution in the countries of Europe and Asia? Isn't it reasonable to say that if we can build a prosperous and remarkably harmonious multi-cultural society in Australia, surely we can find just solutions to the problems which beset the first Australians – the people to whom the most injustice
20 has been done?

And, as I say, the starting point might be to recognise that the problem starts with us non-Aboriginal Australians.

It begins, I think, with the act of recognition. Recognition that it was we who did the dispossessing. We took the traditional lands and smashed the
25 traditional way of life. We brought the disasters. The alcohol. We committed the murders. We took the children from their mothers. We practised discrimination and exclusion.

It was our ignorance and our prejudice. And our failure to imagine these things being done to us. With some noble exceptions, we failed to make the
30 most basic human response and enter into their hearts and minds. We failed to ask – how would I feel if this were done to me? As a consequence, we failed to see that what we were doing degraded all of us. [...]

Imagine if ours was the oldest culture in the world and we were told that

---

2 **to venture** *here:* to risk saying – 3 **stark** completely – 5 **due course** in future at a suitable time – 7 **bearing** influence – 8 **to resign os** to make os accept sth calmly – 12 **indefensible** not able to be protected from criticism – 15 **dipossessed** having had your land taken away – 15 **famine** extreme shortage of food – 17 **prosperous** doing well – 19 **to beset** to trouble – 23 **recognition** the act of recognising

it was worthless. Imagine if we had resisted this settlement, suffered and died in the defence of our land, and then were told in history books that we had given up without a fight. Imagine if non-Aboriginal Australians had served their country in peace and war and were then ignored in history books. Imagine if our feats on sporting fields had inspired admiration and patriotism and yet did nothing to diminish prejudice. Imagine if our spiritual life was denied and ridiculed. [...]

We are beginning to more generally appreciate the depth and the diversity of Aboriginal and Torrest Strait Islander cultures. [...]

We are beginning to learn what the indigenous people have known for many thousands of years – how to live with our physical environment. Ever so gradually we are learning how to see Australia through Aboriginal eyes, beginning to recognise the wisdom contained in their epic story.

I think we are beginning to see how much we owe the indigenous Australians and how much we have lost by living so apart. [...]

I am confident that we will succeed in this decade.

Thank you

---

1 **to resist** to refuse to accept s.th. – 5 **feat** achievement – 5 **admiration** respect for sb – 6 **diminish** make less – 9 **diversity** [daɪˈvɜːsətɪ] variety – 13 **epic** grand heroic

School projects: Questions and answers on Angela

Pupils from Gymnasium Selm in Germany asked the author James Moloney questions on his work, and here are the answers:

While reading *Angela* in class a question came up: Does Mr Malvern feel any guilt about what he did? We couldn't make up our minds whether he knew he was doing something wrong.

Angela's grandfather, Mr Malvern is in the difficult position that many
5 Australians face. He willingly took part in removing black children from their mothers many years ago. He was even prepared to deceive and force the parents to surrender their children. However, at the time, he thought he was doing the right thing. He honestly believed that the children would have a better life if they were removed from their parents who were struggling with
10 poverty and in some cases, alcoholism.

Yet today, those people are being told that what they did was wrong and in my opinion it was. People like Mr Malvern were contributing to the destruction of aboriginal culture, whether they realised it or not. The children who were removed are very angry. They feel their culture has been stolen
15 from them. Family ties are very important to aboriginal people. So Mr Malvern is faced with a difficult decision. He must admit that what he did was wrong even though he thought at the time it was the best thing. He must also admit that what he did has caused great suffering in the long term. That must be a very hard thing to do.

20 **How difficult was it for you to write novels from a girl's point of view? What motivation and intention was behind it?**

Angela is the third book I have written with a girl as the narrator. The first was *Gracey* which you can guess is about the character Gracey. The other was a short, funny book for younger children called *Buzzard Breath and*
25 *Brains*.

I have a wife and two daughters and many female friends. I have learned a lot about the way they think and feel and talk. Other people have said that I seemed to get the female voice right. When I write a book, I often become that person in my mind. It can happen for female characters as well as male.
30 I don't think there is anything to be embarrassed about in this. Do you?

Have you met many Aborigines?

I lived in a small town with many Aboriginal people 20 years ago. I have been sympathetic to them since then.

Have you or your children got indigenous friends?

I don't really have indigenous friends. My experiences with aboriginal people and their difficulties came years ago when I lived in this small town in Western Queensland.

No, my children don't know any indigenous children. Not many live in our suburb and none go to my children's school.

Do indigenous people really have their own actions groups?

In Australia today, Aboriginal people are very keen to show their identity as indigenous people. They don't talk about integration. At University, they can often find other Aboriginal people to help believe in that identity. They are encouraged to do so. It can lead to problems such as I showed in the book.

I liked the novel *Angela* because it shows the problems that Aboriginal Australians have even today. It's very important to realise that racism is not only a problem coloured people in the USA have to face. Racism against Aborigines in Australia is not a theme you hear about very often in the German media. (Nina B.)

I think racism can exist wherever one racial group is in a minority. In Australia, we certainly hear about racism in America through the news and through movies as well. Sometimes we hear about racism in Germany against immigrant workers from Turkey or in France against black people from Africa. Australia does not get mentioned much in the international news but we have our problems with racism. Aboriginal people here have been very badly treated for two hundred years. As a nation we are trying to do something about it but it is not easy. Older people here tend to be very prejudiced. Worst of all, they don't want to recognise that terrible things were done to aborigines in the past. One of the worst things was the focus of *Angela*. Black children were taken away from their parents. In some cases, this helped the children survive the appalling conditions that Aborigines were forced to live in. Some white Australians point this out and say that such Aboriginal people should be grateful. But mostly, black children were taken away because the government hoped this would make aboriginal culture die out. That is what I was trying to get at in my book. It is a different kind of racism from what you come across in the USA or Europe.

Will you write a sequel? (Kevin)

I am not planning another book. *Angela* is the third book in a trilogy about *Dougy* and *Gracey*. You might like to read the first two if you can find them.